THE
BEAST

PAUL DI'ANNO

JOHN BLAKE

Published by John Blake Publishing Ltd,
3 Bramber Court, 2 Bramber Road,
London W14 9PB, England

www.johnblakepublishing.co.uk

First published in paperback in 2010

ISBN: 978 1 84454 884 2

British Library Cataloguing-in-Publication Data:

A catalogue record for this book is available from the British Library.

Design by www.envydesign.co.uk

Printed in Great Britain by CPI Bookmarque Ltd, Croydon CR0 4TD

3 5 7 9 10 8 6 4 2

Papers used by John Blake Publishing are natural, recyclable products made from
wood grown in sustainable forests. The manufacturing processes conform to the
environmental regulations of the country of origin.

THIS BOOK IS DEDICATED TO
THE LOVING MEMORY MR LESLIE
MARSHALL (OUR FATHER) —
NEVER FORGOTTEN, AND TO MY
MUM FOR PUTTING UP WITH IT
ALL — I LOVE YOU PEANUT!

WWW.PAULDIANNO.COM

FOREWORD

My name is Paul Di'Anno. That's me on the front cover, just in case you're a bit fucking slow on the uptake.

Nicknamed 'The Beast', I was first unleashed on an unsuspecting public when I was the lead singer of the rock band Iron Maiden, probably the most successful heavy metal group of all time.

Later, I found a different kind of notoriety when I parted company with said band. Ever since that day, colourful legends, rumours and myths about me have flown around the world of rock music – you've heard them, I've heard them. Drinking, more drinking, drug abuse, sex, guns, prison, violence, marriages, divorces, taking library books back late; you name it, I've done it.

If you're one of those Bible-bashing herberts who think rock musicians are the spawn of the Devil, sent to this world to pollute the minds of impressionable teenagers, this book will probably provide the proof you've been looking for. Come to think of it, you're probably right, in any case.

If the thought of impressionable young girls getting it doggy-style from drug-addled rock stars offends you, well you'd better put this book down now, love. Take a Mogadon and lie in a darkened room for a bit ...

Still here? Hmm, thought so ...

Seriously, if you're a paid-up member of the moral majority, or a politically-correct soul who's easily shocked, Christ Almighty, you'd do well to take my advice and fuck off out of it now, while the going's good.

On the other hand, if you're one of those sickos who's just reading this because you want to hear disgusting, depraved tales of booze, drugs and sex – well, you'd better pull up a chair, old son, 'cos you're definitely in the right place!

Where do I start? Shoving bottles up groupies' arses, birds snorting coke off my dick, prostitutes blowing smoke rings out of their cunts, screwing birds with bananas, sticking a gun up a girl's pussy, getting blow-jobs from middle-aged housewives, getting jailed in America after nearly killing a woman, being busted for possession of an Uzi and a pile of cocaine by the LAPD. It's all here and more.

Almost kicking a band member to death, attacking 15 bouncers at a gig, threatening crowds with guns, falling offstage pissed, chasing my girlfriend through a packed concert hall trying to kill her, starting fights in every continent in the world, getting arrested, being illegally smuggled between countries, and generally raising hell. Need I go on?

You have to understand, most of this stuff was done under the influence of enough Jack Daniel's to float a small yacht, and enough cocaine to finish off an entire country. Millions of pounds has passed through my hands over the years, feeding a habit for all-night boozing sessions, mindless drug abuse and groupies who like to fuck.

I've left a trail of destruction behind me like you wouldn't believe – trashed hotel rooms, vomit-covered groupies, bloodstained sheets, shit-smeared walls – believe me, it's not pretty.

If you're a rock fan, well, you'd better read on to find out how it really is backstage, in the world of concert halls, recording studios and endless hotel rooms. You're going to discover a few surprises, too.

The following book is all true – I know, because I lived it. Some of the names of former band members, ex-wives, groupies, girlfriends, drug-dealers, police officers and general low-lifes have been changed, to protect their identities. Others have been changed because I can't remember them. And if anybody else takes umbrage at what they read, well, that's tough shit.

So forget what you've heard or read elsewhere, because I'm the man behind the legends – the man they call 'The Beast'. And this is my story ...

CHAPTER 1

A lot has been written and said about me through the years – most of it bad, some of it untrue.

I've got a theory – I think the world needs people like me, just so that everybody else can talk about them. Some people just can't help getting into trouble, and others are compelled to watch as they do it. It's like driving past the scene of a road accident – you can't help looking, in case you see something gory. You don't really want to see anything gory in case it grosses you out, but you can't help looking, anyway.

Well, there have been a lot of gory moments in my life, and from the things people say about me, it seems there's always a load of bystanders around when they happen.

Before I agreed to write this book, I thought long and hard about it. Was it really such a good idea? A lot of weird shit has happened to me over the years, and there have been lots of casualties when things have really gone off. Some of them have been innocent victims, others less so. Did I really want to open up old wounds all over again, and stir up ghosts which are probably better left where they are? Possibly not.

Also, I thought the old Iron Maiden legends had been told and re-told so often that everyone's heard them already. Trouble is, they often get more dramatic with every telling, usually with yours truly cast as some sort of pantomime villain.

On the other hand, though, when I started to think about it, I felt I deserved the chance to put my story across. While everyone's got their favourite Paul Di'Anno story, I've kept it shut all this time. When journalists have slagged me off, I've just thought, 'Fuck you, cunt, what have you ever done?'

Some of the Iron Maiden folk stories were invented by gossip-mongers long after I'd left the band and, since then, one urban myth has generated another. How many times had I been married? Did I get thrown out of the band? Did I really end up in prison in America? (Five; no; and yes.)

Yes, I've taken loads of drugs; yes, I've drunk almost every drink under the sun. Do I have a problem? Do I fuck! Where's the problem? I've just had a fucking good time, that's all; and I loved almost every bloody minute of it. Admittedly, when I drink or take drugs, I often cause a problem – both for myself and other people – by going off and doing something stupid, but that's just me.

It makes me fucking laugh when I hear today's so-called 'celebrities' whining on about going into rehab, and conquering their 'demons'. Fucking tossers, all of them! For your information, poverty is the only demon I know of, and that particular demon can be found everywhere round East London, where I grew up. When I go back there now, believe me, I can still see the demons.

For the benefit of the rumour-mongers, I have indeed been to rehab ... it was for anger-management. I was ordered to attend after serving a prison term in America a few years back. My temper has been far more dangerous to me and those around me than booze or drugs ever were. When I get pushed too far, something just snaps, and then it all gets out of hand. I've attacked friends, enemies, wives, girlfriends, band members, police officers, complete strangers – you name it. I'm not proud of it, but there you go.

Sex has also been an equally dangerous addiction for me, too – women have always been attracted to me for some reason, and they've often caused me more trouble than any artificial stimulant ever could. Sometimes it was their fault; more often, it was mine.

I've had three 'legal' wives, and two common-law ones. Yeah, I know – there's not too many of today's so-called 'boy bands' who can make a claim like that – they're more like Christian prayer groups these days.

I met this woman once who read palms or saw into the future, or some shit like that. This bird was some sort of Gypsy Rose-type, telling people how many kids they were going to have, or how they'd find everlasting happiness. She was having a look at all the palms of the boys in the band, giving them a load of shit about finding their destiny and being true to themselves and all that bollocks. I didn't believe a fucking word of it.

When it came to my turn, I shoved my mitt under her nose; well, she took one look at me, and she nearly bloody shat herself. It was like an electric shock had gone through her – she was genuinely terrified. Her face just went white, and she suddenly had this really haunted look about her, like she'd seen something truly wicked. She looked at me as if I was the anti-Christ or something, and said in this strange, strangled voice, 'You ... you've got demons all over you!'

It did freak me out a bit, I must admit. 'Course, the band were falling about, the bastards, laughing and saying, 'Well, we could have fucking told you that!' There you go, that says it all, really. If you ever had any doubt that I was trouble, this book will prove it once and for all.

I've no pretensions of grandeur – my music will never change the world, nor did I ever think it could. At best, it's made some people happy, which is about all you can ask, really. It's also provided me with the biggest and best high known to man, greater than any drug ever invented. That's the feeling of rushing on to a stage, deafened by ear-splitting music, with thousands of fans screaming your name hysterically. It's a feeling like coming face to face with God, or witnessing the birth of your first child – it can't be described in words.

So, this is me putting the record straight, cutting through all the rumours, half-truths and downright lies. I decided that if I was going to tell my story, I'd do it as honestly and frankly as I could.

Read it, and you'll at least get a better picture of the real Paul Di'Anno. You can judge me then, if you like.

*   *   *

You have to remember that most rock bands today, while they like to pose in leathers and look all butch for the cameras, they're about as wild as Girl Guides on a fucking Sunday School outing, really. As soon as they come off the stage or leave the recording studio, they're meeting up with their managers, agents, PR people, arse-wipers or whoever, checking on how much money they've made.

Well, fuck that shit. When I come off stage, I hang out with bikers, drug-dealers, villains, pimps, bouncers – my kind of people. I don't even have to know them. Wherever I am in the world, I can find them:

If you want to make money, at least have the decency to be honest about it. Wear a pair of braces and a stripy suit, call yourself Rupert or Tarquin and get pissed on Chardonnay in wine bars – have the guts to admit what you are. I've more respect for people like that than for those who pretend to be something they're not.

Where bands used to wreck hotel rooms or throw tellies out of the window, now they're sitting at their laptops, checking their share prices. These aren't even real bands, they're just manufactured products, like toilet paper or carpet cleaners. While we weren't everyone's cup of tea, at least with Iron Maiden what you saw was what you got – we were real.

But, of course, I took it a bit too far. Money and fame convinced me I could do whatever the fuck I liked, and the hero worship I encountered just fed a demon which lived inside me, a demon which lurked beneath the surface, ready to burst out at any minute. A couple of examples will give you some idea of what I'm on about.

The guy was fucking pissing me off. I was in this club in the West End, and already I was surrounded by people. Complete strangers, just crowding round me to jabber in my ear. Blokes were going on about Iron Maiden this, and Paul Di'Anno that, it was just mental. You'd think I'd won a Nobel Prize or conquered Everest, instead of poncing about on a stage with a rock band.

Birds were pressing their tits against my face, grabbing my crotch and putting their arms around my neck. Beyond the inner circle of fans, I could sense a bitter, twisted rank of jealous boyfriends and other resentful nobodies, the sort of people who can't stand being eclipsed, even though they should be used to it. So I'm pissing people off, without even trying. Great.

This bloke may have one of these, he may have been a pissed punter, or he may just have been a guy who goes out of an evening to have a ruck. I know that sort, and I can identify with them, 'cos I used to do it myself.

He was a big, tough-looking geezer, crew-cut, earrings, slightly boss-eyed. There may have been some cousins who got it together a few generations back, or it may have been purely a freak of nature that he was born thick as pig shit. Who knows?

Anyway, he was giving me the evil eye. I can spot it a mile off, I've seen it so many times. He'd obviously spent ages practising looking tough in the mirror, after watching too many episodes of The Sweeney or something. You could read his mind – what there was of it – and he'd have been saying to himself, 'Who the fuck does that Di'Anno bloke think he is?'

Well, fair enough, I'd probably have thought the same in his position. But he wasn't dealing with some sort of boy band mincer here, and I shot him a look which said as much. It said, 'Come on then, cunt, you want to have a go, go ahead. I'll fucking have a bit of you ...'

He didn't have the guts to just walk up and twat me one, that would have been too brave, too direct. No, he sidles up amongst the crowd, through the throng of groupies, and deliberately nudges into me, spilling my drink. He's obviously waiting for me to throw the first punch. That's lovely, mate, just give me an excuse ...

Immediately the crowd draws back, as if they're on strings. Have you noticed that most people are born to be spectators? They witness accidents, they give statements, they produce descriptions – all from the bloody sidelines. The minute there's any kind of event or happening that in any way deviates from the soul-destroying boredom of their everyday existences, they're putting up deckchairs and selling tickets. And it's always people like me who're in the spotlight, whether we plan it that way or not.

So they're clearly expecting some kind of show, because they're looking at the two of us like we're the main turn that night. I look again at this guy, and relax slightly. It's obvious he's a weekend cowboy – just a big lump, out on the piss and looking for a bit of aggro.

I looked into his eyes, and there was no real threat there. I've looked into the eyes of the really hard bastards who'd drop you like they were swatting a fly, but this wasn't the genuine article – he was just an amateur playing a role.

And he wasn't even playing it very well. I've been threatened by the real thing in my time and, compared to them, he just looked a bit silly.

There was this exaggerated hush as he lurched towards me, and an even greater one when I smashed the beer bottle I'd been hiding behind my back over his big, stupid head. Glass flew everywhere, blood was pissing from his head like a river, and he just stumbled and crashed backwards, scattering drinks, tables and chairs. He had this sort of dazed look on his face, like a dumb animal that's just been cruelly pole-axed. He was still conscious as he went down, so I was up on him straight away. Once they're down, make sure they stay down. I brought my cowboy boot down on his thick skull as hard as I could. There was a nasty crunch, and the crowd of spectators suddenly looked away.

Assuming he actually survived, that loser probably thought he'd been attacked by some kind of wild animal. Everybody else present probably thought the Paul Di'Anno they'd seen on Top of the Pops was some kind of nutter.

Well, they were both right, weren't they?

The second incident happened a few years later, and while there had been thousands of others in between, this one demonstrated just how far I'd come in some ways, and yet how little I had changed in others.

By this time I was living in LA, with as much money as I could ever spend. Royalties were pouring in, and I've got this really flash apartment in Hollywood. I'm dripping with gold – the Rolex Oyster watch, the chunky bracelet, the earrings. My body is covered with tattoos – my teenage etchings had now expanded into a colourful canvas that covered my arms, chest, stomach, legs, neck and head. All of them had their own story – a glitzy parlour in LA, a bikers' clubhouse in Texas, a backstreet shop in the East End of London.

In terms of experience, the fresh-faced geezer who had joined a pub band named Iron Maiden in the late '70s wouldn't have been able to make me out at all. I'd jetted all over the world, slept (or passed out) in swanky five-star hotels, and basically helped myself to anything I wanted in life: from birds and booze to drugs and flash cars.

If anybody got in my way, I bought them out, so they'd do whatever I wanted. Why go to all the effort of finding a girlfriend when you can dangle a big wad of cash in front of some dizzy little tart, and she'll be on her knees in minutes, sucking you off like her life depended on it. People like that can be bought and sold. If they couldn't be bought (and trust me, nearly everyone can be bought) I smacked them so hard they never got in my way again.

The thing was, though, I'd only changed in terms of material possessions and experience. Essentially, I was exactly the same mouthy little cunt who used to scrap it out with all the other tearaways, running wild through the streets of Walthamstow on a Saturday night. My attitude hadn't changed, my personality hadn't changed. If anything, I'd become much worse, because now I had the money, status and clout to live out any fantasy I'd ever had; it was like being given a special licence to do it. In fact, I think the people around me encouraged it, not only to keep me quiet, but to fuel the Di'Anno legend even more.

Anyway, Di'Anno the flash rock star is sauntering down Sunset Boulevard one night, on his way back from the liquor store. I had a pair of shorts on, with a vest and bandanna, so I looked like any other street guy out that evening.

I turned left off Sunset and cut through a dark parking lot towards my apartment block. It's still quite early, but the light is fading fast. It's a nice, warm evening, and I'm thinking about nothing in particular – just minding my own business. At the edge of my vision, I see a big Hispanic guy walking towards me, his pace quickening. He's dressed much the same as me, and I assume he's heading for a night out on Sunset.

As he draws closer, though, everything seems to speed up, like in a dream; and the next thing I know, his face is pressed right up against the side of mine, with a cold gun barrel pressed against my head. Until now, neither of us had made a sound, which gave the whole thing an eerie, unreal feeling. It was as if I was watching someone else do it in a movie on telly.

Out of the darkness, like silent ghosts, these six or seven shadowy figures slowly appeared, obviously part of the same gang. Their dark, menacing presence just added to the otherworldly air.

Now this I've something I've never understood. Did they just want to mug me? Unlikely – I'd pick on every other fucker on Sunset Boulevard before I started on a big ugly lump like me. Was it the rock star thing? Had they got the hump because of who I was, just like that guy all those years before? Doubt it. If you heave a brick down any Hollywood street, you'll probably hit a couple of members of Motley Crue and at least one of the Van Halens. (Not a bad idea, now I come to think of it.)

No, I think the motive was much more serious. These guys were obviously connected, although I couldn't make out their street-gang colours in the semi-darkness. They'd been around on the LA drug scene, and they'd probably seen me doing the same. They knew people, they knew who was supplying who, and they may have been in on the distribution network somewhere.

All the rock stars and movie stars in LA get through a mountain of cocaine every day, and it's a multi-million dollar business topping up that mountain. It's like a pension scheme for dealers out there. As you would expect, there were some very heavy-duty people behind it, stretching back as far as the Mexican Mafia and La Cosa Nostra. I'd seen and heard things – I knew people who moved in those circles. Anybody who interrupted the supply was likely to be fitted for a pair of concrete shoes.

All of this went through my head in those few seconds as I

stood there with a gun aimed at my head. The thought made the beads of sweat stand out on my forehead, although I gazed levelly into the eyes of the guy who was carrying. It wasn't the first gun barrel I'd stared down, nor would it be the last, but it doesn't do to be too cocky or too fearful. Just keep your cool. Shock takes over, really. Your body just goes into system shutdown, for its own protection.

They'd obviously had me down as some new face on the gang circuit, a guy who was likely to cause some waves. To plead otherwise would have been a waste of breath, plus it would have also been an unforgivable loss of face. I don't beg from anybody, even if they're likely to blow my brains out with a twitch of a finger. Their suspicion would have been enough in itself for a cold-blooded execution, and this may have been what they were building up to. I couldn't tell.

The guy with the gun stepped round in front of me, and stared right into my face. One eye was a sightless black hole, and most of his left ear was missing. To be honest, he looked absolutely fucking crazy. He gabbled some words which I didn't understand, and then sucked in his breath. I thought that was it, and I closed my eyes as I waited for the gun chamber to click, and my life to end.

The side of my head went completely numb, and a split-second later, there was a thunderous crash which made my skull rattle. There was no sound beyond that, as my senses went dead. I fell backwards and my head smacked on the asphalt with a dull crack. Warm blood was in my nose and mouth, and I gurgled as I struggled for breath.

He'd pistol-whipped me, just clouted me around the head with the weapon. It was obviously some kind of warning. I'd obviously really pissed him and his mates off, somehow. I'd had a few death-threats over the past year, mainly from a vindictive ex-girlfriend who'd paid someone to try and put the frighteners on me, but I didn't think this was connected to her.

The gang had legged it, and I rolled over on to my side, still choking on my own blood. He'd obviously opened up quite a gash in my forehead, which was streaming down over my face. I was surprised to find I could sit up, and I numbly climbed to my feet, feeling a bit like a dumb kid who's been knocked over in the playground by the school bully. Eventually, I managed to stagger home, and cleaned myself up as best I could. I looked at myself in the bathroom mirror – as is often the case, the damage actually looked worse than it was. I'd taken a bit of a lump, but I'd live – which is more than I could say for my soon-to-be deceased friend ...

I bandaged myself up – if you go to an Emergency Room in America with anything remotely dodgy, they'll have the cops there before they've broken out the aspirins. Anyway, I had far more important things to think about. Namely, a certain little cunt, whose life insurance premiums were about to go through the roof.

It took me about a fortnight to track him down. I didn't want to seem too obvious, in case I stirred up more hornets' nests than were necessary. But people like that are easy to find. You're not going to find them in the lounge bar of the Regent Beverly Wilshire, or the Franklin Plaza. They're drawn to the biker bars, the pool halls, the tattoo parlours, just like flies are drawn to shit. I should know; he was hanging around exactly the same sort of places as me.

I even found out where he lived. I was a bit like a kind of undercover cop, just casually asking questions of people without raising their suspicions. I didn't want anyone to warn him, I didn't want the bastard knowing what he had coming to him.

For a couple of nights, I hung around outside his apartment block, waiting for him to come home. I just stood there in the shadows, out of sight, with a .38 Special tucked in my belt for company.

Then, on the third night, our friend obviously decides to have an early night. Bad move, pal. He saunters up the pathway, bouncing along on the balls of his feet to an imaginary rhythm. Maybe he was an Iron Maiden fan.

He never got the chance to discuss musical arrangements with me. I sprang out of the shadows like a bullet, and landed a sweet right hook full into his face, with all my weight behind it. He went down like a sack of shit, his nose exploding in a red mist. One minute it was there, the next it had been replaced by this squashed red jelly which was spread from ear to ear.

I grabbed his vest as he fell away from me, ready to give him another one, but it ripped away in my hand, and I was left holding a red silky rag.

As he hit the ground, I swung my foot back and kicked him in the head with all the force I could muster. There was a muted thud as my heavy boot connected with his already-mangled face.

But I wasn't finished. Oh no. I cast a quick look around to check there were no witnesses about, and I pulled the .38 Special from my belt. I put the barrel in his mouth, loosening several of his teeth and drawing yet more blood.

He was looking up at me with his one good eye, absolutely fucking terrified. He obviously thought he was going to die. There was this funny smell, and I realised he'd soiled himself. A big tear rolled down his cheek. Here was a tough street guy, crying for mercy and shitting his pants with fear. To me, that was better than killing him.

I laughed in his face, and rolled him over with my boot. I slowly walked away from the apartment building, and when I looked back over my shoulder, he hadn't moved. He was lying face down on the asphalt, as motionless as a corpse.

Now just hang on just a fucking minute, I hear you say. What the fuck are you playing at, Paul? You don't hear of Ronan Keating glassing someone in a nightclub, or Robbie Williams trying to blow someone's head off with a handgun. Well, no, I don't suppose you do.

But that's me – that's the way I am, whether I'm a penniless tearaway, or a rich rock star. Allow me to explain ...

CHAPTER 2

Funnily enough, I was a pretty wild kid. Yeah, I know that may come as a bit of a shock to most of you, but it's true. East London was my turf, and me and my mates just used to run completely wild in it, like something out of *Mad Max*.

When you're a kid, your worth as a person is determined by how good you are at fighting. If you can handle yourself in a scrap, you're one of the lads – people respect you. It's not that different as an adult really, while you don't roll around on the floor and pull each other's hair (although I have used that tactic in some contract negotiations over the years) people respect you according to how much shit you're prepared to take. If you act like a doormat, people are going to walk all over you, because that's what doormats are for.

On the other hand, if you show you're ready to hurt someone because he's pissed you off, the next guy isn't going to be quite so keen to piss you off. This applies to both kids and adults – they don't like being hurt.

Twenty years later, I was still applying this rule, incarcerated in the bowels of the LA County Jail, California, after a major altercation with the good gentlemen of the LAPD. In there, I was residing among some of the toughest, most evil bastards in America – Cosa Nostra hitmen, Crips and Bloods gangbangers, Mexican Mafia, Colombian drug-dealers and plain old whackos.

I certainly wasn't the hardest guy in the place – not by a long way – but I must have given the impression that if you started with me, I'd go all the way. Whatever it took, no messing.

Fuck with me, and I'll kill you. It might take knives, bats, guns, whatever; but I'll put you away. Piss me off in any way whatsoever, and I'll put a fucking bullet in your head, if I have to.

The law of the jungle was certainly in force on the streets of the East End during my youth – you could see evidence of it on every street corner. Remember, this was just after Ronnie and Reggie (RIP, gents) had become long-term guests of Her Majesty. There were still a few members of their gang at large. Hard-looking guys in smart suits could be seen everywhere, striding around like they owned the place, with bundles of cash and gorgeous birds on their arms.

Did we look up to guys like that? Did we ever! We thought they were the dogs' bollocks. Forget explorers or mountaineers, these were our heroes. There was one guy we knew, he was the landlord of a pub down by the docks where we used to cadge underage lager. He was a big old bloke, built like a docker, with a large, ruddy face.

This bloke – and I won't mention his name, in case he gets in trouble all over again – was always banging on about his friends on 'The Firm', telling us about the wild nights out he'd had with Ron, Reg and Charlie, how they were all really great mates, and what a shame it was for poor old Violet with all her boys inside – he felt for her, he really did.

We'd be sitting there like fucking muppets, gobs hanging open, while this big old geezer was telling us about drinking with George Cornell or playing cards with Frankie Fraser. Talk about wet behind the ears – this was better than *The Godfather* to us, hearing about razor-fights and shootings which took place only a few years before, on the very same streets where we were growing up.

It's funny – if you'd put us in a classroom in front of some arsehole of a teacher while he droned on about Samuel Pepys and the Great Fire, we'd have been flicking elastic bands at each other, or wanking under the desks. But put us in front of a genuine East End hard-man – or so he seemed – and we were all ears. We were just hanging on his every word.

Well, it turned out we weren't the only people he'd been spinning his bullshit to. A while after that, he was razored to within an inch of his life, left for dead on a street corner like a blood-soaked bundle of rags. It seemed a few of the chaps had gotten wind of his Hans Christian Andersen bollocks, and sent a message for him to give the fairytales a rest for a while.

Well, that put the shits up us for a bit, I can tell you. For a while after that, we weren't quite so mouthy in public, and a good deal more respectful to our elders and betters. Lesson learned, you might say.

It showed what power still remained in the East End underworld, if they could cut a guy to pieces just for opening his gob once too often. This wasn't some *Untouchables* movie, this was happening on our doorsteps, for real! Fucking great!

Of course, that's what we all tried to emulate. The great

British tradition of fights outside the boozer on a Saturday night. A good tear-up, fuelled by beer and hormones. Nothing serious, just a sweet right-hander here, and a good bit of boot there. A few bruises, the odd fat lip. Kids' stuff.

The girls used to stand around while we went for it, like some sort of tribal ceremony in which they weren't allowed to participate. The uniform was shaved heads, Doc Martens, braces and Harrington jackets. The etiquette was simply to put your opponent down as quickly and impressively as you could.

Of course, if my mates were the tribe, I was the feudal chief. I was the mouthiest, the loudest, the hardest, the most obnoxious. By a mile. Even then, I had to be the centre of attention. If one of our guys had fattened someone's lip, I'd have to split someone's nose. If they'd knocked out a tooth, I'd have to break a jaw.

And we fucking loved it – I've got to be honest. It doesn't sound very politically correct now, but it was just the greatest thing in the world back then. We'd be in this massive great scrap somewhere in Walthamstow at chucking-out time, and there'd be fists, boots and heads flying. I'd be right in the bloody thick of it, laying into some poor bastard, lacing his face with my fists, and putting the leather in on him when he was down. Shouting, swearing, yelling, bawling. Happy as a pig in shite.

Psychiatrists and social workers will question this aggressive behaviour, pointing to low income, lack of opportunities, poor role models or over-active criminal tendencies. Well, arseholes, I say, we were just kids, having a laugh. Anyway, I'd like to see some poncy bloody psychiatrist take on all-comers on a Saturday night in Walthamstow.

As well as the local reputation we were gaining, there were

more obvious benefits from all this carrying on. I think the
birds used to take a look at this almighty brawl, see which of
the lads looked the most impressive in the midst of it, and if he
survived in one piece, lead him off by the hand when the dust
had finally settled. A bit like *Blind Date* with violence.

If you got lucky (and believe me, I *always* got lucky), you'd
find a nice dark alleyway somewhere, and take up the time-
honoured positions, facing each other up against the wall.
How far the girl let you go depended on the force of your
charm and, more importantly, how much she'd had to drink.

If she'd only had a couple of shandies – the miserable cow –
you'd be looking at a kiss with tongues or a hand up her top,
at best. You'd be told, 'I don't want to go too far ...' and before
you knew it, you'd be walking home with what felt like the Taj
Mahal down your trousers.

A couple of rum and cokes, and you could be talking about
a hand up the skirt and inside the knickers for a quick feel, or
even a bra undone for a furtive nuzzle. It was often -3°C at the
time, but that didn't seem to matter.

On the other hand, if you'd chosen well, she'd have had a
bloody skinful, and you could well see the bra coming off
altogether, revealing little white tits with blue veins and goosebumps. The knickers would be pulled off and stuffed in the
pocket, the skirt would be hoisted up around the waist and
you'd slip yourself inside, holding your partner up by the
thighs as you did her against the wall.

The technique was nothing to write home about, a bit like a
bull charging at a gate, but enthusiasm triumphed over
experience. Many's the night I've stood in some dingy dark
alleyway, banging away at some poor girl, thrusting her back
up against a damp, graffiti-smeared wall. She's shivering with

cold because she's half-naked, her head's thumping against the bricks, and you're humping away like a Jack Russell. Bloody marvellous.

That's what it's all about, really. I haven't really moved on that much since then.

*   *   *

Besides my other talents, I'd always had an interest in music. I don't know where it came from, but I always really got off on it. Buying records, getting the T-shirts, following the groups; it's the same for kids today, I'm sure.

There's a strange story, actually, concerning one of my first experiences in rock music; it's about a guy who's always been something of an idol to me, a bit like a mentor, as we would later turn out to have a lot in common.

I'd skived off school with a mate – like you do – to go and see AC/DC, the heavy metal band from Australia who were just on the verge of becoming really big then. They were playing at a club in London, and we just went along.

They played a great show, and we managed to meet them in the bar afterwards, when we blagged our way in for a few underage beers. Get this – the person who bought me my first-ever beer in any pub, anywhere, was AC/DC's singer, the late, great Bon Scott; legendary singer, womaniser and general hell-raiser.

Talk about an honour – I was just overwhelmed by the guy, and his wild-man reputation. Years later, he came to be a huge influence in my life, not just for his music, but the way he approached everything, just taking it as it comes and living for the day. We both lived life to the full, and aside from a shared appetite for pussy, drink and drugs, we also shared the same down-to-earth attitude and sense of humour, which got us through all the craziness which surrounded us.

Tragically, though, Bon didn't have that much time left with us. He died a few years later in the back seat of a car in a London street, passed out after a heavy drinking session. He'd apparently choked on his own vomit.

There is a terrible coincidence to the day he died, 22 February 1980. That day, myself and the guys in Maiden were making our début appearance on *Top of the Pops*, when I became the first singer to perform live on the show for almost a decade. We'd refused to mime, so they bent the rules for us. So there I am, riding high as a rock singer, and there was Bon, my idol, lying dead in a car, a few miles away across London.

But I'm getting ahead of myself. When I was a kid, heavy metal was what you found in scrapyards, and an Iron Maiden was a medieval torture device. I hadn't the faintest clue back then of how those two quaint terms were going to change my life for ever. Come to think of it, I didn't really know anything at all.

CHAPTER 3

Until my dying day, my name will always be associated with Iron Maiden. There you go – I've said it. A lot of people have said it to me, and it's been both a blessing, and a curse. My various escapades since then have only added fuel to the fire. I'm not knocking it – it's probably why many of you are reading this book – and it's certainly fed all my kids over the years.

OK, you're saying (especially if you're an Iron Maiden fan, Gawd bless you), I'd be nothing if it wasn't for Maiden, I'm still living off it now, etc. etc. Paul Di'Anno, ex-Iron Maiden. You can't mention me without mentioning them. Yeah, I know, I know.

Well, OK, they've helped to make me what I am. But there's one very important factor here – a little fact which everyone seems to forget. That is: I bleeding well helped to make them what they are, an' all. Whether they like it or not, I was a vital bloody part of Maiden, and I helped to create the monster – the same monster which came to dominate the rock world.

All right, they always had musicianship and songs, they were always going to get somewhere, but I was the missing ingredient, the frontman who packaged the whole lot together on stage and on records. I was the face of Iron Maiden. They'll always be a part of me, but I'll always be a part of them, too.

On the one hand, it's opened up a world which I could never have even dreamed of back at the oil company where I worked. Back then, I lived for going out on Friday and Saturday nights, getting pissed, getting laid ... and that was it. (Those fine principles haven't actually changed that much over the years, but you know what I mean.)

I've travelled the world, made lots of money, fucked loads of women, put loads of stuff up my nose and generally had a bloody marvellous time, thanks very much. On the other hand, it's given me a load of heartache, stress, grief, frustration, anger, even violence. Whatever I've had out of the deal, I've paid for in spades, believe me.

Of course, the questions I get asked most often are about my time with the Irons. How did I join? How did we get along? Did my lifestyle upset the others? Why did I leave? Did I jump, or was I pushed? Am I still bosom buddies with Steve Harris? Do I think Bruce is a better singer than me? If you want to know the answers to all of these, you'd better read on, because this is what really happened ...

*   *   *

Like always, I didn't really take it seriously at first, it was all a bit of a laugh. I was a young tearaway, not long out of school, and intent on getting up to a bit of naughtiness, if you know what I mean. If you've heard the song 'Running Free', you'll have already sussed that the lyrics were based on my wild youth, and all the stuff I got up to.

I can't really remember exactly how, it's probably lost in the mists of time, but I think I went from listening to music to actually performing it, almost by accident. Looking back, I think it was a case of me always being the show-off, you know, the 'more front than Selfridges' sort of thing. It just seemed a cool thing to do, to impress girls and that. (Well, that was the idea.) So this cocky young kid, right, who didn't really know anything, somehow ends up as the singer of a punk band called The Paedophiles. (Yeah, I know.)

I'd like to tell you we were really good and we were immediately signed up by EMI ... but it didn't happen that way. To tell you the truth, we were a pile of shite.

Anyway, a mate of mine tells me about this young rock band who were starting to make a name for themselves around the East End pubs, so I go and see them. Me and my mate Loopy (who later became our drum tech, funnily enough) went down to the Cart and Horses in Stratford, East London, where this band are playing, under the name Iron Maiden.

Fuck me, they were even worse than us. It was a very early incarnation of the band, but Christ almighty, they bloody stank to high heaven. We just pissed ourselves laughing at them – they were so bad, I thought they were a comedy act, for fuck's sake.

Their singer at the time, Paul Mario Day, was someone I knew by sight – he was actually knocking off a bird who lived on the fifth floor of my tower block, so I used to see him go past my door from time to time. He left the band after a bit, to be replaced by a singer called Dennis Wilcock.

I saw them again when he was in the line-up, and they weren't that much better. He was doing this weird stuff on stage with a sword and fake blood, pretending to cut his mouth open. It was supposed to be dramatic, like a Kiss type of thing, but to me it looked more like D'Artagnan does heavy metal. Fucking bizarre. Let's just say I wasn't impressed. The future of British heavy metal? More like Hinge and fucking Bracket.

They must have had early versions of a few standards in their repertoire by now, but I can't really remember too much about their set, so they still can't have made that much of an impression at all.

Anyway, later I hear the band are looking for a new singer, and my mate suggested I put myself up for it. I'd got to hear about it through a guy called Trevor Searle, who ran the Green Man pub in Leytonstone. He was a great bloke and, as well as being a drinking pal of mine, he knew Maiden's bass player and founder member, Steve Harris. I must be honest, though, the main reason I used to go to his pub was this fantastic Swedish bird who used to work behind the bar there. She was fucking gorgeous, with an arse to die for, and we were all desperate to give her one. None of us got anywhere, but that's often the way, isn't it?

Anyway, turning my mind back to music for a moment, I wasn't really bothered about the gig. I'd seen 'em and I wasn't bowled over, so I could take it or leave it, really. Like I say, I was a cocky sod. But I was eventually persuaded to go up for the audition, and I sang the Deep Purple song 'Dealer' (which I'd had to learn) and 'All Right Now' by Free, I think.

I thought I'd done all right, but I honestly didn't give it too much thought after that, so it came as a bit of a shock when they asked me to join. The irony is, with hindsight, even then

I still wasn't mad keen. I honestly didn't think they'd get anywhere, which shows you how much I knew at the time. Plus, it seemed a bit too much like hard work to me, and I couldn't really be fucking arsed, you know?

It was only when I sat down and had a cup of tea and a chat with Steve Harris round at his place in Leytonstone that I started really getting into it. I can still picture the two of us sitting there at his kitchen table, with him telling me about all these big plans he had for the band. He must have been convincing, 'cos he inspired me, and that took some doing, I can tell you. Right now, any number of rock fans are reading this, thinking, 'Christ, I'd have given me left bollock to be given a chance like that!'

Yeah, right, only I didn't have the faintest clue of the significance of it all, back then. It was a sign of how things were going to carry on, really.

Even after Steve's pep talk, I think it was only when we starting writing together, rehearsing properly and that, that I really began to think the band had the potential to be something a bit special. My first gig with them was at the Cart and Horses, and we also played some dates soon after at the infamous Ruskin Arms pub, which soon became a home from home for us, really.

I have to give credit where it's due, and say that it was Steve who had the dream at that point; you know, the vision of what could happen for Iron Maiden. Now, everybody thinks like that when they're in bands; they're all wanting to sell out stadiums and have number one albums and all that bollocks, but I have to say it was Steve who was the most committed and the most determined.

He has his faults, as we all do (me more than most!) but he

had the driving ambition, and he really put everything he had into Iron Maiden – it was always his baby really, and I guess it still is. If you cut Steve Harris in half – and the thought occurred to me a few times when I was in the band – he'd probably have 'Iron Maiden' running through him like a stick of rock!

He's a very single-minded, intense sort of bloke when he's got something in his sights – which is borne out by what he's achieved. He had the staying power and the balls to stick with it and see it through. We didn't always see eye to eye – in fact, we had a good few rows with each other towards the end – but we were good mates when we were starting out on this adventure, and there was a real sense of everyone being in on it together.

As I've said, it was definitely Steve's baby, and although we had weekly meetings to discuss plans and things, it definitely wasn't a democracy – more of a totalitarian state at times, in fact – but I suppose that was necessary to get things done without too much fucking about. I was probably one of the main dissidents, of course, but that'll probably come as no great surprise, either.

But when the two of us had our first chat back there in his little kitchen in Leytonstone, neither of us could even have begun to imagine what lay ahead.

CHAPTER 4

The band was starting to attract a really big following, as we were doing gigs up and down Britain, travelling the length of the country through the night, from venues in Scotland and Wales. A lot of people were beginning to discover who we were, and there was this big buzz around us, as more and more people got into this loud, exciting new band. They were loyal fans, too, often travelling miles themselves to come and see us.

The thing is, there was no one else really like us, so there was no one to compare us to. We were a one-off at that time, but it's funny how originality becomes the formula for others to follow, as more and more bands in the same style have cropped up in the years since.

Musically, we were streets ahead of the opposition. We were just in a different league. When I joined, I knocked the daft theatrics on the head and just concentrated on putting on a dynamite show for the fans. Now, we were like a prizefighter who's beaten all the bums and is ready to fight the big boys. Whatever we were doing, we must have been doing something right.

But we didn't half serve our apprenticeship. The road work in those early years was taking its toll on all of us, as we'd be arriving back in London at 5.00am, having stopped to chat with fans, and have a drink with them. I'll say this for us: as well as working hard on our songs and stage shows, we were a band who made every effort to be friends with our fans. We could have left straight after the gig, as a lot of bands did, but we took the time and trouble to get to know people, and it just helped us to become known, really.

It was only the fantastic receptions we were getting at these gigs that kept us going – the enthusiasm and excitement just pumped you full of adrenalin, and drove you on to do more and more.

Trouble was, we'd all be absolutely knackered for the next day, when we had to go to our day jobs. I worked for an oil company, re-shaping barrels before they were sent out to the depots across the country.

I was making really good money there, what with all the little fiddles I had going, such as disappearing down the pub once the boss had knocked off, and then claiming non-existent overtime from him.

I'd been doing the job for a while, and I quite liked it; compared to my other jobs it was a piece of piss, really. I'd been a trainee butcher on leaving school, and I'd been studying for my City and Guilds in that. I'd then worked as a slaughterman in Smithfield Meat Market in London, which I didn't really take to at all.

They were all just things to pass the time and earn a living wage, which is what most people do all their lives, I suppose.

While we're on the subject of work, it was my job at the oil company which was the real reason behind the fact that I was the only one in Iron Maiden with short hair. The others had hair well past their shoulders, and hundreds of people over the years have asked me if this was a fashion statement, an act of rebellion or simply me wanting to be different.

Well, sorry to disappoint you, but it was nothing so glamorous. I'd had long hair for a while, but because my hair is curly, I looked a bit like Marc Bolan. Then I got some green paint stuck in it at work, and I decided to cut it all off. So there you are, the real reason behind Paul Di'Anno's famous haircut!

One of the guitarists, Dave Murray, was working at Hackney Council during the early days of the band, and the two of us shared a squat in Battersea with our girlfriends for a while.

He'd give me a lift in to work after these long nights, when both of us could barely keep our eyes open. Trouble was, he had this old wreck of a car; a little death-trap of a Fiat, which wheezed along at 20mph, so it used to take us bloody ages to get anywhere. I don't want to sound ungrateful or anything, but the car was in such a state, it was bloody lethal. Davey opened the passenger door for me one day, and the bloody thing fell off in the road. Fucking hell.

Such everyday stuff sort of got lost when we began to be caught up on the express train that was the next few years. Things got so out of control so quickly that we were all swept along with it, all of life's little trivialities got brushed aside, and each event we encountered was more bizarre than the last.

There wasn't a single moment I could pinpoint when I realised that we'd hit the big time; it was more like a constant wave of excitement and anticipation, which just kept coming and coming.

I can't really describe those days in words – just to say that they were absolutely fucking unbelievable. For all the fame and recognition we were getting, for it to be happening to a bunch of young lads from East London just seemed to good to be true. The modern-day equivalent would be winning the Lottery every single week.

Typically, I just couldn't believe my luck, and I didn't dare believe it was actually happening, in case anybody came and tried to take it off me. I was always waiting for it to go wrong, to be honest – I just thought it couldn't last.

I've always been a take-it-as-it-comes person – my attitude is, 'If it happens, it happens.' I think you've got to look at it that way, otherwise you'd disappear up your own arsehole.

Both then and now, I get embarrassed when people recognise me and ask for my autograph. My mates always take the piss out of me for it, and I've learned to deal with it over the years, and it's not such a big deal. But back then, I was a young kid, not yet out of his teens and, for the first time in my life, I've got two bob in my pocket, and people know me from fucking Adam. Those two things alone are enough to fuck up your mind for good.

It's a funny old thing, actually, this fame business. For those who've never experienced it, it's difficult to describe. You may feel you haven't changed, you're the same person you were last week, last month, last year; but people's attitudes change towards you overnight. You're like, 'What the fuck happened to you? Where were you last year? Or the year before?'

Now, the attitude of my family and friends towards me has never changed – to them, I'll always be Paul, who makes a living poncing about on stage, making an absolute twat of himself (their words, not mine). My mum has never really felt it was a proper job, even when it began paying the bills; and the only time my dad went to one of our concerts, the poor sod complained of deafness for days afterwards. I send them my albums and stuff – I doubt very much if they listen to them, and there's no reason why they should. They've always been really supportive, and they just let me get on with it, really; you can't ask for more than that.

Although I can't remember the point when the band finally crossed over into the big time, I can pinpoint the exact time when Paul Di'Anno the rock fan turned into Paul Di'Anno the rock musician. It was like one of those moments on telly when Doctor Who changes from one incarnation to another.

I was sitting on a Tube train (going 'up West', as they say on *EastEnders*), travelling from the East End to Oxford Street. I was going to a gig at the Marquee Club – as a paying fan, mind you; I was just going to see the band that was on that night, along with hundreds of other punters.

At the time, Maiden was really starting to get recognised as a band with potential by those in the know – we hadn't actually been signed by a record label yet, but we were getting write-ups in *Sounds* magazine and playing everywhere we could, to bigger and bigger audiences.

With me was my girlfriend at the time, Debbie – we'd been seeing each other for a little while, but she didn't really know too much about the band I was in, or what I was doing. I'd been through a few girls in the very early days of the band, as I didn't really have enough free time to take them out, what with writing, rehearsing, gigging, travelling and all that. Plus, I didn't always have the energy, after that lot.

Anyway, we were sitting on the Tube, as I had many thousands of times before, just chatting away and minding our own business. When the train stops, a group of about 15 blokes get on, obviously headed for the same gig. They're all dressed in black leather jackets and blue jeans – just like me, in fact. They clock me, and immediately do a swift double-take. In no time, they've come up to me, introduced themselves, asked for autographs, found out where Maiden are next playing, and generally overrun me.

I didn't really know how to deal with it, to be honest; I'd never experienced anything like it before. Debbie thought it was great, to be going out with a rock star and all that bollocks, but I was just a bit embarrassed. I didn't really know what to do, so we just made our excuses, jumped off the train at the next stop, which was still three stops away from ours, and walked up the steps to the street, while they were all waving at us from the train. It was really awkward, and it wasn't a situation I'd ever envisaged.

We wandered around for a while, and we never actually got to the gig in the end, because I thought the same thing would happen when we got there. I think we just had a quick drink and went home. I was a bit spooked by it all, I suppose.

Even before my mug became well-known around London, though, I took some diabolical liberties with birds, I really did. There was one I was going out with who used to iron my shirts for me. Now, you can't really ask for too much more than that but, as usual, I took the piss. I was seeing this other girl at the same time, and Miss Shirt-Ironer saw us together near where she lived as she was travelling by on the upper deck of a bus. She had a bloody fit, and when I next came round to her place

4 4

for a cup of tea and a quick one on the sofa, I had some serious explaining to do.

Even back in those early days, I was already getting a bit of a reputation as the 'wild one' in the band, the one who embraced the rock 'n' roll lifestyle to the full. There were a few pub brawls, a few birds here and there, the odd wild party – nothing too heavy yet, but you could see at that stage which of us was going to get the most headlines.

There was a famous incident while Iron Maiden was doing some early recording work, when we found ourselves penniless, and short of a place to stay for the night.

This problem was solved when I pulled a nurse while we were out for the night, and she invited us all back to the nurses' quarters of the hospital where she worked.

Everybody's crashed out, and there's bodies strewn all over the gaff. Me and Florence Nightingale have got the bed to ourselves, and she's stripped off, ready for action. She had quite a horny little body, and she certainly went for it. They're a bit racy, some of these nurses, underneath all that starch. So I've turned her over, and I'm giving it to her from behind, and I hear these muffled giggles in the darkness.

Imagine the scene – there's me and her in the bed, rutting away doggy-style, and there's half-a-dozen long-haired herberts curled up on her floor, trying not to laugh.

The story has an unhappy ending, though, which in the many romanticised re-tellings of this legend, has never been revealed until now. The truth was, I caught a nasty dose of something from old Florence, which had to be treated, and, of course, I had to confess all to my girl back home. Honestly, you wouldn't expect that from a nurse, would you? The dirty bitch. No wonder the NHS is in such a fucking state.

Anyway, once my little rash had cleared up, we were able to concentrate again on the business of becoming major rock stars. People ask me now whether I could see the career path of Maiden back then, if there was any hint of the mind-blowing success that was to come.

I have to be honest and say I couldn't, I was just happy taking each day as it came. The thing was, I just couldn't understand the bloody hysteria everywhere we went. I mean, I'd been a rock fan for years – I'd been to see bands all over the place, but I'd never lost control of my senses and gone absolutely berserk like our fans were doing. They were going fucking crazy, it was getting quite scary sometimes.

At times, you'd wonder what you'd done to deserve it. I remember going on an early tour of Japan, where we played to packed houses every night. I'd never seen such fanaticism. The places we were playing were virtually exploding with the charged atmosphere being generated. I tried my best to take it all in my stride – I can remember having that youthful attitude, 'Well, I might be dead by the time I'm 22, so I'll just enjoy each day as much as I can ...' You have to remember that, back then, 22 seemed quite old.

Mind you, just when I was really getting into the rock star bit, I was brought sharply back to earth round at my mum's. I was a bit out of order, I think I'd complained about the tea she'd made or something, and I copped an unfortunate one – she slapped me round the side of the head. You see, you can be selling records and packing out gigs, but your mum can still give you a slap when you need one!

I think it's been a great help to me, having mates who I've known since junior school, and who've been with me through all of these times, and many more. They let you know if you're getting above yourself, and they keep your feet firmly on the ground.

I don't like the whole 'star' bit; I like being able to walk down the street without being recognised, but you have to realise that's not always possible. It's one of the sacrifices you're going to have to make. It's nice in many ways, having people come up to you, basically wanting to talk to you and be matey, but it ain't half a pain in the backside at times, especially if they catch you on an off-day, or if they're just being a twat for the sake of it. Then, they can wind you up something rotten.

Not long after the Tube incident, I was having a nice meal in Ilford with a bird, just a quiet dinner, nothing too flash. Next thing, this bloke on another table has spotted me and realised who I am. Before I can open my mouth, he's come over, introduced himself to us, pulled up a chair, and is half-way through his bleeding life-story.

I just lost the fucking plot at that point, I went berserk at him, telling him to fuck right off. I chucked a plateful of food at him and screamed in his face, calling him every name under the sun. I mean, I'm accessible most hours of the day and night, but my private life's my own, and yet he seemed to think he could walk right into it, as if he owned me. Wanker.

Another – more dangerous – development on this theme happened a few years later, when this mad bird shows up at the house where me and my girlfriend are living, and she announces that me and her have been having it away (we hadn't – she looked like a pig in a dress) and that we were meant for each other. You can imagine the reaction of my missus when she heard that little gem. The strangest thing is, we actually let her stay for a few days, because we didn't know what else to do with her.

All of these things added to the pressure of writing, recording and performing, so it was no wonder I started going off and doing silly things now and then, just to let off steam, really. It wasn't anything serious at that point; I used to take a bit of speed now and then, and I liked going out for a few drinks with the lads, but it wasn't really a situation which was out of control. I just used to enjoy myself when I could, and that's all there was to it, really.

I think the lads may have started to get a bit worried when I'd go out on a bender and get into a bit of bother, but that was just the way I was, you know? I'd let off a bit of steam, have a few drinks and generally act as if I was taking part in a 24-hour party, which I honestly felt I was.

I'd have still got into scrapes if I was a bleedin' dustman, but I just thought that being a singer in Britain's hottest new rock band gave me a licence to do stuff like that. I felt like it was expected of me. I think as well, my career as a professional singer was giving me the biggest thrill of my life when I was on stage, so I just felt the rest of my existence ought to live up to it.

By far the biggest rush to date came when we played seven nights at the famous Marquee Club, the place I'd visited so often as a fan. But whereas before I'd queued up as a punter, now I was ushered round the back as a performer. All the shows were sold out, and the audiences just couldn't get enough of us – they went fucking crazy like we'd never seen before, the whole thing was just getting totally out of control now.

Inside the club, it was like a bloody sauna, with all those hot bodies pressing forward towards the small stage, and the five of us going at it hammer and tongs up there. At one point during one of the shows, I remember putting my hand up on one of the walls, and it was just sweating moisture because of the incredible heat and energy. Amazing days.

People always ask me how that feels – to rush out on to the stage, when the music starts up, the lights go up, and the crowd are whipped into a frenzy by the atmosphere.

My simple answer is – it makes you shit yourself and throw your guts up. Many's the time I've thought I was actually going to puke, as we're about to go out on stage, especially when I was younger. You get this feeling in the pit of your stomach, especially when you heard the crowd baying out there, and you can feel yourself start to retch.

I used to have a real fear of actually vomiting on stage, just out of pure fright. You're worried about fucking up, you're worried they're not going to like you, you're worried the whole bloody thing's going to go wrong. It's only during the fourth or fifth song that you can start to relax and really get into it, knowing it's going all right.

I wasn't alone in that; the other guys in Maiden used to get the shits as well before a gig. I can remember Steve having to go to the bloody toilet all the time in the first few years of our career, just cacking himself at the prospect of getting out there in front of all those people. I think he's probably got over it now – or at least I hope he has, for the others guys' sake – but I still have a vision of him backstage at some venue, calling out from behind the khazi door, pleading for more bog roll.

When reports in *Sounds* used to call the atmosphere at our gigs 'charged' and 'electric', well, to me, they were 'fucking terrifying'.

Mind you, when it all went right, well, that was something else altogether. Those moments when the band was really in overdrive, when the entire crowd was in the palm of our hand ... well, I can visualise those as if they were yesterday, and they will be with me for the rest of my life. I will never ever forget them.

As I've said, it's like a deeply religious experience, or witnessing the birth of your child; the emotion just floods out of you. It's the best drug I've ever experienced, bar none. To have that power, to have people hysterically screaming your name, it's impossible to understand if you've never done it yourself. Anybody who says they're not affected in some way by that is a fucking liar.

One of my greatest memories of this type of experience happened on stage at the Reading Rock festival in the early Eighties. We'd been asked to appear on the bill there, which was a great honour for us so early in our career, and we were both nervous and excited.

In fact, shortly before the big day, I ran into a bird I hadn't seen for a while, and we got chatting. I mentioned the Festival, and she said she'd like to go. Well, call me Flash Harry if you like, but I told her to pack a bag and get herself down there for the weekend, and I'd come across with some backstage passes.

Sure enough, she comes down with me, and she gets the shock of her life when she discovers I'm in one of the bands playing there. I could tell she was mightily impressed, which was a real bonus, as I had plans of getting into her knickers before the weekend was over. (Yeah, of course I managed it – did you really need to ask?)

Well, she picked a good time to come and see us, because we played the best fucking set of our lives that day, and I felt like bloody Superman. It was just the best day in the world for us. At the end of the set, when we were playing the final song, darkness began to fall, and all these thousands of lighters went up in the air, you could just see them for miles.

It was the most emotional occasion I'd ever known. I looked over at Steve, and he looked back across the stage at me; and I swear if we'd have looked at each other a moment longer we'd have both burst into tears then and there, in front of all of those people. I felt absolutely fantastic, I can't say any more than that. I can remember thinking to myself, 'Fucking hell ... I'm a rock star!'

This idea – which had once been laughable – certainly seemed to turn into reality when we embarked on our first tour of America. Now, as well as being a huge record-buying market to conquer, the States is just the stuff of dreams for any would-be rocker – the limos, the groupies, the parties; I couldn't bloody wait. I was just gagging to get over there and put it about. I was like a kid going on his first school trip.

As it happened, I was to be disappointed. I didn't really take to America at all on that first tour, if I'm honest. I thought the people were loud and over-confident, you know, the big 'I am' – it was a bit of a culture shock, I suppose. I can only think it was all a bit much to take in.

When I say culture, I suppose I mean the lack of it. I can remember thinking that the only thing they had which remotely resembled culture was hamburgers. I think – like a lot of British people – I'd adopted this sort of blinkered patriotism which affects people when they're away from their native country. I bemoaned the lack of good beer (for the record, American beer is gassy shit, OK) and jellied eels, so I'd already written it off in my mind.

That's not to say it wasn't a mind-blowing experience. To be made a fuss of, to be driven here and there, to have women fighting over you, it's all a bit much for a bunch of young lads from East London, to be honest, and we were totally mind-fucked by it all.

It was the first time I'd seen New York, and the skyscrapers and other sights just bowled me over in themselves. I have to say, and this may surprise some people, that I've always been a huge fan of European architecture. I think we have some of the most beautiful buildings anywhere in the world in cities like London, Paris and Rome, but being in New York for the first time, the sheer size and scale of a place I'd only ever seen on films and TV just took my breath away.

Later, I got to know places like Los Angeles, and I began to warm to America, and see it how it really is. Americans are always being told they're the greatest nation in the world, and you'll see precious little international news on their TV channels, so it's perhaps forgivable that they do tend to come across as arseholes sometimes, but most of them are basically OK.

In fact, the more I got to know the States, the more I liked it. I immediately warmed more to the Southern States, and the people down there, but the thing that really won me over was the fact that you can hear rock music being played 24 hours a day on radio stations, TV stations and God knows where else; it's a vast improvement on Britain, where the media don't really give a shit about it. Over there, you've got a real musical freedom, with 50-year-old Grateful Dead fans walking around and not giving a shit. In the UK, the music you like is more of a fashion statement, which says a lot about us, really.

The only drawback is the parents' groups like the one headed by Tippa Gore, wife of failed Presidential candidate Al Gore. Some of them are the dried-up old cunts who burn Iron Maiden records, and claim we're devil worshippers. (Keep on burning 'em, sweethearts, you're making me a fucking fortune. By the way – nice arse!)

But back then, being a happening young band, everybody was practically crawling up our arseholes the moment we got there. They showed us around, took us to do interviews, store signings, public appearances and all that sort of thing.

We had the five-star treatment, and if I said I didn't enjoy every bloody minute of it, I'd be a fucking liar. Besides, you wouldn't believe me anyway, would you?

We were making lots of new friends, doing some really good shows and making a name for ourselves with a totally new audience. Although it was still comparatively early days, we were fast becoming an international band, something we hadn't yet begun to realise.

But as we did interview after interview, I began to suss that people were really taking notice. I realised we were on the right road to really carving out a career for ourselves, but I was far too naïve back then to realise just where that road might end up. (If I had known, I think I'd have turned back!)

I think I was a bit suspicious of it all, to be honest. Once again, I thought things were going too well, that they were just too good to be true, that this sort of gig doesn't happen to a kid from East London, and that all these people were after something. There's no such thing as a free lunch, and all that.

In the meantime, though, I was finding new forms of entertainment. At some point during the tour, I was invited to a party in Los Angeles at the home of a famous film director – I won't say who he is, for obvious reasons. When I got to this bloody great plush drum in the Hollywood Hills, there were gorgeous women practically hanging from the rafters, champagne on tap, and about 20 bowls full to the brim with cocaine, scattered about like those little trays you get in Chinese restaurants.

I was sitting there in this huge soft leather armchair, two blonde tarts by the side of me, looking at me with these huge 'fuck me' eyes, and I've got several lines of coke all chopped on a mirror in front of me. In those situations, all my needs are catered for, and I'm a pig in shit.

*   *   *

They must have really liked us over there, because the shows we were playing were selling out all over the place. America has always welcomed Iron Maiden and its music with open arms, they really seem to get off on the full-blooded energy and aggression of heavy metal music, and that's how it was, even back then.

I think if you're false, if you're putting on an act, people will work you out pretty quickly; but we were the real deal, and we played every gig as if it was the most important one in the world. Certainly, each audience could tell we fucking meant it.

Of course, I'd let it all go to my head a little bit and, by this time, I was a bloody Metal God up there, strutting my stuff in my black leathers every night. I was getting a buzz out of it like never before, just giving it your all on stage, and then driving for miles on to the next gig. It was a big adventure, and I drank it all in.

People were treating me differently as well. They respect success above all else in America; it's not like Britain, where inbred retards get a seat in the House of Lords just because their great-great grandmother got fucked by the local landowner.

I remember one meeting at a record company or something,

there was this bird there who was some sort of executive type. She was good-looking in a Wall Street sort of way; she had really short, dark hair, and wore these small steel-rimmed glasses which tried – but failed – to disguise the most startling pair of powder-blue eyes I'd ever seen.

I'm in this meeting, and she's talking to me about sales figures, market reach, demographics or some such shit. While she's going on, I'm miles away, daydreaming about her peeling off her City suit to reveal a lacy basque and silk stockings.

It was like one of those fantasy sequences when the posh bird decides she fancies a bit of rough, and she takes off her glasses, hitches up her skirt, and shags the handyman.

Well, of course (as if you hadn't guessed) that's exactly what happened. We went out to a club that night, and me and her snuck off to the bathroom together. Far from being the Miss Prim that I'd had her down as, she snorted up a few lines of coke with me, like she'd been born to it. When we're both coked up to the eyeballs, we squeeze into one of the stalls in the Ladies' bogs, and as I close my eyes and thank God for what he's done for me, this high-flying yuppie tart kneels down on the tiled floor in her stockings and high heels, unzips my jeans, and gives me one of the most expert blow-jobs I'd ever had.

I remember I couldn't help thinking that the music business wasn't a bad line of work to be in, as she hastily took the whole length of my cock in her lipsticked mouth, and flicked my bell-end with her tongue. Like the best ones do, she held the base of my dick with her hand, while she moved her head up and down the length of it. I came so hard I saw fucking stars, and her mouth was pumped full of warm spunk. She winked at me, and swallowed hard. Obviously a classy lady.

I turned her around and hiked her skirt up over her arse, revealing these very exotic black suspenders and a tiny G-string. After ripping the G-string aside, I put my cock up between the cheeks of her arse as she bent forward over the toilet bowl.

As I started pumping away, I looked at myself in the mirror and gave my reflection a cheery grin. Perhaps America wasn't such a bad place after all.

Such distractions aside, some of the rumours started about now, saying that I was drinking too much, becoming unreliable, going out every night after the show and causing trouble.

OK, I went out after shows and had a few drinks after hours; it was a way of unwinding and dealing with the pressure. Besides, anybody who didn't like it could just fuck off.

I went out, got pissed, spewed up over the hotel bathroom, got into the odd fight, that was it. It was just the way I was, but I think the other guys were really starting to notice, and I think it began to worry them. It was then that I started becoming 'a problem'. Certainly, I was putting the booze away, and I was getting into coke and speed in a big way. To me, it was just my way of dealing with the microscope we were all living under.

Me and Dave Murray used to be drinking pals when we were on tour, but we didn't go over the top when we had a show the next day and, at that stage, I didn't drink during the day leading up to a gig. Certainly, in comparison with some of my escapades in later years, I was like Mahatma fucking Gandhi.

A far greater problem at that time was the women, who seemed to throw themselves at us in droves, everywhere we went. I'll go into my exploits with groupies in juicy detail later on in the book, but let's just say I was never short of company.

Often I'd go to my hotel room to find girls lying all over the bed, waiting for me.

I'd slide into bed, and I'd immediately disappear under a pile of naked flesh, all kissing, stroking, sucking – you name it. I'd be called upon to service all these tarts, one after the other. As the others watched and waited for their turn, I'd be fucking away all night. Sometimes I was so knackered I could hardly get out of bed in the morning, but I felt my nation's pride was at stake – I was shagging for England, after all.

Quite often, I'd forget where I was, or what I'd been doing. I'd wake up with a pounding headache, a deadly hangover, cold vomit stuck hard to my face and, to top it all off, I'd have a pair of bare tits pressed up against me, or I'd be staring at some spread-eagled beaver.

Apart from getting loads of fanny, though, there wasn't much room for arsing about in the military-style campaign that was our quest for world domination. I think I know what Adolf Hitler must have felt like, invading place after place, conquering it, and then going on to the next. The pressure was on us, so it wasn't only in the bedroom that I had to perform.

We'd always go out on stage in hostile mood, really psyched up for a fight, like we really had something to prove. The thing was, we wouldn't let up, even when we had them right where we wanted them. Song after song after song. Bang, bang, bang. We performed like our lives depended on it, and the guys were playing together like a dream, tighter than a duck's arse. It was a triumphant tour, and it really put Iron Maiden on the map for ever.

I celebrated on one of the last nights by drinking a full bottle of brandy, straight down, for a bet. As a direct result of this, I projectile-vomited all over the polished mirror wall of a top New York nightclub. I kicked a table over and smashed a load of glasses, before throwing some chairs over the top of the bar, smashing all the bottles and optics. I was surrounded by huge bouncers, who fought me to the ground, before chucking me out on to the pavement. They were all lined up outside the door to stop me getting back in, and I stood there screaming abuse and death-threats at them, before I heard the sound of police sirens in the distance. Someone had called the cops. It was time to go home.

Once again, though, if I needed bringing back down to earth after this fantastic tour, I only had to look as far as my mum and dad, who'd taken the bleeding liberty of moving house while I was away!

I got back to London, full of wind and piss about what I'd done and what we'd all been up to, and they'd bloody well gone! The flat was empty! For months, I'd been waited on hand and foot like I was God's gift, and I've come back like the prodigal son, and my folks have fucking moved! What the fuck was going on?

An old dear down the street told me they'd moved out, and gave me a bit of paper they'd left her to give me with their new address on it. The bloody cheek – I couldn't fucking believe it.

If people were now treating me as a celebrity, I certainly wasn't acting like one. There was no poncing around with some supermodel tart on my arm, or attending glittering showbiz premières. No, my nights were spent in places like the Royal Standard in Walthamstow, which would continue to be my local. They all knew me there, and they couldn't care less if you were the lead singer of Iron Maiden, or the guy who emptied the bins on the council estate, they treated you just the same. That is, they took the piss out of you from the minute you walked in the door.

Just like my family would help keep my feet on the ground while all this stuff was going on out in the big wide world, so my mates would help me to keep things in perspective as well. We didn't talk about record contracts, personal appearances or album sales; topics of discussion were far more weighty – whether the barmaid needed a good shagging, if the beer was off, or who West Ham were playing on Saturday.

In later years, I found myself still hanging around my old haunts, still keeping in touch with old mates. It was a way of keeping one foot in the East End, I suppose, even if I was living in an apartment in LA at the time, and was only passing through on a flying visit.

I met Graham Bath, one of the guitarists I'd go on to work with, at one of those haunts, while a few other faces from the London rock scene would also put in an appearance from time to time.

Graham remembers playing a gig there with the band he was with, Persian Risk, when he was a bit under the weather. (It turns out he'd been up all night screwing the wife of a very famous rock star ...)

He says that he was a bit in awe when the lead singer of Iron Maiden strode in beside him in the bogs and started having a piss. I told him he looked like a sack of shit (I realise now he looks like that pretty much all the time) and gave him some coke to perk him up.

Graham was also around to witness some of the legendary nights we used to have out that way; we'd start off at the Standard, and then go on to a club called Oscar's. These evenings would be full-on affairs, with enough booze flowing to sink a battleship.

A few mates of mine around there are bikers and, more often than not, we'd pile back to one of their gaffs, where we would just do stuff you wouldn't believe. Gallons and gallons of drink, every drug under the sun, and some of the dirtiest women you've ever come across. This would go on until six or seven in the morning, when the whole place would look like a giant buffalo had shat on it, with all these motionless bodies strewn across the floor, surrounded by vomit, piss, spunk and God knows how many empty bottles.

I remember one particular night, we've gone back to somebody's house, and there are all these bikers around, and we're pissing it up with them. Everybody's absolutely out of their skulls, and there's this one woman in the thick of it who's just doing everything to everybody.

She's stripped off her T-shirt, jeans, bra and pants, and she's squatting there in the middle of this crowded living-room, stark naked. That would have been bad enough, but they've got hold of this wine bottle, and they're sticking the neck of it up her fanny and up her arse, just fucking her with it as she's crouching there.

And she's loving it — I mean really getting off on it. This bloke is thrusting it in and out of her, and twisting it around inside her, and she's bobbing up and down, moaning with pleasure. The top of the bottle is disappearing up this woman's cunt, and coming back out again, as she gets more and more excited, and starts to come.

So I'm slumped on the sofa watching this, pissed as a cunt, when this bloke beckons me across, and hands me the bottle. He staggers out of the room, and I'm left there like a spare one at a wedding, waggling this bottle around in this woman's arse. She never missed a beat – I doubt if she even noticed it had changed hands.

She came so hard and so loud I thought she'd had a heart-attack. She almost broke the bloody bottle with her thighs – I was well impressed.

Then she ended up shagging a load of them, one after the other. All these bikers are bending her over the settee in turn, and giving it to her up the arse, and she's wailing and moaning like before. The strange thing is, nobody else in the room – apart from the particular bloke who's poking her – is paying the slightest bit of attention. They're all still drinking and chatting away. Meanwhile, she changes hands like they're passing round the bloody crisps.

Fuck me, the sights you see ...

CHAPTER 5

Some of the blokes we had in the band have become household names, playing on the albums and doing the big tours. The others sort of fell by the wayside, especially during the early years, when we used to go through musicians like a labrador goes through bog rolls.

You've heard about my predecessors Paul Mario Day and Den Wilcock, and there are countless others, but there's one guy in particular I remember, and only then because I bumped into him a while back.

He was a drummer, and he used to go by the name of Ron Rebel, believe it or not. I don't know if that was his real name, but I had to turn away from him when he introduced himself to me again, because I was laughing so much.

I think he actually started the band with Steve Harris, way back at the dawn of time, when the earth was still cooling, so he sort of became Iron Maiden's Pete Best, really. Should have stuck with it, old son!

Dennis Stratton was the guitarist on our first album, and he was a really good guitarist, but he parted company after some personal strife between him and Steve. There was a daft rumour going round that he was sacked for listening to The Eagles – I'm pretty sure that's not true, I just think he and Steve didn't see eye to eye, so he had to go. I didn't really know the ins and outs of it, and I wasn't really that interested in knowing, to be honest.

Our paths have crossed a few times since then, and he's always been OK to me. We didn't really have that much to do with each other while we were both in the band, as we were recording at different times. He was a bit older than the rest of us, I seem to remember, but he was and still is a great guitarist.

Before him, we had two guys on guitar – Tony Parsons and Paul Nelson – but I can't really remember too much about them, or what happened to them. They could be playing an acoustic version of 'Wrathchild' outside King's Cross Station, for all I know.

There was another bloke called Doug Sampson, whose drumming can be heard on our famous demo, *The Soundhouse Tapes*; but he left after a while, too, which is when we met Clive Burr.

Now Clive is that very rare animal – he's both a phenomenal musician and a fucking great bloke. I love him to death, and when he walked into our rehearsals at a studio in Bethnal Green, we knew he was the man for us. If there was ever any doubt, he told us he was from Manor Park, so he was one of us all right.

I laugh about it now, because although Clive is very much

one of us, there was a time when we thought he might actually be one of them!

No hard evidence or anything, you understand, but he was always poncing around, brushing his hair and stuff; and, well, you wonder, don't you? So, diplomatic as ever, the whole band sat him down in the dressing room one day and said to him, as sensitively as we knew how, 'Look, Clive, it don't matter to us if you are or you're not, it won't make any difference at all; but come on, are you a poof or not?'

He replied in manly style, 'Fuck off, am I!' and so our curiosity was satisfied. He was soon to provide solid proof of his manliness by going out with an absolutely stunning girl, so we all ended up being bloody jealous of the bloke we'd once thought was a shirt-lifter!

Clive got to play on our first official album, called simply *Iron Maiden*, which was recorded at Battery Studios in West London. The producer was a guy called Will Malone, who'd worked on Mike Oldfield's *Tubular Bells*; and while the production wasn't completely to my liking, nevertheless the energy and enthusiasm of those early playing days really comes across on the record.

We'd signed to EMI, after approaches by several labels, which was a bit of a thrill in itself, to be honest, having record companies chasing us. We'd appeared on the Metal for Muthas compilation album (good name, right?) and there was the feeling at the time that we were reaching new heights, making more and more people sit up and listen.

While we're talking about people we've known and loved, I have to say right here that a bunch of guys who helped us more than anybody could ever have expected were a band we supported on one of our very early tours – Kiss.

Now, the Gods of Rock 'n' Roll were just about the biggest rock act America had ever produced – they were like rock music's royal family over there. Records, films, cartoons, toys ... you name it, those black-and-white painted faces could be found on it.

Obviously, we knew all about them, and although their music wasn't really my cup of tea, it was just the biggest break of our lives to be given the chance to go on the road with them, because they were just about the best in the bloody business at what they did.

Entertainment was the name of the game, and they had fucking great lights, flames, fire-eating, explosions, you name it. And there's us, with just our guitars and long hair, opening the show for them every night. It wouldn't have seemed like a match made in heaven if you looked at it on paper to be honest; you'd have to say the styles of music were quite different. But I think they were impressed by our energy and our attitude – perhaps we reminded them of themselves when they were younger, just starting out.

We could have been forgiven for being in awe of these rock gods as they lived and worked with us, but I wasn't really the type to be in awe of anybody; once again, I just got on with it. I maintained this coolness over the next few years when I met guys like Robert Plant and Jimmy Page of Led Zeppelin; but when it came to people like Joey Ramone, who was a personal hero of mine, well I just about fucking shit myself.

Then, one day on that tour, I realised the world had finally gone mad. I saw Gene Simmons, the Kiss bass player – one of the richest and most famous rock stars in the Western world – wearing a fucking Iron Maiden T-shirt. That was it for me, the lunatics had officially taken over the asylum. I just felt nothing else could happen to surprise me any more. If a bunch of

Martians had landed backstage, playing 'Sanctuary' on Walkmans, I wouldn't have turned a hair.

It was a typical gesture of the living legend that is Gene, and just goes to show why the great ones are so great. When you're a support band, you'll often get treated like the worst piece of dog-shit that ever stuck to somebody's shoe. The sound – perfect in sound-checks – will become mangled and distorted, sabotaged by the headliners' technicians. Lights will mysteriously disappear or be out of action. You'll be given a foot of space between the drum riser and the lip of the stage, so the bass drum is half-way up the singer's arse – these are things that can and do happen. The reason, of course, is jealousy.

A bunch of old dinosaurs don't want a bunch of young upstarts stealing their glory – it's like the male lion realising some young herbert has got in amongst his harem, and the bastard's shagging his way through them, one by one. So they do what they can to fuck you up.

It's a compliment of sorts, I suppose, but it pisses you off no end at the time, and often leads to aggro towards the end of a tour, when everyone's getting on each other's tits anyway. (I'm not going to say which bands did that to us – but they know who they are.)

Kiss, though, were the exact opposite – they couldn't have done more for us. All the space we needed – it was done. They even said we could use any lights we wanted from their mega armoury (apart from the Kiss logo, obviously, but that wouldn't have been much good to us, anyway) and every other type of help and support was laid on for us. I really felt we were in the Premier Division when we were on the road with those guys – they were just the most professional people I'd ever seen.

And when they walked on to that stage, well, there was no doubt why they'd become one of the biggest rock acts of all time. They played like demons, and the show they put on was just stunning – not a bum note, nor a stray light. Professionalism down to a tee. They say there's a reason that the greats are great, and Kiss were the living proof of that.

When the make-up came off as well, they just made us feel part of the family. Despite us still being wet behind the ears in terms of the music industry, they were friendly, chatty; just good fun to be with, and I loved them for it.

Gene, in particular, really took us under his wing, and while Paul Stanley was often away doing interviews, he was a real laugh as well. Their drummer, Eric Carr (who sadly passed away a few years ago) was also a top bloke, and we still owe them all a huge debt of gratitude for everything they did for us. Believe me, when Gene Simmons gives you advice, you'd do well to listen, even if you're a Cockney Jack-the-Lad who thinks he knows everything.

There's always one exception, of course, and that was their guitarist, Ace Frehley. Now Ace's problems have been well documented, and I think he's got himself sorted out now; but at the time he was a bit of a wild man. In fact, when I look back now, he reminds me of what I would soon become.

He strutted around everywhere with this enormous bodyguard beside him. I saw the bodyguard smack a guy in the face in the middle of a crowded nightclub once, when Frehley had gotten himself involved in a bloody great fight. (Like I said, I must have learnt a few tricks from him, without realising it ...)

Another successful early tour was with Judas Priest, another top heavy metal band, whom we accompanied on their British and European tours. I was a big fan of theirs, and it was another great gig for us, putting us in front of the very people we needed to impress.

Unfortunately, there was a bit of a falling-out with them somewhere down the line, when they took umbrage over remarks that I was alleged to have made in the press, saying we were going to blow them off stage. I know I got the blame for it (as usual) but I maintain to this day that I never said any such thing – OK guys?

Anyway, it was a great tour while it lasted; and, once again, we were giving it 110 per cent on stage every night, playing like we meant every note. All of these great tours and fantastic opportunities wouldn't have been possible without one man in particular – our manager, Rod Smallwood. He came on board in the prehistoric days, when we recorded the *Soundhouse Tapes* demo, and he remains at the helm of the mighty Maiden machine to this day.

Now I'm not trying to flatter the guy, because he wouldn't stand for it, but as well as being the best rock manager in the business, he's also an absolutely top bloke; and we all respect the hell out of him. I've bumped into him a few times over the years, once at the famous Rainbow Bar and Grill in Los Angeles, where we had a good drink and a chat. Like with the others, it's always friendly, there's no animosity.

If there's anybody with good reason to get the hump with me, it's Rod, as I must have caused him more arse-ache and aggravation than all the other guys in Maiden put together, but, amazingly enough, he still speaks to me!

Back then, Rod virtually became the sixth member of Iron Maiden really, keeping us all on the straight and narrow (no mean feat in my case). It was him who really put the band on the businesslike footing which was essential in becoming one of the most successful rock acts of all time. I'd compare him to Peter Grant, the manager of Led Zeppelin, or Brian Epstein, who managed the Beatles – that was the sort of influence he had on us. He was far better even than someone like Malcolm McLaren, who often uses gimmicks – Rod was too good for that.

Having said that, my first meeting with him wasn't exactly an unqualified success. He arrived at a gig in London to see us, only to witness me being arrested for possessing an offensive weapon, and hauled off in handcuffs by the cops. They'd searched us looking for drugs, found a knife on me, and all hell broke loose. The incident has become part of Maiden legend, and is illustrated in detail in the next chapter, but I didn't half feel a twat at the time.

While I was down the station being charged (I got a small fine, although it wasn't the first time I'd been in trouble with the police), the band had to carry on without me. God knows what Rod must have thought. He'd only taken charge of the band that night, and Di'Anno's had a run-in with the law already.

When Steve asked him later if he was going to manage the band, he's said to have replied in typical Smallwood fashion, 'Fucking right I am!' He probably felt he needed to keep me out of trouble ... some hope!

He took charge of all the media coverage and really helped to raise our profile in the right way. About the only error he ever made, as far as I could make out, was hiring a publicist to keep the rock mags up to date with what we were doing.

Now this may have been a good idea in principle, but there was one small flaw. One of the blokes he hired was a twat-and-a-half, who got paid about eight grand to feed some half-arsed stories to the press. A classic example of this was the one where I'm supposed to have sat on a pub jukebox while Blondie's 'Heart of Glass' was playing, leading to 'Arse of Glass' headlines. I've no memory whatsoever of doing that, but who would have cared if I did? I ask you! If that really was true, I'd have shat on the bloody thing, wouldn't I?

Another thing Rod did way back was set up building society accounts for us, into which was paid a weekly wage of about £120. This was before we started earning mega-bucks, and it meant that we couldn't go and do something silly, or get massively in debt before we'd even got started. Once again, it was the right thing to do.

Mind you, it was quite a pay cut for me to be honest, because I'd been earning a small fortune at the oil company, what with all the little scams I had going. But it goes to show that rock bands aren't earning millions from day one, as people think. The reality is, it takes at least a year or so for royalties you've earned to filter through from record sales, so you don't get rich overnight by any means.

If you've written a song that's successful, you get a good income from it over quite a few years, as it mounts up. This is why the twats in all these boy bands today are going to find themselves in deep shit after a few years, because most of them wouldn't know the way to hold an instrument (missus!), much less write a fucking song.

It really pisses me off to see good bands and good musicians kept out of the charts and off the radio by talentless cunts who stand around like retards, miming the words to a song which some other twat wrote for them. As for all these endless bloody love songs they sing, well, don't make me fucking laugh. They're all about ten years old! Their voices haven't broken! They wouldn't know a woman's cunt from her armpit!

Guys, if you can't sing, you can't write and you can't play – get out of the fucking industry and don't come back, that's my advice.

CHAPTER 6

Another thing everybody asks me about is the goings-on while rock bands are on tour. Is it really as wild as it's cracked up to be? Well, for most people, it isn't. It can get pretty boring, to be honest – just an endless round of hotel, backstage area, stage, tour-bus, hotel. Over and over ... and over.

If you're Paul Di'Anno, though, there's always some mischief to be made, someone to wind up, something to drink, somewhere to destroy, and so on. You sort of make your own entertainment, if you know what I mean.

I've heard all the 'wild man' rumours about me shagging groupies five at a time, snorting lines of coke and swigging vodka like it was Tizer; and well, I hope you know me well enough by now to know that simply isn't true. I'm strictly a Jack Daniel's man.

I laugh when I hear some of the wild stories about me, usually because they don't even touch the sides of what really went on. It's usually the case that the real story is far worse than what's been printed, but I suppose a lot of stuff I've done isn't really fit to print, anyway. They say truth's stranger than fiction, and it's certainly true in my case. If only the rumour-mongers knew what they were missing out on!

While I can't always recall chapter and verse on who said what or did what to who back then, some of the sights, sounds and smells from that era are still etched in my memory, and they'll stay with me for ever.

On one of our very early signing sessions in America, I managed to disgrace myself in spectacular style, much to the annoyance of the tour promoters. We'd done one of these in-store sessions a few days before, in Cleveland, and it was a fucking disaster. I think the dates had got mixed up or something and there was this almighty cock-up. It was like that scene in *Spinal Tap* where they're all sitting round looking at each other. I don't think we even had an album deal at the time, so no one knew who the fuck we were.

Anyway, on this second date, which was in New York, I'd been out the previous night on the mother of all benders. If I hadn't drunk it, I'd snorted it or screwed it. I'd gone fucking wild in the Big Apple, discovered some exotic drinks I'd never tasted before, and even-more-exotic women who did things I'd never even heard of before. I can remember being carried out of one club, being sick in another, and ending up screwing some tart up against a wall in an alleyway somewhere, still half-covered with puke. Beyond that, the details are lost, I'm afraid. Trust me, it was a good night.

So I've gone back to the hotel at about seven in the morning, pissed as a cunt, and to say I'm not at my best the next day would be a bit like saying Leyton Orient are outsiders for the Champions League.

I spent the entire day vomiting over anything and anyone that came near me, which isn't ideal when you want the singer of the band you're promoting to meet the fans and sign records. The other guys are chatting and signing away, and I've got my head down the bog. I spewed and spewed, until there was nothing left to come up. I was chucking up blood, it was so bad. Then I just passed out on the floor. Bloody hell – no wonder they used to get so pissed off with me.

Then there was the time in a Huddersfield hotel, when I 'married' our guitarist, Dave Murray. Now don't get me wrong – me and Dave were just good mates (I remember we used to call him 'Smurf' for some reason) and besides, he wouldn't be my type even if he was that way. For some reason, though, he thought it would be a great laugh to 'borrow' a wedding dress which had been on display in the hotel, and try it on. As far as I know, the ceremony went ahead, but I can't remember much else about my 'big day'. Always good for a laugh, Dave, especially after a few sherbets.

I ended that particular evening by destroying a carefully-constructed display of wedding gear; I think the hotel was having some sort of wedding exhibition or something. In my pissed state, I smashed the shit out of it, taking the expensively-dressed mannequins and throwing them off the top balcony, so they shattered into tiny pieces on the stone floor below. The hotel management were so pissed off about it, they called the police. Once again, I was forced into hiding.

Dave Murray and myself were among the allied forces in the guerilla warfare which broke out at many hotels where we stayed, when opposing sides would take up arms (well, fire extinguishers) and go to war. They were the type that spray out a thick mist – highly-efficient, and deadly at close range.

'Course, I was in the thick of these bouts of civil unrest, leading my troops into battle. There was one time, though, at a hotel in Berlin, when I was forced to beat a retreat into my room to take cover from an ambush, when an enemy 'sniper' sprayed the bloody thing under the door, as part of a rearguard action. Bastard!

This stuff went all over everything – the furniture, carpets, everything was sprayed white. It was a really posh suite, and practically everything in it was totally destroyed. I think the bill for the damage came to about £10,000. To say our manager, Rod, was not best pleased would be a bit of an understatement. To say he went fucking loopy would be somewhere nearer the mark.

People who run hotels must think that rock musicians are like some sort of animals. They must spend their whole time clearing up shit, piss, vomit and cum from their five-star rooms, and each time they probably think, 'Fucking hell – never again!'

We also used to have fun and games with these little cap-guns, that shot dried peas. We'd bought a few of these somewhere, and used to amuse ourselves by stalking each other through hotel lobbies, airport lounges and God knows where else, playing commandos. We were like bloody kids with these things, getting on everyone's tits.

The damage I caused with mine was unbelievable – I was a crack shot, sort of like the Green Beret of the band. I could cause havoc in a crowded hotel lobby with a single shot, because if you let off anything that sounds like a gun anywhere in America, everybody within a half-mile radius immediately shits themselves.

There was one venue we played – I think it was in the West Country somewhere, – and the band were sound-checking, to make sure everything was OK for that night's gig. I can't be arsed with all that bollocks, so I got an airgun I had with me, and I ran around the empty auditorium, shooting up all the strip lights overhead. I was running around yelling and firing away, and the guys all shat themselves, ducking down on the stage like they were under attack. As they cowered behind the speakers, I was still running around the hall, with broken glass and light bulbs shards raining down around me. Funnily enough, I got a right bollocking for that, too.

One of our earliest gigs as a band was also marred by my bad behaviour, and that was a show we played at Glasgow University on the *Metal for Muthas* tour. Because they didn't have proper dressing rooms for us to get changed in (the hardships we had to suffer in those days!) they unwisely gave us the students' common room to get togged up in. Bad mistake.

Luckily there weren't any students in it at the time, 'cos someone of learning would have been fucking appalled at the bloody stupidity that followed. Me and the guitarist from the support band, Rob Angelo, had a bottle-throwing competition, which is just as dangerous as it sounds.

They'd left some bottles of beer for us, so I'm pretty pissed already, and I thought it would be a great laugh to throw the empty bottles at a nearby television set, to see if I could put one through the screen. When I eventually succeeded, there was a hell of a smash, broken glass everywhere and a beer bottle languishing inside the telly, which made me piss myself all the more. Silly fucker.

Then I turned to the lights that were hanging from the ceiling, and started heaving bottles at them. They were slightly harder to hit, but several got smashed once I'd got my aim, with the result that there's now a huge carpet of broken glass all over the floor.

With a few more drinks inside me, I then got completely out of control. I went on a rampage through the University, smashing every fucking thing I could lay my hands on. They called the police, and their security guards were chasing me, but I didn't give a shit – I just ran away, screaming and yelling, while people locked themselves into rooms and hid under tables and chairs.

While they were looking for me, I broke into the shower room, and set about causing as much damage as I possibly could. I smashed all the windows, tore all the mirrors off the walls, and pissed all over the floor. I would've shat on it, but I'd already been that day – very regular, me.

There was this huge chrome and glass weighing machine in there, a bloody massive great thing, and I managed (with some effort) to kick that over, sending it toppling on to the hard stone floor with one almighty crash. There was bits of glass and shit strewn everywhere, and a rancid smell of piss that was ninety-nine per cent lager. The floor of this place looked like the Battle of the Somme.

I was about 20 at the time, yet acting like a fucking ten-year-old. Rob was in on it as well, mind you, we were like a pair of naughty schoolboys together. And if we were the bad boys of the class, our manager was the headmaster. He went fucking ape again when he found out what we'd done, as did the people from the university. The shit storm that caused, it took weeks to sort it all out, apologise, and pay for all the damage. Was I remorseful, or embarrassed in any way? Was I fuck!

I don't think they'd had much experience with heavy metal bands up there, and it must have looked like a pack of wild animals had run amok in the place when I'd finished. Certainly I think we were probably the last band they booked for a while! I had to avoid Rod for the next few days, 'cos he was still ranting and raving about it — I can remember hiding under the seats of the tour bus at one point, to keep out of his way.

Talking of backstage shenanigans, there's one particular legend about me which every Iron Maiden fan knows, 'cos it's been told and re-told a thousand times. It's the one I mentioned in the previous chapter, where I'm arrested at one of our early gigs, by police who're apparently looking for drugs. They don't find any (by pure chance, I'd taken the last of a batch of speed earlier in the evening) but they do find a large knife I had on me.

Now, the legend goes that it was a flick knife, which sort of fits into the 'wild man' image. The only trouble is, it wasn't anything as glamorous as that — it was a tooling knife, which I'd been using at work in the refinery, and which I'd forgotten to take out of my pocket. Like I was really going to stab somebody with that — I didn't even know I had it on me!

The upshot of that story was that I pleaded guilty to possessing an offensive weapon, and the coppers did manage to bail me out in time to get back to the gig, where the band were almost finished. I did the last two songs — well, Steve Harris had been doing the singing, and I reckoned the crowd had suffered enough.

While I'm talking about life on the road, another war-story

comes to mind, and it's one which really shoots down the myth that a rock musician's life is one of endless glamour.

I'm ashamed to say this one didn't actually happen that long ago either, so I haven't the excuse of being young and stupid to hide behind. Frankly, at my age, I should have known better.

Anyway, we're playing some dates in Germany with my solo band, and we're staying in a hotel which is also a brewery. At least, that's what I remember, but as you can imagine, my brain is a bit fuzzy on the details, which is perhaps just as well for all concerned. If I had total recall of all my drunken exploits, I'd be psychologically scarred for life.

So we've finished the gig and we're really hitting the hard stuff. Beer is flowing down my neck – in case you haven't tried it, I should point out here that the beer in Germany is bloody strong – and as if that wasn't bad enough, the bloke who owned the brewery (or, at least, he seemed to be in charge at the time) gave us a load of tequila, bottles and bottles of the stuff.

Well, once I get started on that it's Goodnight Vienna. Put your tin hats on and take cover. Things got really out of hand pretty quickly, with me staggering around and insulting people (mainly my band members, who probably deserved it).

I can remember getting into a heated argument with one of the guys, and getting up from my chair to hit him, only for him to dive under the table like a startled rabbit. (He was obviously used to being on the road with me.) To get my hands on him, I upturned this massive great table, which was laden down with everybody's drinks, so there's bottles and glasses flying all over the place.

The general ambience of the occasion isn't really helped by these two groupies who start hanging around. Now, they're a bit rough (I did say the beer was bloody strong) but, frankly, you're not going to worry when you're in that state. If you say otherwise, you're a liar.

They came over to have autographs signed, and when they'd given me a pen, they both whipped up their tops and pulled down their bras, so I could scribble my name on their tits. (If I'd had a pound for every tit I've signed, it'd be like winning the Lottery.)

They're showing off these autographed tits to everybody in the bar, so I figure they're in the mood to get friendly. (You learn to recognise the signs!)

Anyway, I got paired up with the marginally less grotesque of the two, and she's sitting there on my lap, trying to suck my face off. I've got my hand up her skirt and inside her panties – remember, we're in the middle of a crowded bar – and I'm fingering her vigorously, just to get her warmed up.

That doesn't seem to be a problem, because she's got this look on her face like she's just about to come, and her cunt is sopping wet. She's got her hand down inside my jeans, and she's got my erect dick in a vice-like grip, so she's obviously up for it.

So, we've gone upstairs for a session. When you pull a groupie, there's no need for social niceties like making small talk, buying her flowers or shit like that. There's no need. You both know what you want, and it's almost a businesslike atmosphere. We didn't say a word to each other as we went up the stairs or opened the door to my room.

Once we're inside, she walks straight over to the bed, climbs on to it and kneels there on all fours, pausing only to pull her skirt up over her waist, and tug her panties down around her knees. There's this big white arse facing me, as I walk across the room. She'd obviously been around the block a few times with rock stars – there weren't any starry-eyed nerves with this girl. (Some of them look at you and say, 'Was that OK for you, Paul? Was that OK?' – it's fucking pathetic, really.)

Anyway, this tart must have had almost as much to drink as I had, and she proved it before very long. I gave it to her up the 'Gary' with as much energy as I could, and the force of me banging away at her from behind obviously upset her stomach a bit.

I shot my load inside her, and I withdrew, putting my dick away and zipping up my jeans. She just remained motionless, kneeling there with her bare white arse sticking up in the air.

She turns around to look at me, and she looks really green. Now I do sometimes have that effect on women, but this is a bit extreme. Suddenly, there's this guttural growling noise, and she spews her guts up right in my face, spattering me from head to foot in diced carrots. It was like the girl from the Exorcist, she just pukes all over everything. It was fucking disgusting.

I'm standing there looking at her, with warm vomit dripping off my chin, on to the floor. Picture that scene (if you can bear it), and tell me rock 'n' roll ain't a glamorous business.

But before I really strayed from the path of righteousness, the stuff we used to get up to in the very early days was quite innocent, in comparison. Quite often, someone would get a custard pie or a bucket of water on the last night of a tour, if the others thought they deserved it.

Iron Maiden played the Rainbow Theatre in London on one occasion, a gig which was recorded on film for the live video we released soon after. While we're getting ready to go out there, I discovered that some bastard (or bastards) had filled my high-topped leather boots with shaving foam and confetti, which meant I had to squelch my way around the stage all night, walking like a bloody crab!

Incidentally, many people who saw that video have asked me why the lyrics on the song 'Killers' are different to those on the record. The answer is, we'd written it not long before, and we hadn't finalised the lyrics then, so I had to make some up specially for the occasion!

Steve was the victim of another gag, this time during a long journey on a tour-bus across North America. He'd fallen asleep, and was happily snoring away. Now, Steve's eyebrows join up in the middle and, while he was asleep, the rest of us painted on eyebrow extensions to our faces, so when he woke up he was surrounded by them! He was still waking up, when he looked around, and slowly realised what we'd done. Then he starts yelling what cheeky bastards we are! Who, us?

We were just kids really, having a laugh. When I started to get really out of hand, as I got more famous and the band got bigger, my behaviour got a lot more serious, and nobody really knew how to handle me. They still don't.

*　　　　　*　　　　　*

By far the liveliest guys to hang out with on any tour are the road crew. They're the ones who'll lead you astray, because they're the ones who always know where the action is. Most of these guys are battle-hardened road warriors, they know every bar in every town. They're also very familiar with the international groupie circuit, so it was no surprise that I was attracted to their company almost from day one.

The rest of the guys would be writing, rehearsing or sound-checking, and I'd be off pissing it up with the road crew!

I worked with one in particular, a guy we called Radar, for the simple reason that he was the worst navigator in the history of travel, and was forever getting us lost. This guy couldn't find his own arsehole with two hands and a flashlight, and whenever he had a map on his lap, you'd know you were in trouble. You'd hear the band shouting, 'Where are we, Radar?'

If you needed to go to Copenhagen, he'd take you to Amsterdam; he was a fucking nightmare. This failing was more than compensated for, though, by his skill as a blagger. This guy could blag his way into anything, anywhere in the civilised world. He'd ring up hotels and talk them into giving us a 25 per cent discount, just by giving them a load of old flannel. He could get you just about anything you wanted, wherever you were in the world. I think if you'd asked him to get you some nuclear weapons, he'd have been loading them on to the lorries by the next gig – he was a star.

He was a wild fucker, too. I remember one night during a really competitive (and life-threatening) drinking contest, we mixed up a highly-toxic cocktail for him, which contained whisky, curry powder, chilli powder and all sorts of other stuff too disgusting to mention. We bet him £10 that he wouldn't drink it, and the crazy bastard downed it in one. He didn't spew either – the mark of a real man!

Of course, me and Radar were as thick as thieves, sharing the same outlook on life. We had some wild times together when we went down to St Tropez with another roadie, Karl, just hitting the bars and chasing women. I don't think I've ever seen so many fannies in such quick succession before – black, white, big, small, just opening up before me. Great stuff.

Radar also went into touring history for another feat he

pulled, and this one is, I have to say, still one of the most impressive I've seen in 25 years of touring. He walks into this nightclub in Sweden, when we were on tour there with Kiss, and he spies this pair of birds, chatting at the bar.

Now it soon becomes apparent in conversation that they are not only lesbian, but also an established couple, having been together for about 20 years. Short hair, sensible shoes – they'd definitely come from the island of Lesbos all right, no point wasting your time there. Quite a challenge for any man, you might say. Not Radar.

He chatted them up, got them to buy him a load of drinks, and then invited himself back to their place, where he proceeded to shag the pair of them to within an inch of their lives. It was like a scene from a porno movie, he said later, with the two of them clambering all over him and each other.

While he was giving it to one from behind, the other one would be kneeling alongside, frigging herself off with a giant dildo, as he sucked her tits. Good man.

Because he (rightly) knew we wouldn't believe him, he brought these two pairs of soiled panties on to the tour-bus the next morning as proof. Like I say, a real man.

We used to pick up some unlikely passengers on some of these tours. I remember I picked up a prostitute in Amsterdam, who joined us on the tour-bus for a while, as we completed a European tour. Nobody knew who she was, where she came from, or what the fuck she was doing there. She was a game girl, though, and ended up staying on for about a month, helping me with my stage costumes.

The other guys would be reading, chatting or playing cards towards the front of the bus, while I was getting a blow-job from a prossie in the back seat. I think that speaks volumes, really.

There was another girl who found fame for a very different reason – and a far less pleasant one at that. I pulled her in Rome while I was on holiday there in the early Eighties (which in itself was still a bit of novelty – where I grew up, a holiday meant a weekend at Southend in a caravan).

Can I start off by saying for the record that this girl was the fucking dog's bollocks, to coin a phrase from the beauty industry. Didn't speak a word of English, but there was nothing to say, really. I think she understood all there was to know about me within a few minutes of our first meeting.

She was a bloody stunner, with a great body and this massive pair of tits. They were the real kind as well, not the plastic cones you find on birds in LA. These babies were the full-blooded variety, capped by nipples the size of large saucers! Those experts amongst you will know that it's a rarity to find all the top-of-the-range components on one model – usually it's one or the other, but she had 'em all.

From the minute I saw her, I was like fucking wood. If I'd have tripped over, I'd have broken the Olympic pole-vault record, for sure. I was so up for it, I just couldn't wait to get stripped off and get stuck in. I give her a load of old bullshit, which she doesn't really understand anyway, but by then we're past caring.

But when I get back to her place, I discover there's a problem. Now I'm not normally a fussy sort of bloke. If a bird's half-decent, I'll usually be up for it, do you know what I mean? If she's got all her own teeth, that's good enough, and if she's had a wash, well, that's a bonus; just so you know where I'm coming from.

But this woman ... well, I made the astonishing discovery that she had something very seriously wrong with her plumbing. In fact, she sounded like an old boiler that's badly in need of maintenance.

She strips off her jeans and top, to reveal a tiny black G-string and a black lacy bra, which is straining under the weight of those two massive great breasts. So far, so good.

I tear her underwear off her, and lay her down on the bed with her legs over my shoulders. I had a bit of a fiddle about, and everything seemed to be where God intended – she wasn't a transsexual or anything frightening like that – so first I stuck my fingers inside her crack and waggled them about; then I let down my undercarriage and prepared for landing.

That's when she let rip the loudest fanny fart I'd ever heard in my fucking life. It blasted off like a bastard shotgun, and I almost hit the ceiling in shock. I think the force of it must have blown me off the bed.

Once I'd realised I hadn't been shot, I just looked at her in amazement, as if to say, 'What the fucking hell was THAT?' I was standing there, half-dazed, with this massive erection at half-mast in front of me; and she's lying there on the bed with her legs wide apart in the air, and this hairy beaver winking at me. I think she was wondering what all the fuss was about. She didn't seem the slightest bit embarrassed, she just sort of shrugged her shoulders and gave me a sort of half-smile, as if to say, 'It wasn't me ...'

But when I climbed aboard and tried to get inside her again, fuck me if she didn't let go another one. It was like trying to mount a bren-gun. By this time, I was in fucking hysterics. I was laughing so much I forgot what I was supposed to be doing, and gave up the assault on her tubes altogether. Well, the magic of the occasion had sort of passed really, hadn't it?

It wasn't all sex and bad behaviour back then, though. I can remember me and Clive, our drummer, spending endless hours on the tour-bus listening to Derek and Clive tapes, the comedy act of Peter Cook and Dudley Moore. There we were, these two wild rockers on tour, laughing away at these tapes like a pair of kids in front of the telly.

When you're cooped up in confined spaces with the same people round the clock, every day of the week, the smallest things like that can provide some much-needed light relief from all the tension and shit that went on.

The childishness did sometimes go a bit far, though, when we wound each other up. Perhaps the worst of these happened at a hotel in the north of England, when we were about to return to London to play at the Hammersmith Odeon.

I'd gone into my room, and noticed an unusual smell in there, which seemed to be getting worse. I pulled back the shower curtain, and stopped dead in my bloody tracks. Some dirty bastard had only gone and shat in my shower!

Now, a joke's a joke; but you don't shit in a man's shower, not if you want to keep your fucking head on your shoulders, especially if it's my shower you've shat in. The smell was fucking unbelievable, and there's this fucking great turd languishing in the bottom of my shower stall, like a dead dog. What the hell he'd been eating, I don't know. I found the culprit – the sick fucker – and went completely off my trolley, calling him every filthy name under the sun and giving him a good battering.

Unbeknown to me, though, one of the others was tape-recording my rant, and they played it to the audience at one of the next gigs. Like fucking animals, honestly ...

Don't get me wrong, we were serious about what we did; and we certainly didn't piss about (too much) when there was work to be done; but it was these moments which kept us sane when we were in each other's company 24 hours a day. They were certainly far safer than the other distractions I was now discovering on later tours, ones which would present a serious threat to myself and everyone around me.

I did manage to get myself into a bit of serious trouble even during the early days with Maiden, though, usually because of my big mouth. There was one night in Bristol I think it was, when I'd gone out to a few clubs with some fans I'd met after the show. I've had a skinful to drink and I'm doped out of my head on speed, so I'm like a firecracker ready to go off, really.

Well, this particular firecracker ignited before the night was out; we got set upon by a crowd of skinheads, who seemed to want nothing more than stamp our faces into the tarmac.

It was the usual thing — young lads, beered up, full of piss and wind. If someone's really going to smack you, he's just going to do it without warning you; he's not going to spend 20 minutes yelling at you first. I've been in enough fights to know that the most deadly ones are over in seconds. That's when one of you is usually on his way to hospital, or worse.

So there's this tribal thing where everybody yells in each other's faces for a while, there's some pushing and shoving, and then there's one little flurry which sparks it all off. It may have been a butt or a punch, but everyone's committed then. It's gone past the point of no return, and no one wants to be seen to back down.

The other band members were safely tucked up back at the hotel, and it's a fair bet that the manager would not have been best pleased if he'd known the singer of his band was out on the streets of the city centre, brawling with the local tearaways.

Anyay, in the middle of all this mêlée, this one lad grabs me by my lapels, obviously trying to pull me round in a headlock and then batter the shit out of me. No chance, son. I'd been around a long time.

We tussled around a bit, pulling this way and that, both holding on to each other's collars. He was a bit bigger and heavier than me, so I'd have to put him down in a hurry.

I can see his face now – ginger, lots of freckles – and remember how his eyes opened wide with surprise in the split-second before I crashed my forehead down on to his, splitting the skin wide open, and leaving what was left of his eyebrow dangling down over his eye. He'd got so much blood gushing down from his forehead that he looked like he'd got a red hankerchief tied across his face. Nasty. Bet that stung a bit.

I've no idea whether he was an Iron Maiden fan, or whether he'd ever even heard of us back then – maybe not. I just wonder, though, when we were on the telly over the next few years, Top of the Pops or whatever, if he ever looked at the singer, and said, 'Fuck! That's the guy who twatted me!'

A nice thought, that.

CHAPTER 7

I was in a band which I absolutely loved, and the first album had been a testament to that. I was travelling the world and getting paid for it – the sort of stuff you dream of when you're farting around pubs and clubs in East London. But at some point during the run-up to the second album, *Killers*, something, somewhere, had changed.

It was very slight, and I can't put my finger on when it started, even looking back now, but I just felt that our style of music was becoming more polished, and more commercial. We'd lost something of the punk-type edge we'd had, and we were in danger – to my mind – of just getting a bit too arty-farty, if you could ever call Iron Maiden arty-farty.

When we played the new songs as part of the live set, I felt that they stood out, that they were different. I could see that the songs being written were going more and more that way, and I wasn't too happy about it, if I'm honest.

Because I didn't believe in that musical direction 100 per cent, I wasn't giving it 100 per cent any more, as I once had. I tried to throw myself into work, as I had before, as I like to be full on or not do it at all; but my heart was no longer in it. I knew it, I think the rest of the band were starting to realise it, and I started to become more and more unhappy with the situation.

I started to withdraw into my shell a bit; I didn't talk to the other guys about how I was feeling – which I certainly should have done – and I just felt things were starting to change. In particular, me and Steve started to get a bit niggly – I think he could tell I wasn't really that pleased with the way things were going.

Whereas I'd used drugs – mainly coke and speed – for recreation before, I now started to look at them in terms of numbing my feelings, which meant I became more and more isolated. I never drank on stage, and I was never drunk on stage, but more often now, I'd stay up later and go out for a few drinks on the nights before shows, whereas before I hadn't. If drugs were offered to me in the club or bar, I'd take them.

I was probably starting to get even more out of hand, and I'm sure the others must have had their doubts about me by now. The thing was, I was starting to care less and less about how they felt. My behaviour was getting worse and worse, which was gradually bringing everything to a head. I had these two demons with me now – drugs and alcohol – and wherever I went, they followed.

I remember one night at a club in Munich, when I was propping up the bar. It was getting late, and there was a gig the next day, but there was loads of coke being passed around on trays, and I just helped myself. I ended up staying most of the night, during which I took more cocaine than I ever had at one time before. I can't even remember getting back to the hotel, I was so out of it.

I felt bloody rough the next day, my nose was really sore, and you can't really think straight when you're not looking after yourself. If you feel tired and hungover at the start of a tour, you're going to feel absolutely fucked at the end of it, I can tell you.

The travelling really gets to you after a while, just being ferried from hotel to hotel, from one concert hall to another. I seem to have spent half my life in a plane, I may as well have been a bloody bird, for all the time I've spent in the air.

Ironically, instead of calming the problem and dulling the pain, my increasingly heavy drinking and drug-taking definitely made things worse, and put more distance between me and the other guys, because Steve hardly drinks at all, and I don't think he liked me going out like that in the middle of a string of dates and getting out of order. I'm a bit of a handful at the best of times – you may have already gathered that – but when I've had a drink or a snort of coke I'm a hundred times worse, and I must have been a fucking nightmare to deal with.

If I didn't want to do something, I wasn't going to do it, and anybody who said otherwise could just go fuck themselves. If they persisted, they'd get a fucking slap. Perhaps subconsciously, I was uneasy with all the fame and attention, and I was trying to get shot of it without even realising I was doing it – I don't know. But relations between me and the rest of the band deteriorated more and more as the tour continued.

We did have to cancel a few shows because I'd lost my voice, but the real problem lay far deeper than that. I just didn't care as much any more.

The Killers era had started really well – we'd basically gone out and done exactly the same as we had with the first album, wowing audiences and winning over new legions of fans. It had been produced by Martin Birch, who'd worked with Deep Purple. Now Martin's a really nice guy, and a very good producer, but the overall sound of the record just wasn't to my taste. I thought it just sounded too polished, that it didn't sound 'live' enough.

But I was in a minority. The fans loved it, and it went straight to Number One, as the first one had done. To kick off the Killers tour, we first supported Judas Priest at the Palladium in New York and, once again, we played our arses off. On the bill that night alongside us and Priest were Humble Pie, while Whitesnake were the opening act.

It was an especially great honour for me to do a show with Humble Pie, as I'd been a huge fan of Steve Marriott for years and years, he was a bit of a hero of mine actually. Here was a guy from round our way, an East End boy who'd made good. I suppose I was trying to emulate him, really, and I was chuffed when we hit it off, even though he used to call me 'Terry', after Terry Downes, the boxer, who he said I looked like. (I bloody didn't.)

Later on that tour, we enjoyed a jamming session at a bar in Lubbock, Texas, which is where Buddy Holly was born. I can't remember too much about it, other than we were all there, drinking and having a laugh on stage, so it must have been a good night.

I shagged a bird that night, who I'd picked up in the bar, and that was all a bit of a blur as well, really. The only thing I can remember from that encounter was that she had the biggest pair of tits I think I'd ever seen. They were like two skinheads fighting under a blanket. Back in my hotel room, when I tore her bra off her, these great things flew loose, and nearly took my bloody eye out. Ah, happy days.

But for me, good times like that were gradually becoming few and far between, in amongst the rows and recriminations. I certainly wasn't happy with the new musical direction, and I can't stick with something if I'm not 100 per cent happy with it.

I was getting more and more depressed all the time, and I remember ringing mates back home, and telling them how I felt. I should really have been talking to the band about it, because they may have been able to help, but instead I kept it bottled up. My mates' reaction was fairly predictable: 'Are you fucking mad? Leave Iron Maiden? Just shut up and think of the money!' But I've never been able to do that, and to this day I'm not sure whether that's been a blessing or a curse.

My only outlet was getting more and more pissed and fucked-up, but things were coming to a head on that front, anyway. It was clear we couldn't carry on like this.

Towards the end of the tour, it just became unbearable. If you'd asked me why, I wouldn't have been able to explain it to you, but I just felt I'd had it with the band as it was. It was all in my head, I never told any of the others, but I was convinced it was all over.

I remember finally thinking that I owed it to the fans either to give it 100 per cent every time, or just fuck off out of it altogether. Then, something happened that finally pushed me over the edge. It was one of the worst things that's ever happened to me, and I find it difficult to talk about it, even now.

My grandfather, my mum's dad, passed away. We'd been

really close, so much so that it was like having another parent. In fact, he inspired the song 'Remember Tomorrow', because it was a favourite phrase of his. The song took on a special meaning after his death; and I re-recorded it later in my career, because I wanted to pay a tribute to my grandad.

I'd been flying to and from the hospital when he was ill, because we were touring in Britain at the time; but when the news came, it just knocked the wind out of me. After all that had happened, I just didn't have the strength to fight on any more.

I was just devastated that I wasn't there with him when he went, and I still can't really deal with that. I'm not the most intelligent person in the world, but I'm not stupid, either. I just wish I could have rectified some things in my life before it was too late, and that was one of them.

People will laugh if I tell them I've got a sensitive side, but it's things like that which have made me tough – turned me into a hard bastard. I've been hurt so many times that I've just closed the doors now – you can't touch me.

I've been shot, stabbed, punched, kicked, you name it, it's made no difference. But the loss of someone close to me is like the worst thing that can ever happen.

One of my best mates when I was at school was a kid I used to hang around with in Walthamstow. We'd been booting around one day, and we'd said goodbye to each other as normal, and made our separate ways home. I found out later that he'd broken into a block of flats after he'd left me, and climbed up to the roof, from where he'd thrown himself off.

It was like my worst nightmare – you can't prepare a kid for something like that; you can't really explain to them why their friend's killed himself. And likewise, after losing my grandad, being in a rock band just didn't seem so important any more.

*   *   *

The city of Copenhagen was the place where rock history – if you want to call it that – was made, as it was to be the setting of my last ever concert as the singer of Iron Maiden.

After the show, I took myself off with a mate of mine, who'd just left the Army, and we just went off on a massive all-night bender. I drank and drank, like there was no tomorrow, which sort of rang true, really. But it felt like I was celebrating, that I was free. It was relief, I suppose – I'd made my decision, and that was that.

The meeting had started like any other, just general chit-chat about tours, record releases, album covers, whatever. We used to meet like this every week in our manager's office in London, where we could go over any plans for the future, and just keep everybody informed about what was going on.

But on this particular occasion, the agenda was looking pretty full. I'd come to lay my cards on the table, and say that I was unhappy with the way the band was developing. What I didn't know at the time, however, was that the other members of the band had decided to sack me.

I must have read hundreds of accounts of my leaving Iron Maiden, and they usually involve some dramatic bust-up, handbags at five paces or whatever. The people who write these things have usually got some agenda of their own, and they certainly weren't present at that meeting. Well, I was, and it wasn't like that at all. It was more along the lines of a civilised discussion, and a mutual decision that it would be best for both me and the group if we parted company.

It was literally a case of Rod saying to me, 'Paul, we think it's best if you leave Maiden,' and me saying, 'That's all right, I was going to resign anyway!'

So, the decision was mutual, and easily reached. There were no tears, fights or hurt feelings. Now, I know people say that all the time, and it's usually football managers or business leaders who've been kicked out on their arse who say it the most, but in my case it happens to be true. Like I say, it certainly wasn't a shock to my system, I really wanted out by then.

I can't remember the exact dialogue as I left, but it was something like, 'Well, good luck, Paul. Take care of yourself, mate ... I'll see you around, yeah?' Not a punch thrown, nor a nail broken.

I think I was pretty disillusioned with the rock industry altogether at that point, and I'd half a mind to get myself out of it for good. Whatever had affected me during my time with Iron Maiden was still with me. It's hard to imagine now, but I didn't feel like playing music any more.

When the news broke about the split, the music press went berserk. While rumour followed rumour, all the fans were talking about it. And what was I doing while all this gossip was going on?

Well, I was keeping out of the way. At the time when the news broke, I was actually in Oslo, energetically shagging this bird who used to be one of Maiden's catering staff. I'd packed my toothbrush and condoms, and just pissed off out of it for a while. I stayed in Oslo for a few months, just until the heat died down.

And while I lay in bed with my young culinary friend, and pondered what to do with the rest of my life, back in the UK, a young singer was chosen to be Iron Maiden's new frontman. His name was Bruce Dickinson.

*   *   *

There's one question I get asked a lot, and I'm sure Bruce does, too. It's the obvious bleedin' question – who was Iron Maiden's best-ever singer?

Opinions vary, but you've got to remember that opinions are like arseholes – everyone's got one. In fact, it might surprise folk to hear me say this, but I'm gonna put down on the record here that Bruce is absolutely the best singer the band have ever had. I'm not being modest when I say that, but I think he's got a bloody great voice, and it was just what the band needed at the time, when I left.

You can't really compare my voice to his, and I wouldn't want to. We're two very different animals (well, I'm an animal, anyway ...) and that's all there is to it. The fact that my voice is better suited to the old songs, and his is better suited to the newer stuff, just proves my point that the band was progressing in a different direction.

I know people would really love me to slag Bruce off, or say we hate each other's guts, but I've no reason to pick a fight with him. (Especially if he had one of his fencing swords in his hand at the time.) We're grown-ups for God's sake, both doing a job, and both hopefully enjoying it, so good luck to him, I say.

I went along to see Iron Maiden at the Hammersmith Odeon, not long after Bruce joined, and I thought they were all right, actually. It was a bit of a weird feeling, of course, watching somebody else front the band you'd been in for so long – a bit like watching somebody else shag your bird, I suppose.

I know many people still tell me they prefer the band when I was in it, but everybody's taste is different, and everyone's entitled to their say.

If I'm being asked about Maiden's guitarists through the years, I always have to say – with respect to the other lads – that for me, Adrian Smith will always be the best all-round guitarist Maiden have had. He can make a guitar do stuff most people couldn't dream of, let alone do.

And as for my relationship with Steve Harris, well, he's still a fantastic bass player, and while we don't really see each other that much, we're not at each other's throats, either. When we meet, it's always, 'Hello, how are you?' There's never any hassle. There's no reason why there should be – we're not in competition with each other.

A couple of years after I'd left the band, Steve's daughter was born, and he invited me to the christening, which was a nice gesture. I wasn't able to go, because I was off abroad somewhere, but he'd made the effort to keep in touch, and I was pleased he did. I've bumped into him a few times over the years, at a local gig in Essex, over at his bar in Portugal, and we always have a bit of a chat.

We've both come a long way since we sat in his house back in Leytonstone, planning the future over a cup of tea, and maybe we'll get together for another cup of tea – or something a bit stronger – before we're too much older.

Another question I get asked all the time is: am I a multi-millionaire, having written and performed some of those famous songs? Well, the answer to that is a definite no, although my name does still appear on the credits.

The truth is – and not many people know this – I sold all my royalties back to the band a few years back. What did I get for them? About 50 grand. I've since been told we should probably have asked for more, that I could have got up to a million, but it's not worth worrying about, really. I've made money from my other records and tours, so it's not like it was a life-or-death thing. It felt like getting rid of a millstone round my neck, to be honest with you.

If I have a regret, it's only that my kids won't get those royalty payments as they get older, as it would have been a nice thing to hand on to them.

I don't resent anything they've achieved since I left the band, as I say, we're not in competition. I got in trouble a little while back for saying on stage that I would be playing 'some old Iron Maiden shit'. For the record, I meant the word 'shit' in the American sense, when it just means 'stuff' — I certainly didn't mean that Iron Maiden songs were shit — I wrote some of them, after all.

I also copped some flak just recently for recording a compilation of Maiden songs — people accused me of selling out, you know, trading on my past. Well, if I don't receive royalties from them, I'm not exactly doing it for the money, am I? Nah, it was just something that I wanted to do, just to put that whole thing to bed, really.

What would have been a fitting epitaph to my time in Iron Maiden almost happened a little while ago, when they were playing the Rock in Rio festival in Brazil. As I spend a lot of time over there now, they were apparently asking people whether I was around. The idea was that I would get up on stage with them and do a few of the old numbers, for old times' sake. Christ, can you imagine what the fans would have made of that?

CHAPTER 8

Booze. As you read this book, you'll probably discover that this one word flows through most of the narrative, like a thread holding it together. 'I was pissed when I hit him ...', 'she was pissed when I shagged her ...' that sort of thing.

OK, it's not exactly *Harry Potter*, but then you never expected it to be, did you? Did you honestly pick up this book, look at the picture on the front cover, read the title and think, 'Hmm, that sounds like a sensitive, thought-provoking read ...' Did you?

You fucking liar ...

Anyway, I make no apologies about it. Booze is like the lifeblood of rock music. We pour it down our throats until they overflow, then we go and spew over a roadie, just so we've room for some more.

Personally speaking, it's played a significant role in some of my most celebrated outrages, from smashing every stick of furniture in a hotel room and carving swastikas on the walls, to carrying out the most demonic sex acts on the pert young body of an unsuspecting groupie.

I've been told that it brings out an inner demon in me, and it's a demon which certainly makes the blood of band members and road crews run cold. When this demon manifests itself, evil is amongst us, my friends. And when that happens, a relaxing evening after a show can turn into the darkest day in Hell...

One particular time I'd been out on the piss, me and a mate had been down the West End at this unlicensed drinking den we knew. I think we'd both drunk our own body weight in whisky. Anyway, there's something of a fracas at the club, as is often the way. I'm vague as to the exact details, but the two of us started fighting everybody else in the club, and somehow ended up fighting each other. Don't ask me for reasons, because there aren't any.

The establishment took the right and proper view that it would be better off without our patronage, so several bear-sized bouncers chucked us out into the street. We carried on fighting for a while, but we soon got bored, so by about four in the morning we're staggering around the streets, both pissed as cunts.

Bearing in mind that I'd been kicked out of America a few days before (don't ask – you'll hear the full story later) I was in a pretty good mood, all things considered.

At one point, I remember deciding that I needed to take a piss. Normally, if I'm in a hotel room or a bar or somewhere, I'll just piss where I stand, 'cos I can't be arsed to go to the bog, but as there were still crowds of clubbers walking past, I thought I'd be a bit discreet. I'm nothing if not refined. So, lurching unsteadily across the pavement, I lean on a shop window, get the old chap out, and start spraying away like something from *London's Burning*.

Talking of men in uniform, it soon dawns on me that I've got an audience. Two boys in blue, a couple of London's finest, have come up behind me and are looking disapprovingly at this – admittedly unsavoury – spectacle. I can't remember their exact words – as I believe I've already mentioned, I was as pissed as a cunt – but they let it be known that they took a dim view of my toilet habits.

Unfortunately, when one of them asked me just what the hell I thought I was doing, I turned around with the old chap still in my hand, and Old Bill got a golden shower he wasn't expecting. I know it's the oldest gag in the book, but I swear it's true. He wasn't best pleased.

Wallop, I was wrestled to the ground, and clapped in handcuffs. They then unceremoniously carted me off in the back of a police van to West End Central, where they informed me I could use the bathroom facilities free of charge. Having recently spent some considerable time in a prison cell in the States, I wasn't mad keen on going into another one, and I told the copper this, as diplomatically as I knew how.

I kept shouting that I needed to call my lawyer. I didn't tell them that he was in Los Angeles, or that he was still dealing with my conditional release terms from the LA County Jail – well, it wasn't exactly the time or the place, was it?

As we drove to the station, I loudly protested my innocence and repeated my calls for a lawyer, which probably caused me more harm than good, as I was rapidly beginning to piss everyone off. The bigger copper said to me, 'Look, mate, never mind calling your lawyer, you've been watching too much fucking TV. You're as pissed as a twat and, more to the point, you've pissed all over my mate here, so we're taking you in for the night.' Well, he was no Dixon of Dock Green, but he had a point.

As we drove through the London streets, I weighed up the pros and cons of my situation. On the negative side, I'd only been in the country a few days, and now it looked like I was going straight to prison. Also, if they found out about my recent spell as a guest of the US Federal Government, that might cause some grief with any charges I might be facing here.

On the plus side, I'd managed to chuck away two grammes of coke I'd had on me, and they were hardly likely to find out about the America business unless they were planning on ringing Interpol at that time of night. They didn't even know who I was.

So, I decided to keep quiet and, sure enough, they never found out. I could have been Carlos the Jackal, for all they knew. They just thought I was some drunk, which is an outrageous assumption, when you think about it.

I paid in other ways, though. I chucked up all over myself in the night, so I awoke on the cold floor of this cell, caked in stale vomit, and smelling like a cess-pit. I had to take a dump on the filthy hole they called a toilet, and when you've had a skinful, as I'm sure you know, it just rots your insides. The whole bloody place smelt like nuclear waste after that. There I was, an idol to rock fans across the world, slumped in my own filth, like a bloody tramp. If I'd told the coppers who I really was, there's no way they would ever have believed me.

There was a bit of a hiccup when they found one-sided razor

blades in my wallet – I'd been using them for chopping up cocaine. I told them we were professional electricians, and that we'd been using them to strip electrical wires!

They obviously thought I was a pain in the arse, and so they couldn't wait to see the back of me. They chucked me out in the morning with only a telling-off, a blinding hangover and a rather funny smell to show for my trouble. There's a moral to that story – you can lead a life of hell-raising across the Western world if you like, but when you're in England, don't piss on a policeman, all right?

*   *   *

Before you decide that I must be a fucking alcoholic of the bed-wetting, pants-shitting variety, can I just say a few words in my defence?

I can go for long periods of time without drinking at all, it doesn't bother me. However, if it's put in front of me, I'm going to drink the fucking lot, OK? Everything to excess and all that. Moderation just isn't in my vocabulary.

When I do go on a bender, that's when it does all tend to go a bit tits-up, to be honest. Grown men run for cover, people flee the streets and everybody boards up their doors and windows. When I'm really on a big one, all but the most battle-hardened end up littering the floor.

If it's a binge over a number of days, well, you'd just better alert the local cops right away. Just let them come and take me away now – it'll save a load of hassle and grief later on. That's when stuff gets smashed, people get abused, and my fellow musicians end up embroiled in the mother of all brawls.

To be fair, I've always tried not to go overboard before a

show; although it's also true that I haven't always succeeded. There was one gig I remember a few years back in Europe when the show was about to be cancelled, because of some technical problems they'd been having backstage.

This put me in a fucking bad mood straight off. I was fucking steaming. Once you're psyched up to do a gig, you're ready to get out there and slaughter them, so when something like that stops you, you've got no escape for all that pent-up aggression. The promoter was hiding from me – having been cut off in my prime, I would've ripped that cunt's head off, and shit down the hole.

I've always said that the two hours on stage makes up for the 22 hours of boredom that you've had to put up with on tour. If you're denied that, you've nowhere to go to, really. It's a bit like pulling some cracking bird, ripping her pants off, and then not being able to get it up when you're ready to get inside her beaver, you know? You're going to go a bit mad, aren't you?

So I'm in the frame of mind to kill someone, and this is made worse by the fact that, with no show to do, I get as pissed as it's humanly possible to be, and still be conscious. I'm absolutely wankered. I've got vague memories of causing mayhem backstage, screaming and roaring at anyone who came near, but the details are a blur, to be honest. The only visions I can recall are completely out of focus, and tinged with a red mist.

Finally, after all that, the announcement comes that the gig isn't going to be pulled after all. Luckily, I'm too pissed to realise the seriousness of the situation, but the band are fucking shitting themselves. They've got a show to do, in front of an arena of rabid rock fans, and their singer can't even stand up, let alone sing. I'm semi-conscious, fast fading into oblivion.

On top of this, there was an unfortunate episode that night when a fan accosted me, and I went back into the dressing room, got a gun, and chased after him with it. Event security and my road crew had to intervene before I shot him.

Like the true pros, though, natural instinct soon took over. Once I'd been helped on to the stage, we did the most rip-roaring fucking show you've ever seen. We tore them to pieces. I think the adrenalin just started pumping, and the old routine just sort of kicked in. OK, I was a bit out of control, I fell over a few times, and I had to do most of the show on my knees, but who cares about that? The kids went mad – they loved it. I might be pissed, but I can still turn it on when I have to. To anybody who says I'm an alcoholic, I'd say that I'm still the best, all right? Anyway, why don't you come back and tell me what the fuck you've ever done?

While I do have a reputation for hard drinking, it wasn't actually that bad during the very early days with Maiden. It was only later that the boozing got heavier and the drug abuse became more serious. That's when all the trouble started.

Mind you, I probably seemed a bit over the top to Steve Harris, as he hardly ever used to drink anything. I've only ever seen Steve pissed twice (on one of those occasions, I've got vague memories of him trying to climb a tree) and he doesn't generally get out of control, he's just not that sort of bloke. He wouldn't touch drugs if you paid him – he wouldn't even trust aspirin, I don't think.

With me, though, if it was on offer, I'd take it. A line of coke, a few pills, a large drink, a wet fanny – yep, ta very much, mate. To me, that was part and parcel of being a rock star. If you couldn't enjoy yourself with it, what was the point?

One of my earliest memories of being on tour with Maiden

was a show we did at Hammersmith with Judas Priest. I spent the evening with the guys from Priest and their road crew, and we were playing this drinking game, where you'd have to take a gulp of a drink as a forfeit. Unfortunately I lost, and I got as drunk as I'd ever been before in my life.

I was still really young then, and I must have nearly died from alcohol poisoning, I was that bad. I left every available surface in my hotel room sprayed with vomit. It was sprayed up the walls, down the curtains, all over the telly – everywhere. The entire place looked like it had been pebble-dashed. I must have staggered around, blind drunk, just puking up all over everything. I can't remember anything about the rest of the night, it's just a complete blank. It was a sign of things to come, really.

I've found it's when I drink Jack Daniel's that things do tend to get a bit out of hand. I must be one of their best customers, but people have told me that it has an evil effect on me, that I become a different, darker person, and certainly that's when a lot of skirmishes have happened over the years, whether they've been with wives, girlfriends or innocent bystanders.

If I have Jack with some cocaine, they sort of cancel each other out, and I'm still pretty calm and mellow, but if I have a load of Jack by itself, I turn into my alter ego, who the band christened Fuckeye Jones. Now Fuckeye Jones is a really nasty piece of work, so-called because one eye closes up almost completely. That's when the shit really hits the fan. He's a scary fucker, and no one wants to get on the wrong side of him.

He starts all the fights, trashes all the hotel rooms and backstage areas, and he just has this devastating effect on his surroundings wherever he is, like a cyclone or something.

Let me put it this way – if anybody messes with me or gives

me any shit, I'd punch them or knife them, no trouble. But if anybody gave Fuckeye Jones any shit, he'd not only cut them up, he'd carve his fucking name on their head afterwards, know what I mean?

But when it starts, it really starts. We've been touring in the most godforsaken places on earth – the wilds of Buttfuck, Indiana – and we've taken over a bar, made complete drunken twats of ourselves, pissed off the redneck natives no end, and it's all ended in a massive brawl out in the parking lot, like something from a Western movie. I'll still have been on a high from the show, and I end up battering the shit out of some poor cunt who's made the mistake of looking at me sideways. Well, fuck 'em, that's what I say.

Just recently, at a party after a show, I drank two bottles of whisky straight down, one after another, like I was drinking Tizer or something. For about an hour, I was the closest thing you've ever seen to a devil on earth. I was aggressive, offensive, violent, loud, obnoxious – and I was just getting warmed up.

I spent the evening causing absolute fucking mayhem in this hotel where we were staying. There was so much carnage, it was like a Stealth bomber had fired a missile into the lobby. After chucking some vases on the floor, I ended up throwing a bottle of Cognac through a plate glass door, sending shards of glass skimming across the polished floor, and putting everyone nearby in fear of their lives. There was this snooty, middle-aged couple frowning at me from the lounge, so I ran over and screamed at them. Apparently, I threatened to put the woman over a table, hitch her dress up, and give her one up the arse, right there in the middle of the room. They both just sat there and stared at me, open-mouthed.

After that, I got up on to a huge mahogany table and

challenged the entire room to a fight, before the band finally surrounded me and dragged me down. Everybody else within a half-mile radius was just shitting themselves – they were terrified.

It's a bitter irony of being in a rock band that you tend to stay in posh hotels. Now, posh hotels, by and large, tend to be populated by posh people. These poor people have to witness scenes of vile degradation as someone like me drinks himself half to death, abuses everyone around him, challenges everyone present to a fight, gets some groupie's tits out in the lounge bar, and generally leaves everyone around him wishing their spleen would rupture.

When I eventually passed out on the floor of the bar, they couldn't find a pulse – I think all my bodily functions had shut down in protest. So they decide that I must be dead, but instead of calling an ambulance – or an undertaker – they decide to leave it until the morning. (Well, they were all pissed, too, and it was getting late...)

They carried me to my room like a corpse, and just dumped me on the floor, where I apparently sprawled lifelessly. It came as a hell of a shock to them all when I surfaced the next day, like Frankenstein arising from his crypt, only not quite so pretty. They honestly thought I'd snuffed it.

No such luck.

CHAPTER 9

I suppose I wanted to do something different. Different to what I'd done before, and certainly different to what Iron Maiden were doing. It had to be something that I found interesting, because if I was going to launch a solo career, it had to be because I actually wanted to do it, not for reasons of money, fame or whatever.

I found what I was looking for when I put together a bunch of musicians to form the band Di'Anno. Now I was never keen on using my own name in a band's title, but most record companies insisted on it, because of the Maiden connection, I suppose. I've actually never been comfortable with that, because I just think it adds to the responsibility and stress of the thing – if it's your name that's on it, it's you that's in the firing line, after all. I've got enough aggro when I release a new record, without taking that sort of risk.

There was further confusion with this particular group

because it was known on various occasions as Lone Wolf. The names often changed between recording and touring, depending on who was calling the shots, which didn't really help much.

But the music we were putting together was certainly different – still with a hard rock edge, but with keyboards, time changes and a more progressive feel. I tell people now it was sort of like Rush meets Duran Duran, which gives you as good an idea as any of where we were.

The developments were part of my philosophy of constant change – I wanted each album to sound different to the previous one, in order to keep people guessing.

We signed a record deal with the FM Revolver label, and they gave us loads of money, and told us to go off and make an album. We ended up in these recording studios in the middle of Monmouthshire, miles from anywhere. It was the same place where Rush made their famous album 2112, and despite being in the arse-end of nowhere, it had a good feel about it.

I was determined to work hard and try to make a real go of it, so I did my best to behave myself for a while.

We got the drummer from Sad Cafe in to help out, and I was pretty pleased with the results, although I didn't really have anything to judge it by, because we were trying something that was completely new to us.

It sounds like an old-fashioned concept, but I think a musician should try to stretch himself, rather than playing the same type of stuff year after year, and that was the thinking behind what we were doing, really. The album actually did quite well – it went to Number One in Japan, and I think it made people think again about me, and what I was capable of.

One of our earliest tours as a group was supporting Thin

Lizzy, who're one of the greatest rock bands of all time. There was an added connection there, because we were being managed by Christine Goram, whose husband Scott was Thin Lizzy's guitarist.

I got on especially well with their singer, Phil Lynott, who would die of a drug overdose a few years later. Phil was a damn fine human being, and there aren't that many of those about. I spent a lot of time with him, and we shared some good times together. The fact that he died so young was a tragedy for the world in general, and rock music in particular.

The experience of putting a band together and going back out on the road was a bit like being in therapy, I suppose. For one thing, it showed that I could still do it – but this time, the onus was on me, rather than a group.

The band were great guys, and we had a real laugh together. We had a guitarist, Slasher, who was a complete lunatic. We were playing this club in Essex one night, and we've finished the set, and gone backstage. We're changing out of our stage gear, and he's completely stripped off. So we grab him and throw him back out on to the stage, slamming the door on him. So these punters leaving the club were confronted with this bollock-naked guitarist coming flying out at them.

We must have been doing something right as a group, because we played this gig near Folkestone once, and all these people travelled across from France to see us. We were good on stage, and we were getting better as we got more road experience together, and learned how we fitted together, musically.

I enjoyed working with the band, and I still think we did some good recording work together. I also enjoyed it on a personal level, which was quite a relief, as I'd seriously considered quitting the music business altogether after the split with Maiden.

But – yes, there is a but – I must be completely honest and say that I never considered it to be a long-term thing. Now I may hurt a few people's feelings when I say that, such as the people who bought the album and saw the shows, plus everyone who worked on them.

But I'm not gonna bullshit you – it was an experiment, really, just to see what happened. I have to say that the progressive, sort of melodic-rock approach we took, with the keyboards and that, were never really my thing.

I can remember thinking at one point that I didn't want to be making that sort of music for ever, and that I'd rather be a chimney sweep, if it came to it. Bit brutal, but there you go – that's how I felt.

Most importantly, I think the seeds of the music which lay ahead were sown at that time. Having decided what I didn't want to do, now it was time to find out what the alternative was.

*   *   *

Battlezone. Not a description of my life – although it's as good as any – but the best solo band I'd put together to date, and one which really put me back in the Premier League of heavy metal music.

For a start, I was able to call on the services of some very talented musicians I'd come across, including characters like John Hurley and John Wiggins, both of whom would play an important part in the Di'Anno story as it unfolded over the next few years.

Wiggins had come from a band called Deep Malice, who were really good, and there was this pair of Danish guys we had on drums and bass, but don't ask me where we got them from. (For some reason I could never work out, we seemed to have an endless stream of Danish guys in the group – God knows why.)

Just as important as the guys' musical talents, though, was their attitude. This band was really a return to my musical roots – we were a punky, thrashy sort of outfit, having stripped away all the keyboards and layers, we were down to the raw basics.

And fuck, we kicked arse. Really. We sounded pissed-off and angry, which is pretty much how I've been for a lot of my life, and when we got on to that stage, we went for it like I never had before. We were just in your face from the start of a show to the finish, every concert was like going to war.

We had this sort of vaguely futuristic, sort of Mad Max theme running through our songs, as I can remember being convinced at the time that the world was heading for a nuclear holocaust, I can't remember why.

All of this stuff we were doing must have made waves within the music business, because we were signed up by the record label Castle, and we did loads of press interviews about who we were and what we stood for. We had good people working with us behind the scenes, too, which was and still is one of the most important factors in any rock band.

Our manager at that time was a guy called Mickey Keys, who's a bloody brilliant bloke, and really well known in the business. Mickey was right behind us from the start and, believe me, you couldn't want anyone better in your corner.

Our first album was called *Fighting Back*, which just about said it all, really. It summed up how I felt about getting back into the ring again, after Iron Maiden. It did really well, particularly in America, where it seemed to be going down an absolute storm. They're very open to powerful rock music over in the States; there's less of the sterile shite which infects our charts and airwaves over here. I think people recognised the power and fury we had in our songs, and they just lapped it up.

So, we headed off to America to get stuck into some serious touring. This was really to support the album, so we were prepared for some heavy-duty roadwork in order to get ourselves known again.

And, I have to say right here, that this was really where things started to get a bit crazy. In fact, let's be honest, it went totally psycho. It's no exaggeration to say we went absolutely fucking mad on that tour – we thought we were the bloody Sex Pistols.

One of the Battlezone tours was christened the 'Slap the Flaps' tour, for pretty obvious reasons, in honour of all the girls we were servicing every night.

One particular lady, an Australian if I remember right, was responsible for the unofficial title of another tour, the 'LOUTS' tour. During a bout of particularly violent foreplay, this classy Sheila said: 'I'm on the blood at the minute, mate, but you can lob one up my shitter if you like!' What a fucking gem. So the 'Lob One Up The Shitter' tour was christened. Lovely.

On that note, there was an unfortunate incident during one leg of the tour where we were all invited back to someone's house after a night of partying. Instead of sitting around eating crisps and sausages on sticks, like normal people do at a party, we decided to have a shit fight. That's a bit like a food fight, but with one obvious difference.

I shat in someone's baseball cap (I don't know whose, but put it this way – I don't think he wore it again) and we starting flinging this cap around the house. Well, it was a bit like that scene in the film *Trainspotting* where the young lad's shat the bed at his bird's house, and the evidence ends up flying across the kitchen as her parents are having breakfast.

The place was fucking trashed. To say it looked like animals had run wild in there is a gross insult to animals. You wouldn't believe human beings were capable of such filth. There's shit all up the walls and all over the furniture, and the whole place looks like D-Wing after a dirty protest. Add to that the bodies strewn about the place in little pools of shit and vomit, and you've got an idea of the party we had, really. I guess you had to be there.

Unfortunately, that started a trend on those early tours. I used to think it was a great laugh, while pissed, to open up one of the drawers in a hotel room and take a bloody great shit in there. Fuck knows what the chambermaids must have thought when they opened the drawer to find a huge great turd lying there – it must have stunk to high heaven.

Another unfortunate habit, while I'm confessing my sins, was to wake up in the middle of night and just take a piss in the middle of the room, spraying the furniture, carpets and everything. Not surprisingly, our management got some stick from hotel managers, and everybody flatly refused to share a room with me after I started doing that.

Bad toilet habits aside, on that first jaunt we started off at the Palladium in New York, where I'd supported Judas Priest a few years before and, after that, we embarked on a schedule which would see us going twice around the entire country.

When you think about what a huge country America is,

you'll get an idea of the scale of what we were doing. We lived with each other day and night during that time, and although we were playing under the name 'Paul Di'Anno's Battlezone' – which I still wasn't that happy about – we had the sense of being in on something together, like I had with Maiden in the early days. It was an adventure, in every sense of the word.

We got on pretty well, considering, and we did the business on stage, night after night after bloody night. The music was just so hardcore and intense, you had to give it 100 per cent all the time, there really was no other way.

As I said, this 'fuck-you' attitude spilled over into our daily lives as well, as we continued to lay waste to some of the major cities across the US, in a haze of drugs, sex and booze.

If I'd got a bit out of order during the later stages of my last tour with Maiden, I got totally out of fucking order this time. I was just completely out of control, really – it was like a bloody riot, day and night. The groupie situation just got totally out of control – I was overdosing on it.

In fact, among all the other names flying about, it could have been called 'The Venereal Disease Tour' because it seemed as if I was making a significant contribution to research into sexually transmitted diseases. Due to me sticking my dick wherever I fancied 24 hours a day, we were having to stop off at clinics on a regular basis, you know, to get the old chap sorted out.

One guy caught a dose of crabs at one point, and we were all having him on that he'd have to shave off all the hair on his body to get rid of them. So off he goes, shaving his chest, legs, arms and that. When we finally told him we had some cream which would work just as well, you should have seen his bloody face!

There was one girl in Seattle who insisted on being handcuffed to a hotel bed on all fours, before taking it doggy-style from anyone who fancied it. I think we took some pictures of her there, stark naked, just being given one bloody good shafting after another. One would shoot his load up her, groan, then withdraw and do up his trousers, while the next moved into place, unbuckling his belt. The English love queues, after all.

Mind you, there were plenty more who didn't bother with such niceties, preferring to get straight to it. You'd be sitting having a beer, chatting to someone, and a groupie would perch herself on your lap, get your dick out, and start bouncing up and down without so much as an invite. Often, girls would just roam from one hotel room to another, half-naked, just looking for someone else to fuck.

Others would sneak into the backstage area and go down on the entire road crew without batting an eyelid, just sucking off one hairy-arsed roadie after another, without question. These young girls, many of them in their teens, would be kneeling there with their jeans and knickers peeled down to their knees, and their T-shirts and bras up around their necks, with their tits hanging out. Meanwhile, a group of ageing, overweight men would be forming an orderly queue with their cocks hanging out. It's a sight to behold, believe me.

While all this was going on, I was getting as many drugs up my nose as humanly possible, which just fucked me up completely. I'd have to stuff loads of tissues up both my nostrils every morning, as the amount of cocaine I was snorting meant they were just bleeding constantly. I didn't know then that I was permanently damaging my septum, something which still causes me problems now.

We were playing shows for five or six days on the trot, and then taking a couple of days off, during which we'd just have a non-stop party.

The schedule was gruelling enough anyway, and all our carrying on made it even more so. We were absolutely fucked, but we were getting fucked as well, which sort of made it all right.

We left a trail of destruction behind us, like we were some kind of Viking army, pillaging our way across America. Of course, whenever there was any trouble, yours truly was right in the thick of it. We'd stopped one night in Raleigh, North Carolina, after we'd been travelling for bloody miles. I'm pissed as a cunt, and I'm bloody desperate for a slash, so I jumped out of the tour-bus while it parked up at the hotel. I nipped round the corner and, with a great sigh of relief, started pissing up the window of a JC Penney store. Nothing against them, it was just the nearest place available. When you gotta go, you gotta go, right?

Anyway, so I'm standing there pissing away with this fucking huge grin of relief on my face, when this police cruiser purrs up behind me, and stops. These cops get out, and I can tell by their faces they're not happy, so no sooner have I shaken the last few drops off, than I'm spread-eagled over the bonnet of their car, being given the third degree.

Thank Christ I didn't have any drugs on me, but they were going to take me downtown anyway, just for pissing on the window. Once again, my illegal pissing was going to land me in the slammer.

I managed to talk them out of it in the end, telling them who I was, and explaining that I was staying in the hotel round the corner. I think they couldn't be bothered to arrest this mad Englishman, who was obviously just guilty of having a weak bladder.

As it turns out, they should have hung around, because that night we had the mother of all parties at the hotel. There were naked women crawling all over the beds, and an orgy of Biblical proportions erupting around them. Booze and drugs were everywhere, it was like Sodom and Gomorrah. At one point, I was giving this bird one up the Gary, and she was sucking off somebody else, while two others were wanking over her. When I'd finished, I turned her over and sprinkled a little bit of coke on her pussy. When I slowly licked it off, she went crazy. I saw her a few minutes later, giving somebody a hand-job in the bathroom. It was that sort of do.

Just to give you a flavour of what a classy occasion it was, there was this one bird who was absolutely cracking. She'd been giving one of the guys the come-on, or so he thought. Anyway, he's tried it on with her, and she's knocked him back, just completely blanked him.

This particular gentleman was pretty well off his face by this time, and he's pretty fucked off. He stamps off, but then he comes back a minute later, undoes his flies and proceeds to piss in her face. Her hair and dress are soaked, she's standing there screaming and crying, and he's still pissing all over her, as we're falling about laughing. Well, it seemed funny at the time.

On another occasion, our drummer got so completely pissed he fell out of a hotel room window, and very nearly did away with himself. I think it was only the fact that he was blind drunk that saved him, because they say the body is extremely relaxed in that state. Well, he was as relaxed as a newt, so he survived. Mind you, this was a guy who'd already lost the sight of one eye due to an accident with a stray drumstick, so it was only to be expected, really, the silly fucker.

As our epic journey went on across the US, a continuing theme of the tour was one of mindless violence. If we weren't fighting other people, we'd be fighting each other. It just took the slightest thing, while we were standing around waiting to go on stage, and we'd all go for each other. The promoter or tour manager would wonder what the row was, and come rushing in, and we'd be rolling all over the floor, kicking seven shades of shit out of each other. There'd be broken ribs and stuff, dressing rooms trashed, debris everywhere ... it was just wild.

There'd be words, then fists would fly, and everybody would wade in. The whole room would just be consumed by this massive brawl, and they'd have to call the venue's security staff in to break it all up and restore order. Sometimes, they just called the cops.

When we got some extended time off, that was when we'd get into the worst trouble, especially yours truly. In between the two trips across the country, we had a bit of a break, just so we could physically recover from it all, really. I was feeling pretty good, because the tour was going so well, and I'd met up with this bird who lived in Austin, Texas. We hooked up for a while, and I stayed at her place, while the guys headed off in separate directions before the tour resumed.

I don't know whether I was a bad influence on her, or if it was the other way around, but we used to get up to some bloody wicked partying. We knew a lot of Mexican guys who lived in the area, and one in particular became our regular drug-dealer.

One time he'd supplied us with about four grammes of coke,

which cost me just over $100. When I'm fully wired, this woman says she wants to go see a rock show. Now you may think that after all that touring, this was the last thing I needed to see; and in this case you'd be bloody right, because on the bill were two of the worst bands in the history of rock music – Ratt and Poison.

When you say the two names together you've sort of got the flavour of their music – they were part of that LA Glam movement, where the guitarist's eyeliner is better than the women's in the audience, that sort of thing. The whole bunch of them should have been taken to an island and nuked years before, but there you go.

So I've been dragged along to this gig, and I'm doing line after line of coke in the car on the way over, just to numb my senses for the horror that awaited me. When I get there, I duly drank most of a bottle of tequila, and took even more drugs.

The bands come on, and my bird's shouting to me, 'Aren't they great?' I'm smiling back at her, thinking, 'Thank Christ I took all that coke ...'

At some point that night, a guy offers me a line of crystal meth. Now this is a particularly potent drug, which will just about blow your bloody socks off, and after all the booze and coke I'd done, it was likely to do away with me altogether. Me and my bird took some, and just carried on raging and partying into the small hours.

At last, it was finally time to go home. Unbelievably, I drove the bloody car back to the apartment – yeah, I know – and we just crashed out. But this is the weird thing – neither of us was able to even think about going to sleep, we just lay there like zombies.

We were there for three days, like two corpses on their

death bed. Motionless, just staring at the wall. It was like time had stopped. Finally, we started to get the craving for something to eat, and we dragged ourselves out of bed, ordered a load of Mexican food, and just stuffed ourselves. As the drug started to wear off, we just felt sort of warm and dreamy, as if everything was in slow motion.

After we'd come round properly, I think we slept for two days solid. It was a weird experience, a bit like taking a holiday from your body. It felt like I'd been floating around in the air, watching myself. In fact, pretty much the whole of the time I spent at this house passed in some sort of drug haze. God knows how I ever managed to get out alive.

When we eventually got back on the road, a popular pastime was wet T-shirt competitions. We'd been to a few clubs in Chicago where they held them, and the lads were going bloody berserk.

I was even invited to be a judge at one, which was staged down in Florida. Once again, I'd bought a load of coke off a mate that night, and I'd probably snorted three or four grammes of it, washed down with a huge bottle of tequila.

Well, talk about judging women's tits, I couldn't tell a big tit from a blue tit, I was so off my face. They were walking up and down this stage with their giant boobs waving from side to side like they're gonna put someone's eye out any minute, and I was just sat there grinning like the village idiot – I couldn't see a thing.

When they got up close to me, they'd give me a quick flash of these massive silicone tits, and whisper things like, 'You can see a lot more later, if you like ...' I can't remember what the prize money was, but it was probably fuck-all. And these girls were prepared to give it up just like that, so they had a better chance of winning.

Before you ask, no, I didn't take any of them up on their offer, because I was too out of it. And, anyway, I do have some standards.

Partying aside, I realised by the end that it had been a bloody good tour, and it had done me a lot of good over there.

We finished up with some massive shows in Daytona, Florida, and another good one at the Palladium in New York, which was covered by MTV and attended by various bigwigs from the record company.

We took another short break afterwards, during which there was a bit of fannying around with line-up changes. One of the guitarists had become a bit of an egomaniac, so he was out, and the drummer at the time had become a bloody liability, so he was down the road as well.

Graham Bath joined us on guitar, while Steve Hopgood, who used to be in Persian Risk, took over on drums. Steve and I became partners in crime, and I must say here, he was busy egging me on during many of the exploits you'll read about in this book.

Once we'd got our shit sorted out, we recorded our next album, which we named *Children of Madness*. Again, it was released on the Castle label, and we immediately started gigging again across Europe, in support of it.

We were driving to a show on the *Children* tour, and I can remember that we had a long drive between stops, something like 48 hours. Now, if you've got any sense, you'll get your head down on those journeys and get some rest, otherwise you're going to be absolutely wrecked when you get to where you're going.

Instead, yours truly spends two days and two nights snorting coke from this bloody big bag I'd bought. I must have been a bloody drug-dealer's dream. I bought this great stash, and just snorted my way through it, while watching videos on the bus, and drinking beer.

Joining me in this escapade was the singer of the band who were supporting us, and we just lay there, day and night, me doing coke and laughing. Of course, when we finally get to the gig, we discover that neither of us can sing a bloody note, because we're in such a state. I sounded like Kermit the Frog. Sorry, guys.

Actually, that episode had one benefit – I stopped doing coke for about 18 months afterwards, although I was still taking speed on a regular basis.

The late-night boozing was getting worse by this time as well. I remember me and Graham went for a night out in Toronto, after we'd finished a show there. We went out to eat – always make sure you eat, before starting a session – and we stopped in a bar on the way back to the hotel, where we had a beer and a shot of Jack Daniel's.

I think I said to him, 'I'm not really tired yet, are you?' and we agreed to go on somewhere for a few more drinks.

Anyway, we end up at this club, where we meet a bunch of guys who were without doubt the worst possible people we could meet, if we'd wanted an early night. The entire New Zealand rugby squad was out on the town, and we ended up drinking with them until about 7.30 in the morning – all of us absolutely legless.

Later that morning, we have to check out of the hotel, and get back on to the tour-bus. I'm feeling bloody knackered, but I've taken some Pro-Plus, just to stay awake.

Graham, meanwhile, is still laid out in his room, stretched out on the bed with only his underpants on, trying to go back to sleep. The tour manager's trying to rouse him and, in the end, he tore the underpants off him as he got up, leaving him starkers in the hallway. At that moment, this little chambermaid comes by, and is shocked to be confronted with this bollock-naked rock musician.

It wasn't the only time Graham came to grief on that tour. While we were staying at another hotel, he'd got so pissed he managed to lock himself out of his room. He tried to climb out on to the fire escape to break in that way, and only succeeded in falling off, dropping about ten feet into deep snow.

He had a habit of falling off things for some reason – at one gig he fell off the stage into the orchestra pit, nearly knocking himself out. As you'll find out later, it wasn't the only time he would come to grief on one of our tours, but the next time, it would result in something a bit more serious than a bruised ego.

CHAPTER 10

She was giving me that come-hither look that birds do, the
dirty bitch. She was obviously fucking gagging for it.

Well, I didn't need an official invitation. I got her up
against the wall, pushed her skirt up around her waist, and
gave her a fucking good seeing to. No big deal, you may
think, Di'Anno probably does that stuff every night of the
week. Well, right enough, but I only mention the above
because we were both 12 years old at the time.

She was called Sharon, and she will go down (ahem!) in
history as the first-ever woman to succumb to the legendary
Di'Anno charm. It was my first sexual experience, and it
happened in her dad's garden shed in Walthamstow. I can't
really remember much else about it to be honest, so it
probably wasn't that mind-blowing.

Unfortunately, though, her dad soon found out about my
little foray into his darling daughter's knickers, and he gave

me a good clumping as a result. That sort of sets the scene for the way things would go from then on, really.

So the lovely Sharon was the first, but you'll probably have guessed that she was by no means the last. Since that happy day, I've shagged thousands of women, all over the world. I just don't know what it is about me and women – they've caused me more grief over the years than booze, drugs and bands put together, but still they come back for more, and still I snap 'em up when they do.

As a whole, my love life has always been like a fucking war zone. My five marriages have all gone the same way, while the number of casual and serious relationships which have crashed and burned, well, I lost count many years ago. The marriages have given me at least six children that I know of (there are probably a few more elsewhere) and I would happily die for them all, but it saddens me that they're not around me all the time.

Women have always been drawn to me for some strange reason, and this is still true to this day. I'm not boasting, just telling the truth. I was in Los Angeles a while ago, chatting over a few drinks with a mate of mine, and we were talking about this very subject – women we've known and loved, and all that.

Well, it was quite a lengthy conversation, but we worked out that I'd slept with well over 1,000 women (and this was a few years ago now). Friends have since said I've sold myself short, that the total's nearer 2,000, but I've no way of knowing.

There have been passionate love affairs, casual flings, drunken one-night stands and drug-addled quickies. There have been cosy, house-in-the-suburbs marriages and violent, drug-fuelled encounters. One of these ended with me being sent to the County Jail in California for five months, following a famous incident in which I almost ended up killing one particular woman; more of that later.

My trouble (or one of my troubles, at least) is that in my position, you can get girls with a click of your fingers. It doesn't matter if you've got a face like a badger's arse; if you're the singer of a rock band, there will be birds lining up to be fucked by you. You'll be fighting them off. You can have a face like Nora Batty's beaver – no problem, they'll be over you like a rash.

And while I've never been slow to take advantage of the many impressionable young nubiles who press their bare tits into my face after every gig, the truth is, I've got zero respect for the vast majority of them. I know they get off on it, sleeping with a rock star, but I'm sure it's made me treat women like dirt, just because they act as if that's the way they want to be treated.

I think that whole scene has turned me into this monster that summons women like some Roman emperor, calling on slaves to do his bidding. I've had them down on all fours giving me a blow-job within minutes of first meeting them. The perverted stunts I've pulled would turn your stomach – just because I was bored. It gives me a real thrill just to see how far women will go, the things they'll let me do to them, so they feel they've pleasured the great Paul Di'Anno. If I have to make any sort of effort with them at all, I just tell them to fuck off, 'cos I can't be bothered.

My favourite little trick – and we're not talking Paul Daniels here – is to have a bird snort a line of cocaine off my dick, as it stands erect. I've had hundreds of them do this, just lining up the powder on my old chap, and slowly run their nose along the length of it. I don't know why, it just gives you a kinky thrill as some bird you've never met before just bends down over your crotch and starts snorting away. Mind you, if you start to deflate, you've got $100 worth on the floor, and she'd better start clearing it up.

But before you think women who have sex with rock stars are tragic victims, let me put you straight. Most of them are game for anything. Some are into kinky stuff, like whipping, spanking, walking over you in high heels, licking your arsehole out, or having you piss over them; but others will just lie there like a sack of spuds with their legs in the air, and let you do what the fuck you want. You take it, because it's on offer. You'll be there in your hotel room at night, thousands of miles away from home, knocking the arse out of some tart, just for something to do, really. If you were at home, you'd turn the snooker on; out on the road, you give a groupie one.

It's a bit sad, really. They'll be lying there in the bed underneath you, with their tits bouncing back and forth as you're thrusting away, and this really dopey smile on their face, just because they're being fucked by Paul Di'Anno. Like I said, sad fuckers, most of them.

In fact, sometimes I couldn't even be arsed to shag a groupie – I'll have got one of the roadies to do it, while I watched them. It's like having your own live sex show, in the comfort of your hotel suite!

There were these two sisters that I met once in Phoenix, Arizona. Nice girls, eager to please, and they were promising all the extras. They were giving me the green light, you know, 'We'll do anything you want, Paul ...'Anyway, I've taken both of them back to my hotel room, and I've got all their kit off, so all three of us are completely naked, and I'm ready to give them a really good seeing to. They've got these fantastic bodies with really big tits and these huge, dark-brown eyes. They may even have been twins, they were so similar.

They're side-by-side on my bed, and I'm kneeling between them, having a bit of a fiddle around with both of their tits, tuning into Radio Moscow and all that. After a bit of that, they've let it be known that they're ready for the real action. Flaps down, ready for landing, as they say. I hadn't actually taken any drugs that day, so I was quite clear-headed, for once.

I can remember persuading them to do the cocaine-snorting trick and, sure enough, they took turns in lining up the coke along the top of my dick and snorting it up, one after another. I don't think they were really used to doing coke, but they were both eager to please. It was like a scene from a porno movie, as they leaned over my crotch in turn. I had a stalk-on like a fucking railway sleeper – you could have hung a wet donkey jacket on it. I was really getting off on the whole thing, especially as they'd gently tickle my balls as they were doing it, to keep the old fella up there like wood.

Of course, the reverse is true as well; if you sprinkle a little bit of coke on to a woman's pussy and then lick it off, it makes them tingle all over, according to my exhaustive research. A handy tip, there – you can't say this book isn't educational. So we did that for a while, they both spread their thighs to reveal their inner workings, while I spread a little bit of Peruvian marching powder over the little pink bits. I licked both of them out as best I could, and while I tasted the coke on my tongue, they writhed and sighed on the bed. As one got the treatment, the other knelt over us, watching.

In my role as on-the-spot correspondent, I can also report to you that if you smear your dick with cocaine (should you be that way inclined) you can fuck for England, hour after hour after hour. It seems to keep you hard – you can just go on for ever. If you don't believe me, you can ask those two sisters, they'll tell you.

I've still got a mental image in my head now, it's as clear as if it had just happened. I can see me getting inside them and pumping away, while these gorgeous birds claw my back, moaning and squealing at the tops of their voices.

Who'd be a rock musician, eh?

*   *   *

Another romantic experience – and one that Mills and Boon almost certainly wouldn't have dreamt up – occurred on my birthday one year, when I had a surprise visitor at my hotel. This girl had been hanging around with the band that night, and somehow, when the party had finally broken up in the early hours, she'd found her way to my room.

There was a knock at the door and, when I opened it, there she was. As naked as the day she was born, wearing just a wicked smile. She flounced past me as if she was on the Paris catwalk, and lay down on my bed with her legs spread wide. 'It's your birthday, and I'm your present,' she said. 'Do whatever you like with me!'

Well, I didn't need asking twice. I flipped her over, and had her on all fours so bloody fast her feet didn't touch. She's giggling away, just kneeling there on the bed, with this sweet little arse stuck up in the air and this tight little fanny inviting me in. I was offering up thanks to God and Allah as I kneeled up behind her, unbuckling my belt.

Not being one to stand on ceremony, I spat on my hand and fucked her hard up the arse. I think it was a back-door delivery she wasn't expecting, and I think she'd previously only been used to one-way traffic, shall we say; but that's a birthday present I won't forget in a hurry. Certainly better than any Marks and Spencer gift set, anyway.

In fact, I tried for a second helping, but unfortunately I'd drunk enough to drown a dwarf that evening, so I couldn't get it up again. I think she was probably grateful, though – she'd probably had about as much as she could take for a while.

Once you've had years and years of getting a different girl – or girls – every night, you think up little sex games to experiment a bit. You name it, I've done it – I stoop at nothing. Some of the things I've done would just blow your mind.

As well as putting my dick up each and every available orifice that was offered to me, I've also used broom handles, bananas, bottles – even guns. Front or back, it makes no difference to me. If they wanted a wild time with a rock star, they certainly came to the right place; although some probably got more than they bargained for.

Many's the time I've had some tart biting the pillow, with her arse in the air, and a Jack Daniel's bottle-neck shoved right up her ring-piece. I've brought them to an earth-shattering climax with nothing more than a shampoo bottle and a bit of elbow grease! Quite often I've felt like James fucking Herriott, standing there with my bloody hand up some tart's snatch. In some cases, you'd be in danger of losing your fucking arm.

There was this silly bitch once in LA who said to me, 'I can do everything – no one's ever really made me come!' She was the quiet, retiring type – she'd spent the entire evening at this bar getting her tits out, and challenging all the blokes there to take her 'up my ASS'!

Well, I like a challenge, so we've gone back to the hotel and I've had a go at her. I'm hammering away like a jackhammer, and she's screaming at the top of her voice, scratching my back, sticking her fingers up my arse and squeezing my balls. I'm a bit wary, because she's got these long nails like red talons, but she's certainly keen. If she wasn't a pro, she was certainly an enthusiastic amateur.

So I'm banging away, and she's certainly well up for it. I'm sticking my length right the way up inside her, and she's moaning, 'Fuck, fuck ...' in a low voice. It all seems to be happening all right, and her face contorts as my thrusts get harder and harder. She sighs deeply, her head falls back, and her body relaxes, so I guess she's reached the big O. Right on cue, I shoot my load inside her, before rolling off, panting.

While I caught my breath, I watched while my mate had a go with her, and it seemed to happen again. He had her doubled up like a deckchair, ramming it into her while her ankles rested on his shoulders. Between the pair of us, I think we fucked the poor cow to within an inch of her life that night. She was nothing special, really. I just think those Hollywood boys hadn't been doing the job properly, to be honest with you.

Anyway, she wasn't the best fuck I've ever had, and when we'd finished with her, she showed no signs of realising she was no longer wanted. As well as outstaying her welcome, she was a real mouthy cunt anyway, so I lost my rag with her in the end. I was a bit out of it, so perhaps I wasn't really thinking straight when I decided to sort her out. I'd told her to shut the fuck up, but her gob just didn't stop screeching on.

I got a handgun which I'd had in the hotel room, and grabbed her with my other hand, shoving her back on to the bed. She only had a hotel bathrobe on, which fell back to reveal her naked thighs. I prised her legs apart, and shoved the gun up her pussy, screaming at her, 'If you really want to be fucked, I'll fire this fucking gun, you'll be fucked then!'

Not *Pride and Prejudice*, I grant you, but it livens up a long tour.

Another groupie experience almost had an equally tragic ending, but this time it was me who had a near-death experience. I'd picked up this pair of girls, and taken them back to the hotel.

They're both wearing heavy metal T-shirts and jeans, so I ordered them to strip. While I lay on the bed, they peeled off their clothes, unhooking their bras and stepping out of their little G-strings. In doing so, they've let it be known they're game for anything. In a matter of minutes, one's on her knees sucking my cock to within an inch of its life, while the other's kneeling beside me on the bed while I nuzzled her huge nipples.

After a while, the two of them are sitting astride me on the bed. One is bouncing up and down on my groin, riding my cock like she was in a rodeo; the other is sitting on my face, as I lick out her (large) pussy. The only trouble was, the one sitting on my face was quite a big girl, and she was slowly crushing me to death. In fact, my head had disappeared completely under her meaty thighs, so I'd lost all senses. The world was a dark, silent place to me at that point.

I realised I was fast running out of oxygen and, as she bobbed up and down, I couldn't even scream, 'cos I didn't have enough air to make a sound. When I tried to call out, I just got a mouthful of pubes.

She was too heavy to push off, so I was just lying there with this giant hairy pussy going up and down on me, like a bloody great hoover bag. I suffer from asthma, so my chest was getting really tight, and I think I was just turning purple when she finally got off, the dozy cow. Still, what a way to go ... you can just imagine the obituary in *The Times*, can't you? My mum would have been so proud.

Another Di'Anno conquest who stands out in the memory was this beautiful Italian bird I met over in America. She was gorgeous, a bit like Madonna, but better looking. The only trouble was – and there's no polite way to put this – she was as thick as pig shit.

A goldfish would pass a GCSE exam before that soppy tart, I promise you. She was from Salem, Massachusetts, and I think she tagged along with us for a while, after hooking up with me backstage.

I can remember lying in bed with her back at the hotel, and I started bullshitting her, 'Look, I've got something to tell you ...'

She's all wide-eyed innocence. 'What?'

'Well, it's my old chap here. It may not look much now, but when it gets going, good God, girl, it's enormous. It's a medical condition I'm afflicted with – I've got an absolutely massive dick. That's why they call me the Italian Stallion!'

She's like, 'Really? Ooh, Paul!' Her gob's hanging open, and she's already looking a bit uneasy, bless her. She obviously thought she was going to be tortured by this freak of nature. So I go on to explain to her that before we can get down to it properly, I'll need to break her in gently, so she's ready. Amazingly, she agrees, and I look around the room for something I can put up her.

As luck would have it, there was a bowl of fresh fruit on the sideboard, and I grab hold of this big old banana and brandish it in front of her. Her eyes widen a bit, obviously, but she doesn't complain, so I ease her back on to the bed, pull her legs apart, and slowly slide it up inside her.

Imagine the scene – there's me in this posh hotel room, with this young girl lying in front of me on the bed, with her legs spread out as far as they could go. It looks like I'm giving her a gynaecological examination, as I move my hand up and down inside her. I'm stuffing this big old banana up into her as far as I can, again and again, while she's lying back, rocking back and forth, like it's the most normal thing in the world. Fucking hell.

The same girl came to grief a bit later on that same tour, if I remember rightly. We were staying at a Holiday Inn in Minneapolis, and it's something like -32°C. Whatever part of your body is exposed to that sort of cold will drop off, believe me.

Anyway, this daft tart wants to go across the road to the 7-11 store, but she realises she's lost her ID. Now, in America, you need to be at least 60 (and a particularly old-looking 60, at that) if you want to buy alcohol without any ID. The legal drinking age is 21, and they're really fucking paranoid about it. You can buy a semi-automatic weapon in any old store, or score heroin on a street corner, but you better not try to buy booze.

So, Soppy has lost her ID, and we're all hunting for it. I was even out on the roof of the hotel at one point, in case it had blown out of the window. (Yeah, I know, but it seemed quite reasonable at the time.) She decides to look around outside, but hasn't got any bloody shoes on, so she cuts her feet to fucking ribbons on all the ice, and there's all this blood everywhere. That's how smart she was.

Yet another Mastermind contestant was a Portuguese girl I met somewhere. Once again, mind-blowingly beautiful, yet just as unlikely to trouble the scorer in a pub quiz.

I've met her backstage and, yet again, I've managed to persuade her to come back to the hotel with me. She's a bit reluctant, playing a bit hard to get. She obviously didn't want the delicate flower of her womanhood being sullied by the likes of me just like that, so I had to be a bit clever with this one.

I'm plying her with drink and coke and everything, and we're just sitting there in my room, chatting. Anyway, it's getting late, and she starts to talk about leaving. She doesn't have any money for a cab, and I tell her I haven't got any currency on me, adding that my credit cards are on the tour-bus.

As if it's just struck me, I say, 'I know, why don't you stay here tonight? It'll save you trying to get back on your own! It's very dangerous out there you know!' (Like I'd know ... I'd spent a grand total of about seven hours in the place.)

So she says, 'But I've nowhere to sleep here!' So I assure her that she can sleep in my bed, that I'll be a perfect gentleman, etc. etc., and that she's perfectly safe. (About as safe as a turkey at Christmas!)

She seems to be happy with this, and we carry on chatting. I was giving her a load of old bullshit that I was making up as I went along. I told her that my Dad was a photographer for *Penthouse* magazine, and that he was always on the look-out for new glamour models. (It almost goes without saying that he isn't!)

Just as I thought she might, she piped up, 'Ooh! I've always wanted to be a model!'

I pretended to look her up and down, professionally. 'You know, I think you might be a great model but, of course, I'd have to see in you in a proper pose, I can't tell while you're sitting here fully clothed like this.'

Would you believe it? She seemed to be swallowing all this rubbish, because although she looks a bit nervous, I can tell she's tempted. I suppose it wouldn't be that impossible to believe, that a rock star could help get you a modelling job, so it must have seemed like a golden opportunity to her.

Anyway, she overcame her shyness, and while I'm encouraging her (and trying not to chuckle) she's slowly peeled off her skirt and top, until she's standing there in the middle of the room, all self-conscious, with just her bra and knickers on. She looks fucking gorgeous, all vulnerable and ready to be taken advantage of.

I'm still desperately trying not to start laughing, and now I'm also trying to quell a hard-on like fucking iron, but I'm pretending to be undecided as to whether she's got what it takes. 'I don't know,' I tell her, 'I suppose I really need to see you without any clothes on at all.'

There's a tense stand-off for a few minutes. I can tell she's wrestling with her conscience – she obviously doesn't want to stand completely naked in front of this depraved rock singer she's only just met; she probably came from quite a strict religious family, after all.

On the other hand, the promise of fame and fortune can turn pretty much any girl's head, so she was obviously giving it serious thought. In the end, her defences crumbled. She slowly took off her bra, and then pulled off her knickers, until she was standing there awkwardly in the middle of my hotel room, naked as the day she was born, with her tits and bush in full view.

You'll be glad to know that this tense thriller has a happy ending, as not only did she spend the night there with me, I fucked her half to death. Lovely.

*   *   *

From the start of my career with Iron Maiden, when we were still a fledgling pub band, I realised almost straight away that the whole girlfriend issue would be, to say the least, a bit tricky. Often it was for honourable reasons; we'd be away touring, or locked in a rehearsal room or recording studio somewhere. Just as likely, though, I'd be tempted by one of the young birds who waited for us backstage, and I'd soon have some explaining to do.

When I was a wild youth, even before becoming a singer, I used to two-time girls when I thought I could get away with it – what young lad doesn't? I'd be out with one when the other would see me from a bus, or I'd walk into a pub and they'd both be there. Either way, I'd end up in the shit.

Even before fame and all that bollocks came along to make my life complicated, I'd already found ways to complicate it for myself, without any help from anybody else, believe me.

Girls were always attracted to me, even then, for some reason – I could just charm them out of the trees.

For those who've never encountered it, the situation with women and rock bands takes some believing, and I think it caught us all by surprise when we started out. There we were, a bunch of lads from London, going abroad for the first time, having people make a fuss of us, playing these barnstorming gigs every night, and moving from one hotel to another. It just wasn't something any of us had an experience of.

On top of all of this, you have a never-ending stream of young women who want nothing more than to tear your clothes off. Talk about a fox in the chicken coop, I was like a predator, fucking for England. If I said it wasn't fucking marvellous and I didn't love it to bits, I'd be a bloody liar.

On our first tour of America, I often had three or four women climbing all over my bed, romping around – it was every male's fantasy, come to life. They'd do anything you want, just for the honour of fucking the singer of their favourite band. They'd be blowing me, frigging each other, wanking themselves off, you name it – anything I told them, they'd do without question. It was like those sex slaves where their only purpose in life is to please their master. That's not the way I saw it, but fucking hell, if some bird wants to stick her arse in my face, I'm not going to say no, am I?

With the forbidden fruit, though, came hidden dangers. Namely those nasty little rashes which can put a man's pride and joy out of action for a while. This was a constant hazard for me on the road, especially as you didn't know if the girl sharing your bed had done the same for the last rock band to pass through town, and the one before that.

A good way of telling, I used to say (and listen to Dr Paul, now) would be to squirt a little bit of lemon juice on to your fingers. When the groupie's stripped off and ready for action, open her legs and stick your fingers inside her. Have a bit of a fiddle around, and see what happens. If they winced, it was probably best to steer well clear... I'm not Dr Ruth, but people who know about these things swear it's true.

As I got more and more famous, so the nightly girl action got more and more intense. Backwards, sideways, swinging from the chandelier, every which way – I couldn't get enough. I saw more beavers on those early tours than your average zoo-keeper does in a year.

Being young and single, I think we all enjoyed the pleasures of the flesh at one time or another, especially me, Dave and Clive, who were like kids let loose in a fucking sweet shop.

I remember a particular night on one of our first tours, when we secretly taped Steve Harris in the throes of passion with a girl he'd met. We'd bought these remote-controlled tape recorders in Japan, which could be activated from outside a room, so we were all outside, giggling, as we heard all this moaning and groaning. This girl was saying, 'Ooh, Steve, you're so hairy ...' – we bloody cracked up!

I think that memorable incident took place at a hotel in Sheffield, which was to be the scene of many outrages on subsequent tours, with fire-extinguisher fights and multiple shagging. Ah, happy days.

I can imagine there'll be women reading this thinking what a sexist bastard Paul Di'Anno is. Well, fair comment, but if I can say a few words in my defence, I can only point out once again that the women who queued up outside my hotel room door were there of their own free will – no one forced them.

In fact, if my memory serves, they all seemed to be bloody gagging for it!

If I was taking advantage of them, they were certainly taking advantage of me as well. They would probably boast to their mates back at work on Monday that they'd slept with the singer of Iron Maiden, and good luck to them, I say. It was honest, direct and above board, without all the usual pissing about and 'getting to know each other' bollocks.

In fact, you'll be glad to know that at one point in my solo career – admittedly when I was old enough to know better – I did make my own special contribution to a more equal society, by introducing the 'Humanitarian of the Year Awards'.

These prestigious gongs were presented to the musician or roadie who copped off with the woman who matched the description required for that particular day. For instance, you'd get ten points for sleeping with a lovely blonde-haired bird if it was a Monday. On the other hand, a Friday may mean that a giant, skinny bird would earn 50 points. Mind you, you'd have to bring their underwear back to the tour-bus as proof – rules are rules, after all. If it was bloodstained underwear, the points tally would go off the scale.

The specifications were planned in advance during the tour, and competition was pretty fierce. If the woman in your sights was a dwarf, or had some other physical deformity, you'd be doing your points average no harm at all.

Top night of the week for the Humanitarian of the Year Awards was Wednesday night, when the ugliest bird in the pub or club was a highly-prized asset. We were touring in Spain with my band Battlezone one year, and we were in a club which without a shadow of a doubt boasted some of the roughest-looking old tarts I've ever seen, and that's saying something.

I spotted one lurking by the bar which would have clinched me the title there and then. She was such a beast, it wasn't true. She wasn't just ugly, she looked genuinely scary. Thinking back, she looked as if she'd had a toucan's face grafted on to her own, with this great hawklike beak sticking out of her face where her nose should have been.

I strolled over, cool as you like, and casually informed her that her luck was in. However, I'm ashamed to say, dear reader – and she must have been a fucking lesbian or something – she just wouldn't go for it. Whether she'd got wind of the competition and got the hump when she found out she was odds-on favourite to be the ugliest bird of the evening, I don't know. The Di'Anno charm – even when applied at full blast, with both blowers on – had no effect.

Still, you'll be pleased to know that this story has a happy ending. Guess who won the Humanitarian of the Year Award for seven years on the trot? Yeah, that's right ... who else?

Someone who gave me a good run for my money, though, was our drummer, Steve Hopgood. Me and him used to have various women on the go all the time out in LA, six or seven each. Quite often, we'd go to a bar and they'd all be in there – which was when you needed to make a quick exit, of course.

Talking of Mr Hopgood, there was a famous incident involving him, which happened in New York while we were both in Battlezone. This fat bird has shown up at the stage door after a gig. When I say fat, I don't mean pleasantly plump; I mean she looked as if her mother had mated with a hippo – bloody enormous. Anyway, she was dressed to kill, with all her make-up on and her hair teased out and all that, and she was obviously up for a good time.

She obviously thought a lot of herself – as an awful lot of American women seem to do – and she was trying to blag her way backstage. In doing so, she makes it clear she'll pretty much do anything that's necessary, if you know what I mean. So, someone says, 'All right, bitch, if you want to get back here, this is what you do. First you give me a blow-job, then the guitar roadie, then the drum roadie.'

Well, she doesn't turn a hair. She's down on her knees in a minute, doing them all, and I think she did a couple of the boys in my band for afters, giggling all the while. They're all queuing up in front of her, as she sucks one cock after another. The cum is all dribbling down her chin, but she's so fucked-up on coke, she doesn't even notice. While she's doing it, we're all pissing about, grabbing her tits and putting our hands up her skirt, sticking our fingers inside her snatch – it was really getting out of hand, but she didn't seem to care. I doubt if she even noticed.

In fact, I think one of the lads may have lost control of his faculties altogether, and just lifted her up on to a table, ripped her skirt off, and starting giving it to her right there across the tabletop. She was loving it – she had her legs wrapped round his waist as he was pumping away between these great fat thighs, and I think the fact that we were all watching just made her all the more enthusiastic. As she was lying back, taking it from him, we pulled her shirt and bra up and got her tits out, which just made her even more horny.

Then everybody started wanking over her, so her tits are splattered with warm cum. She smears it all in and starts rubbing her nipples, like she's in some private fantasy. It must have been for her, I suppose, 'cos she was no oil painting. They say the big ones are always grateful, don't they?

I didn't fancy it – not after that lot – but as soon as they're all finished, Steve comes in the door. We've pointed him out to her – bastards that we are – and she's run up to him, still with spunk all round her mouth, squealing, 'Ooh! Steve! Steve Hopgood!' and she's given him this big, wet sloppy kiss.

She wasn't the first woman to disgrace herself in my company, and she sure as hell wasn't the last. You got the strangest types turning up backstage – from burned-out crack whores to nervous teenagers attending their first gig.

There was one girl at a gig somewhere in the West Country – she came backstage to get some autographs or something after the show. Battlezone had done a fantastic set, just flayed 'em alive, so we're just buzzing, bouncing off the walls and ceiling with pure adrenalin.

This girl was about 19 or 20, quite plain, and a bit on the chubby side – a buxom country wench. She was wearing one of our T-shirts, so she's a bit in awe when she gets to meet us, which is always a good start, really. Her boyfriend is out in the main hall, but security haven't let him in, so she's there on her tod.

She's OK, not the brightest thing on two legs and with a decidedly dodgy perm, but you can't always be that choosy in these matters. We've given her a drink of Jack Daniel's, and she's obviously not used to it, because she's as pissed as a cunt within minutes.

The next thing I know, she's sat there snogging one of the guys, just wrapping herself around him. While he's kissing her, he's slowly lifting up her T-shirt and fondling her tits with his spare hand, in full view of all of us.

As her shirt is lifted up, you can see this hefty old-fashioned white bra, the sort of thing that a middle-aged Sunday school teacher might wear (I'd imagine). I don't think she'd been dressing to impress in the underwear department, so it's a fair guess that her boyfriend probably wasn't getting that much, I'd say.

After a short fag-break, and a bit more to drink, she's slumped back in the chair, and before long he's undone this sturdy great bra, and her massive great tits are hanging out. He's getting more and more passionate, we're getting more and more interested in the proceedings, and she's let it be known that she's game.

So he undoes her jeans, revealing a pair of white knickers roughly the size of North Somerset, and slowly slips them off, as the vultures gather. So there's this girl, who had probably been out in the crowd shyly holding hands with her boyfriend less than half-an-hour ago, now lying back in a chair almost naked, while half-a-dozen long-haired men stand around her with their dicks hanging out.

And she did all of us, one by one. We took it in turns to get between her legs, and between us, we fucked her every which way. When we'd finished with her, she was a right mess. She was stark naked, covered with spunk, lipstick smeared across her face, and her hair stuck out like a scarecrow. We slung her out of the backstage area, but I can't think her boyfriend would have been that happy to see her.

There was another girl who came along to several shows here in Britain, and liked to pretend she was a cut above the typical groupie. While they usually wore the standard 'rock chick' garb – leather mini-skirt, cut-off T-shirt, leather jacket, stilettos, etc. – this bird liked to wear long summer dresses or skirts, like something out of a Laura Ashley ad.

She talked really posh, and someone said she was the daughter of some big nob somewhere; it was ironic, really, because she encountered enough big knobs when she was with us to last her for the rest of her life, I'd say.

When there were other people around, she'd put on the big 'I am' act, acting like she was superior. But when there was just a few of us from the band there, and she'd got a few drinks inside her, she turned into a raving fucking nympho. She would literally beg for it.

The flouncy skirt would be hoisted up over her waist, the delicate little lacy knickers would be hastily tugged down to her knees, and her bare little arse would be stuck up in the air like a cat on heat. Within minutes, one of the lads would be rogering her from behind, as hard as you like, while she howled and screamed for more. Once the party really got going, another one of the lads would be putting his cock in her mouth, while someone else would take over at the other end. Between us, we'd all get through her like this.

Night after night, she'd be there between all these guys like a kind of spit roast, just lapping it all up. Five, six, seven, eight guys one after another – she'd be game for everything we could throw at her.

If she really was related to the aristocracy, I wonder what Daddy would have thought if he'd seen his darling daughter being ravaged and defiled in this way by morally bankrupt rock stars? It doesn't bear thinking about.

*   *   *

It could have all been so different ...

You may be surprised to know that I was once a happily-married family man, living a relatively normal life in suburbia. No, I'm not kidding – it was just after the split with Iron Maiden, when the dust began to settle.

I was still unsure about what I was going to do with the rest of my life, so I had a bit of time on my hands. The royalties from the Iron Maiden records were still coming in, and I just had a bit of an extended break, before I started my solo career.

The seeds of the band that would later become Di'Anno were being sown, as I was meeting up with a few musicians around that time, talking about songs, lyrics and stuff. It was early days, but I had a few ideas that I wanted to try out.

In the meantime, just as everything was starting to calm down a bit, I go and turn everything upside down again ... by falling head-over-heels in love. Her name was Beverley, and she worked in a bank. She must have been very different from the sort of rock chicks I'd been hanging out with up until then, because I just lost my head completely, and asked her to marry me.

She was – and still is – a very beautiful woman. They say you'll only find true love twice in your life, and she was my first real love, there's no doubt about that. Even after all the women I'd slept with, I just wanted to be with her.

After we were married, we went on honeymoon to Antigua, which is a place I really loved. I wrote a song about it, which later turned up on my first solo album. It's absolutely stunning there, with all those beaches, and we should have had a fantastic time together. The only problem was, Bev got really sick almost straight away, which soon turned out to be the first wave of morning sickness. She was pregnant – and Paul Di'Anno was going to be a father.

In fact, I was well up for the whole family bit – I put down a deposit on a house in Billericay, and we moved in with my parents while builders did up the place, renovating and extending it.

We just saw ourselves living this idyllic lifestyle out there, which is pretty much what happened, really. It was lucky that I was out of that whole recording-touring-recording treadmill, and I could actually spend time at home with Bev while she prepared to have our baby.

As the big day drew nearer, I was out one night, playing darts at our local pub with my father-in-law. Now Bev's dad is just one of the best human beings you're ever going to come across, he's just a smashing bloke, and we got on like a house on fire. So we're there playing darts, as we did quite often, and suddenly we hear, 'Quick, Paul – Bev's waters have broke!'

I can remember it took a few minutes to dawn on me – I think I carried on throwing darts – and then I pulled up sharp, and said to myself, 'Fuck – I'm having a baby!' It was like the whole thing had just hit home.

Now, any father will tell you, it's the worst feeling in the world when your wife first goes into labour, because you're hanging around like a spare one at a wedding, while she's in pain. The thing about it is, there's absolutely nothing you can do, apart from hold her hand a bit – you just feel bloody useless.

After about four hours, the big moment arrived, and my son, my baby boy, came into the world. When his little head popped out, it was just the most amazing feeling I'd ever had. And when I held him in my arms for the first time ... well, I just cried. It is one of the most incredible feelings you can ever have in the world – it's like 100,000 fans are screaming at you for an encore, that's the best way I can describe it.

And so, for the first couple of years, I was at home with Di'Anno junior while Bev went back to work. I was getting a few things together and playing the odd gig, but I was a full-time house husband for a while, and I enjoyed the time we spent together. It was the nearest thing I'd ever had to a normal life, and I should have made the most of it, because it wouldn't last for too much longer.

*   *   *

If the world of marital bliss and the world of rock 'n' roll were far removed from each other, they would soon collide. The crunch happened when I was away recording at these remote studios in Monmouthshire.

They were in the middle of fucking nowhere, so we had a lot of time on our hands, without the temptations of city life. I was abstaining at the time, being happily married and that, so I just let the others get on with it when we did go to the nearest town.

I threw myself into the work, because I wanted to get the job done as well as I knew how, and then go home to my family. I missed them so much in the weeks I was away – I just hated being apart from my new baby, not being there for him.

I just wanted to sleep in the same bed as my wife at night, knowing we were all safe and happy together. The fact that I was miles away on my own just broke my heart, it really did.

When they came up to see me, I just felt blessed to have such a family, and it was fantastic to see them again. They arrived just as we were finishing off the album, and I remember having a really good feeling about life in general at that point – I was pleased with the record, and thought it'd do well, and I was optimistic about the future we all had together.

If anybody asks me now why I put myself through that, being apart from my family for long periods just to make a record, I think I'd say that it was my family who were making me do it, in a funny kind of way.

I wanted to prove to them that I could still do it, that I could make successful records, even without the backing of Iron Maiden. I can remember thinking that I didn't want my little boy growing up hearing bad things about his father. I suppose I was doing it for him really; I just wanted him to be proud of me.

In case you're wondering, this particular story doesn't have a happy ending. Me and Bev broke up a while later, which is something I regret to this day. I still feel she was a true love of mine, and it saddens me that we weren't able to make a go of it, and be a real family.

We're still best friends, and I still care about her a lot. I still feel as protective of her now as I did back then. If anyone _as ever to try and hurt her ... well, God help them. I'd rip their fucking heads off and shit down the hole.

I mentioned earlier a passionate love affair which took place while I was living in Los Angeles, and it's an affair which has given rise to one of the most popular legends about me.

The legend is that I was sent to Los Angeles County Jail for assaulting a woman with a deadly weapon, while in a cocaine-fuelled frenzy. This is something that people usually shy away from mentioning in front of me, and it's not something I'm generally happy talking about, even to my closest friends and band members. The unfortunate thing about this particular legend, though, is that it happens to be true.

It was around 1990, and I was living with this girl in LA. She was Texan, and she was also pretty wild, and in my experience, those two things very often go together. Our relationship was what you might call 'stormy', and what could more accurately be called 'a fucking war zone'.

The slightest little thing, and she used to go fucking ballistic. Any excuse, and she'd be off. We used to have the mother of all fights, on a regular basis. Whereas some couples go shopping together or do the garden, we'd have a fight. She was like a bloody hellcat – she used to smack me right in the mouth during an argument, and if you've never had the pleasure of being smacked in the mouth by a big leggy Texan girl, take my advice and don't bother. I blame myself for the arguments, and I can't blame her for retaliating.

Now, we didn't need Jerry Springer to tell us what was at the root of all these problems. The fact that I was doing cocaine morning, noon and night made our already volatile relationship like a powder-keg, ready to blow at any moment.

So much so that during one particular 'domestic', we made so much noise that the LAPD were called to our home. There'd been a massive fight involving a knife, and I was seconds away from fucking killing her with it.

When the cops burst in, they found me with this knife, and that was that. My feet didn't bloody touch. I was arrested, taken downtown and thrown into jail. The charge was assault with a deadly weapon. I think they found out who I was, discovered my reputation, and just decided I was going down for it.

What put the fucking tin hat on all of this was the fact that cops searched the apartment and found a huge stash of cocaine, and my Uzi gun. I may be a rock star, but once they'd copped that little lot, they weren't about to ask for autographs.

What seemed like the entire LAPD riot squad were called out to drag me away, and I was slung in jail. So while she's still on the outside, I'm in the slammer. I had to make various court appearances, all shackled up and dressed in an orange boiler suit, like Hannibal bloody Lecter.

They appointed a State Attorney for me, so I get sent back to jail, and I'm in the middle of this bloody nightmare.

These places are bloody tough; the best thing to do is to keep your head down, and your gob shut. Needless to say, I didn't do that, but it's the best thing to do. I actually had quite a card school going before long, and there were a few hairy moments during arguments over cards, I can tell you. I also had a good trade in flogging cigarettes, which I used to shift for $2 a go. Only problem was I had to hide them up my arse, but my clientele weren't exactly fussy.

If you've ever seen a movie where someone gets sent to jail in America, and it's a really tough place, and he gets fucked up the arse by a 20st black guy, don't believe it. That doesn't even begin to describe it. They're 20, 30 times worse than that.

The other problem was that the band were trying to write and record an album over in Britain, which wasn't helped by my being indisposed for the time being. I actually wrote some of the lyrics while I was in jail, and we called the album Menace to Society, which is how the judge described me at my trial (and on which my band agree with him.)

I think it came as a bit of a shock for the guys in the band when they found out what had happened, to be honest. They'd seen me get into trouble before, but charges of assault with a deadly weapon and assorted firearms and narcotics offences are a long way from having one too many and twatting someone. I don't think they realised at first just how much trouble I was in.

They'd never liked that particular girlfriend, really. A few of them had said it was like a 'John and Yoko' situation, where she came between us all. I think something was always bound to happen in the end, because that whole situation had been so tense for a while, ready to blow up at any minute. I just don't think any of us expected it to happen so dramatically. I'll describe that whole relationship in more detail later, but let's just say it wasn't a walk in the park – more like a stroll on the Gaza Strip.

In all, I was in the County Jail for nearly five months, and while it didn't scar me psychologically, as many would have you believe, relations between me and the good old US of A would never be quite the same again. But that's another story.

CHAPTER 11

I've seen a lot of aggro in my time. That's not some kind of boast, it's just a fact. If you grow up in East London, you're not gonna be mixing with choirboys, know what I mean?

From the streets of the East End to the ghettos of Los Angeles and a load of places in between that you don't even want to know about, I seem to have an uncanny knack of finding trouble. The way I am means I lose my rag now and then and, more often than not, I've paid the price for it.

There was a saying round where I grew up, 'It'll kick off if it has to' – and I've never been one to walk away when bother flares up. If I reckon someone needs a bloody good slap, believe me, they're gonna get one, and I don't give a shit who or where they are.

People say Paul Di'Anno could start a fight in an empty house, and I must admit there is something to that, but I see it slightly differently. I take shit from no one. Ever. If someone gives you a V-sign at a traffic light, you'll probably shrug and say to yourself, 'Well, OK, perhaps he was in a hurry, and perhaps I was in his way ...' If someone shouts across the street at you on a Saturday night, you'll most likely think, 'Was he shouting at me? Ooh, I won't say anything, I don't want any trouble ...' In other words, you'll turn the other cheek, which most right-minded people would say is the right and proper thing to do.

Well, fuck 'right and proper'. You can shove 'right and proper' right up your fucking arse, because if someone gives me a V-sign, I'll be out of the car and on their windscreen. Someone yells at me across the street, I'm gonna walk right over there and beat a tattoo on their fucking head.

I do what you'd like to do, if you had the guts. What if they've got a weapon, or I'm outnumbered? Fuck it, I'll give a good account of myself and go down fighting. I'll take a good few of them out before they take me out. It's not the size of the dog in the fight, it's the size of fight in the dog. The most dangerous guy in a brawl is someone who doesn't care about cuts, bumps or bullet wounds. That's the guy who's going to keep coming at you and coming at you. And that's me.

I've probably been in thousands of fights over the years – somebody's said something to me, and I've gone off on one at them. It can be a minor irritation, where I've thrown the backstage buffet all over the walls, or a major beef, where I've wrapped a mike stand around a roadie's head. Nothing personal – just don't piss me off, OK?

OK, it's got a bit scary at times for innocent bystanders – I've reduced hardened tour managers to tears when I've gone on a rampage, but it's not something I do deliberately, or even have any control over. The really worrying thing is, I simply don't know when I'm doing it. The red mist comes down over my eyes, and I just want to destroy every living thing in front of me. If a barman refuses to serve me because I'm drunk, he's going to get a bottle over his head. If some music journalist's pissed me off in some way, he's going to get a good kicking.

People are genuinely scared of me, because they're afraid of what I'll do. I'm not saying that like it's something I'm really proud of, but their fears are based on my past history in this area. Most people can't take any form of verbal or physical abuse – they just crumple up in front of you. That's fine with me.

A classic example of this happened just last Christmas – a guy in Slovenia came up to me after a show and started mouthing off, giving it the big 'I am'. Now, I'm expected to listen to this guy, just because he's bought my records? I don't know him – I couldn't give a fucking shit whether he's alive or dead. He keeps on, so I just smacked him in the fucking mouth. I've done all his nose and mouth in, and he's gurgling blood, so I just put my face up to his, and screamed, 'DO YOU WANT SOME MORE?' He just tried to slink away into the background, the yellow cunt.

Some of the early Maiden gigs were in the sort of dives you definitely wouldn't take your girlfriend to (or anybody else's, for that matter). Believe me, you took your bleeding life in your hands when you went on stage. Gawd help you if they thought you were crap. More than once, we had to fight our way out when it all kicked off, barely getting away in one piece. I know the Maiden guys probably blame me for most of the rucks (and again, they may have a point, there) but they certainly didn't complain back then when I put a bottle over some wanker's head.

In the years since then, I've still managed to get myself into bother, even when I've not been looking for it. A few years ago, I'd just come back to the UK for a visit from my home in LA. I'd only been in the country a few hours, so it wasn't as if I'd had time to upset anyone. I'm walking down Oxford Street in broad daylight and, before I know it, a row has started with these six blokes.

There's pandemonium in the street. Passers-by are scattering, and people are running inside shops to get out of harm's way. In the meantime, I'd waded into these guys like a bloody pro. I smacked one in the mouth, and he went down like a sack of spuds. I'm a fairly big geezer, so when I hit you, you're going to feel it. He was well out of the way. One grabbed me from behind, and I jabbed my thumb into his eye, which made a lovely squelching sound.

That still left their four mates to contend with, though, and as if the odds weren't good enough, one of them pulls a blade and, remember, we're rucking in broad daylight on one of Britain's busiest streets here, he plunges it into my throat.

The shock of it made the world go silent. For a few seconds, all I could hear was the blood rushing around in my head. I staggered back, and discovered I have a deep-crimson torrent of blood pissing out all over me like a fucking burst main. I honestly thought my bloody throat had been slit, and that I was a goner. In fact, it was the side of my neck that had been cut, rather than my throat, although it wasn't for lack of trying on his part, the bastard. I keeled over, crashing into a display of shoes outside a shop. They obviously thought they'd killed me, so they all legged it towards Tottenham Court Road.

I managed to stagger to my feet, pulling myself up with a painful effort that brought stars to my eyes. As I staggered up

Oxford Street, soaked in claret, have a guess how many people came to my aid, showed concern or generally gave a shit about me in any way whatsoever? Yeah, that's right – none.

Having just flown from supposedly one of the most dangerous cities in the world, I'd almost been done in permanently by a brave little herbert with five mates and a knife. Even I deserve a warmer welcome than that.

Another of my war scars looks just as impressive, but in this case, the story behind it is one of bloody stupidity, rather than aggro.

I've got a really ugly-looking scar on my right leg (just by my Hammers tattoo, actually) which I tell people is from a bullet-wound which I got in Los Angeles. Now that sounds like I must have been part of a drive-by shooting in South Central LA, or something.

In actual fact, like a lot of disasters I've suffered, it was me who was to blame. I'd been messing around with guns – yeah, I know – near my place over there, shooting targets with a few mates. Anyway, one bullet caught a nasty ricochet, and found yours truly on the rebound.

'Course, it seemed quite funny to everybody else, seeing me go down like something out of High Noon, but I wasn't laughing quite so much on the way to the Emergency Room. I'd been well and truly kneecapped by my own gun. Ever since then, I've been able to tell when it's going to rain the next day.

Another shooting spree had far more dangerous consequences and could easily have ended in tragedy. This particular time, I was absolutely fucked up on cocaine – I could barely see, let alone shoot straight.

I'd been doing coke all afternoon at my apartment, and I'd done so much that my nostrils were bleeding. So, high as a kite, me and three mates had gone off on another of our gun-toting escapades. As you can probably imagine, this was quite a common occurrence and, yes, it is as dangerous as it sounds. We used to drive out into the desert and shoot up the odd cactus, always assuming we were sober enough to actually hit one. More often, we'd run around like Clint Eastwood on speed, firing at anything that moved, and laughing like banshees.

Now the thing about being out in a California desert is that you don't tend to get too many passers-by, so no unsuspecting member of the public's likely to catch any friendly fire.

On this occasion, though, we were so absolutely out of our heads that we decided it'd be a great laugh to go up into the Hollywood Hills for the latest round of gunfights. Of course, this ended in mayhem, but it could easily have ended in carnage. Get this – we actually started firing randomly at passing cars as they drove by. Four drugged-up maniacs, spraying live ammunition on innocent motorists. It's a miracle no one was killed, or even hit. It's no defence I know, but we honestly weren't capable of hitting a barn door at five yards, much less a series of moving targets.

When I remember that now, and people ask me what possessed me to do such a thing, what the hell was I thinking of, am I out of my fucking mind, etc. etc. – all the things people usually ask me, I can answer with only one word – cocaine. Say no more.

Mind you, it wasn't the first time that my love for firearms – preferably illegal ones – has got me into strife, and I didn't even have drugs to blame this time. As a young kid, I put one of the windows of our local church in with an air rifle.

Now, before the moral majority (you know, those who're

convinced we're devil worshippers – yeah, right) jump in and accuse me of an early Satanic act, I can tell you the only reason the pellet went through the window was 'cos I was such a bloody awful shot! Believe me, I couldn't hit a bull's arse with a banjo.

I'd been pissing around with this thing, and despite divine intervention and all that bollocks, it was our local place of worship that copped it. This grand old building had survived the Blitz, only to get shot up by the young Di'Anno!

Anyway, you'll be glad to know God got his vengeance on this evil young sinner almost straight away – my nan had seen what happened, and as little old ladies did in those days, she laid into me and gave me one hell of a clout. I went fucking reeling – I didn't even see it coming. Good right hand, my nan, she could've turned pro.

*   *   *

Whether you're talking about guns, knives or fists, it's a fact of life that there are people around who just spend their lives asking for a good kicking. I remember one occasion in particular on one of my solo tours, when I found one of these people.

It happened during a tour of the States, and me and the band were going out a lot after shows and getting into trouble. I was drinking a lot and taking a lot of drugs at that time, and the fights we got into were horrendous. We'd be in some bar or somewhere and someone would say something – before you know what's happened, it's all kicked off, and we're all laying into some poor bastard.

There are a lot of poor white trash in America who see rock

bands as being the spawn of Beelzebub, and see it as their moral mission to kick the living shit out of them. If the band are in their local bar or club, terrorising the female population, there's even more reason to run their asses out of town. Let me just say that if any cross-eyed, in-bred fuckwit wants to take me on, he's going to be picking bits of glass out of his face for some time to come.

Anyway, I think it was towards the end of our tour, and so we were all a bit frayed and frazzled from being on the road so long. I was in LA, and my girlfriend was flying up from Texas to meet up with me, so I was probably a bit emotional to start with.

Anyway, this complete wanker – who was from some TV station or other – kept following me about, with this camera on his shoulder. Now, I'm not keen on dickhead journalists as a rule, and this guy's really getting on my tits, 'cos I'm trying to lose him before I go to the airport to meet the flight from Texas.

Trouble is, I just can't shake him off. Everywhere I go, he's there waiting for me. We were staying at the Radisson Hotel in Beverly Hills, and I went out to Rodeo Drive to do some shopping, buy a few presents and that. I've come back to the hotel, and who do I see waiting there, but this twat again.

I've stormed up to him, and screamed in his face, 'What part of "Fuck off" don't you understand? I don't fucking want you here, so disappear before I fucking kill you!' Not Oscar Wilde I know, but I was pretty pissed off by this time.

Anyway, he's still refusing to get lost, and that's when the red mist really descended. I snatched this big TV camera from him, and just chucked it in the swimming pool. When he protested, I just laid into him like a man possessed.

Thinking back now, I hope I didn't hurt him too much, because what happened next is all a bit of a blur. He went down, and I just rained fists and boots on to him as he writhed on the ground. I can remember at one point picking his battered and bleeding body up by his collar and belt, and trying to throw him headlong into the traffic on the freeway. All right, perhaps he didn't deserve that, but I'd completely lost my rag, and I just wanted to kill him.

Another dickhead got similar treatment, this time in the middle of a concert. This 'fan' had been in the middle of the crowd at a gig in Berlin, and insisted on booing and whistling at one particular track, just because he didn't like it.

He shouted up at me, 'Your new songs are shit!'

So I shouted back at him, 'Well, you're fucking German, so fuck off!' (Yeah, I know, a career in the diplomatic service beckons, right?)

He's still ranting and raving, so I just launched myself into the crowd, and dived in amongst the mass of bodies. He's still having a go, so I just smacked him in the face, and he went down like he'd been pole-axed. Silly fucker. Of course, there's chaos as everybody's screaming and trying to get out of the way, and security are wading in to try and get me off him. Funny really, because security are usually employed to protect the band from the fans, not the other way around.

'Course, the band are like, 'What the fuck are you doing? What's wrong with you?' Once again, I'm the cunt, aren't I?

Somebody else who was stupid enough to pick a fight with me – and he, of all people, really should have known better – was the guitarist in my band, Graham Bath. It happened during yet another American tour, after a show we'd played in South Carolina.

I had a stinking hangover, due to drinking what seemed like a bloody crate of vodka the night before, to celebrate the bass player's birthday. In this state, it's really best to leave me well alone. Like I've said, you're bound to get on each other's tits every now and then when you're on tour; you're living in each other's pockets every minute of the day, after all. I'd taken some more coke and drunk a shitload of Jack Daniel's as well that day, so I was still pretty wasted.

We'd had a funny couple of days, and everyone was in a really weird mood. One roadie had accused another one of drugging and raping him, so we had to sack the geezer, and drop him off at an airport. So there's just a bad atmosphere around us, to start with. I'm coming down off the coke, and the drink is kicking into my system, so my nerves are frazzled. It's not going to take much for me to descend into madness.

I'm lying across these two seats at the back of the coach, just minding my own business, listening to a Walkman and drinking a beer, when Graham starts. He comes up to me and says something, which of course I can't hear. He gestures to me to take my headphones off, and I give him a gesture in return, one which leaves him in no uncertain terms that I want him to fuck off.

He takes the hump at this, and starts rearing up, yelling and shouting. When I take no notice, he jumps on top of me, pinning me to the seat. I'm trapped between the two seats and can't move, while he's holding me down. He's yelling that I'm a cunt, and whether or not that's a fair comment, it's certainly fighting talk.

I finally get him off, and the fight spills out into the parking lot. It's gotten really nasty by this time, and we're both screaming at each other. Suddenly, I just snap, and I lay into him with my fists. A very ugly brawl develops, with me swinging punches at his bobbing head. I crack him a good one across the jaw, which sinks him to his knees, and then I slam my fist full into his face, which drops him on to the tarmac.

So, one of my best mates is sprawled lifelessly in front of me on the ground, thanks to me; and this is where any reasonable guy would have walked away, but he'd wound me up so much, I was thirsting for blood. I ran at him at full speed, and kicked him square in the mouth, with as much force as I could muster.

There was this horrendous crunching noise, and blood spurted up my leg. I was wearing these big heavy biker boots (part of a $10,000 shopping spree at a Harley Davidson store the day before), and my steel toe-cap just smashed his face to pieces. His jaw was in bits, all his front teeth were broken, and his nose was gaping open.

The others waded in and pulled me off, and there was pandemonium for a few minutes, as everyone was shouting at once, while I was still screaming with rage, and struggling like a wild animal. Meanwhile, Graham's just spread out there on the ground, with a huge pool of dark blood gathering around his head.

In the confusion, I managed to wriggle free, and what do I do but go and lay into poor old Graham again. He's unable to move, absolutely defenceless, and I stamp my heavy boot down as hard as I can on top of his head. That's when I was finally wrestled away, like a beast being captured.

It was at this moment that the cops arrived. They'd obviously heard all this carrying-on, and wondered what the hell was happening. Imagine the scene – there's a load of long-haired blokes standing around pushing, shoving and yelling, while another bloke lies motionless on the floor covered in blood. Fuck me, it's a wonder they didn't throw the bloody key away.

We managed to convince them that it was a family matter (yeah, right) and because of my Italian name, I think they thought it was some sort of Cosa Nostra shit going down, that they really didn't want to get too involved in. So, amazingly, they fucked off and we were able to get back on the bus.

We were able to carry Graham back on to the bus, and we took him to hospital in the next town.

He needed a lot of surgery to put him right and, of course, I felt bad about it immediately after I'd done it. But there you are, he'd taken me over the edge – and you can't turn back the clock. To make matters worse, Steve Hopgood had been filming the whole episode, so the moment when I very nearly killed one of my band members has been immortalised on film. It's a scary thing to watch, believe me. The crunching sound it makes when my boot smashes into his face distorts the sound on the video, it's so loud.

The funny thing is, Graham was so pissed that he didn't remember a thing about it after he came round. It was only when the effects of the booze wore off and his face started to hurt like buggery that he realised there was something wrong. We stopped at a roadhouse so we could clean him up properly, and he got one hell of a fucking shock when he looked in the mirror. There was this monstrous, unrecognisable face staring back at him, swollen to twice its normal size. He's no oil painting at the best of times, but he looked like the bloody Elephant Man. The strange thing is, we were all the best of mates again immediately afterwards when we'd all sobered up.

Graham was even well enough to play the next show, in fact, but he didn't volunteer for any backing vocals.

While I'm not backward in coming forward when it does kick off, I have to say there are several episodes of my life when this has been a miserable bloody curse, rather than any kind of blessing. This was when my being a bit handy with my fists inflicted pain and hurt on some of the people I love, and it's something I'm really not happy talking about, even now.

I regret hurting Graham in that way, but at least he's a big boy, and we shook hands on it afterwards. Other violent episodes haven't been quite so easy to resolve.

I'm not blaming drugs; they're OK if it's only you that's affected. Don't get me wrong, I'm a big boy, and I can look after myself without having a wet-nurse telling me what to do. If you want to put something in your arm or up your nose, then that's up to you, but don't come whining to me if it all comes on top, 'cos you're the one that took it, no one forced you – that's always been my attitude.

And that's all right as far as it goes, but when drugs fuck up your mind so badly they make you turn your wife or girlfriend into a punchbag, then it's all gone very wrong, and it ain't ever coming back. When I think of myself punching those people in the face as hard as I could with the same hands that are typing this, well, I want to chop them off, and that's no lie.

I find it bloody painful to even think of it now, and it's still one of the few things I really regret about this life I've led. I'd give anything to be able to change that memory, to make it go away, but I can't; and I'll take it to my grave.

Yeah, I can hear you yelling, what about the poor cows who took the hidings? Yeah, I know. Believe me, I know. There's nothing you can say to me about this that I haven't already said to myself over and over, twice as loud, and for twice as long. I know what I've done, and I've got to live with it.

It's a long way from a kid's romantic vision of a rock star, but I'm being honest. It's part of my life. It happened. Trust me, it'll never, ever happen again.

*   *   *

On the opposite end of the evolutionary scale, though, as I said before, there are some people for whom a good slap is the only solution. It's like they're drawn to the sort of people who'll do it for 'em, as well.

I was signing autographs backstage after a gig one night, and I happened to be wearing an Italian football shirt, sort of a tribute to my ancestry, if you like. Anyway, I'm signing away for these fans, when this big guy appears in the queue. He's obviously a football fan, as he's wearing team colours himself, and he clocks mine.

In this loud, mouthy sort of way, he turns around and says, 'Italy are shit!' Just like that, backstage at my gig, just gobbing me off.

In an instant, I fucking saw red. It was like I accelerated from nought to sixty – 'mellowed-out' to 'homicidal' – in the space of a few seconds. I leapt across the table and launched myself at him, while people scattered in all directions.

Before anybody could get in between us, I'd head-butted him full in the face, and followed up with a solid right-hander to his jaw. His legs just crumpled underneath him. I think the shock of it pretty much bowled him over. He went crashing down on to some chairs and tables, spark out.

'Course, once again, everybody's on me like a rash. There's all this clamour, people are fussing around, the venue are going mad, my management's going mad. Yet again, everybody's like,

'Why did you do that? What were you thinking of?' More to the point, why did he do that? What was he thinking of? Some people will just take a liberty with you, and when they do that, they've got to expect the consequences.

If you'd mouthed off like that around the pubs and clubs of the East End when I was a kid, you'd have lasted about five fucking minutes. Just because I'm famous, people think they can take the fucking piss out of me. Well, here's a newsflash – try it, and see what happens. I'll split your fucking head wide open.

I was talking before about aggro in small-town America? Well, a case in point was this fucking redneck down in Baton Rouge. This guy was a fucking classic Southerner, the sort who'd have been wearing a white pillow case over his head not too long ago – the sort of boss-eyed retard who's happy to be an ignorant shit-kicker all his life.

This bloke was the living proof that cousins shouldn't be allowed to marry – I think his second cousin was probably a sheep. Anyway, me, the band and crew are having a bite to eat at Hojo's restaurant, en route to the next show.

We're all dressed in the usual way – denims, leathers and that – and while I shaved all my hair off a few years back, most of the lads have got barnets well past their shoulders. Mr Shit-kicker obviously takes an instant dislike to us, and he leans over to his mates and starts giggling.

'Tell me,' he said, in an exaggerated whisper, 'Are they girls or boys?' They all have a laugh, in that slow, dim-witted way, as if that was the funniest thing since old Billy-Bob caught his dick in the hay-bailer. They're all there laughing and admiring their buddy's great wit.

Well, their buddy was lucky he didn't get the jagged edge of a beer bottle shoved in his fat face and skewered round 'til his fat jowls dropped off. I could have kicked that lardy fucker to death, right there on the restaurant floor.

Instead, I got up slowly from my chair, and walked over to the self-styled comedian. You could have heard a fly fart in that restaurant, as all my lot thought I was going to throw a schizo. His mates have edged back slightly in their chairs, and they're looking at me in that slightly cross-eyed way.

I put my face right into the leader's, and I can see he's a bit worried now, as there's a little nervous tic around the side of his mouth. He's lost a bit of his colour, too. Calmly and quietly, I said to him, 'Listen to me, you fucking inbred cunt. Say one more word, and I'm going to rip your fucking throat out. Then I'll come after your family.'

He looked down at his cowboy boots; it was obvious he didn't want to continue this pleasant social intercourse. As I made my way back to my seat, there's still this awful silence in the room. It was like the atmosphere of barely-suppressed violence was still hanging in the air.

All of a sudden, I heard this plummy English voice pipe up from the other side of the restaurant, 'Oh, hello! You're English!' Turns out it was this bloke who'd moved over there a short while before, and was keen to meet up with some of his own. I expect the Deliverance posse had been giving him a hard time, too, so he'll have been well pleased to see all that kick off. All part of the service, mate.

*   *   *

The guys in the band say they've seen me get into 1,000 skirmishes over the years, especially when I've had a few. They

Top: Eighteen months old and already showing a dislike of paparazzi…

Bottom left: Posing for an early publicity photo.

Bottom right: Snappy dress sense, for a four-year-old! Anybody who says I look like the kid from The *Omen* will get a fucking slap…

The young
rocker –
aged 15!

An early Iron Maiden concert. You can just make out Thin Lizzy's Phil Lynott in the wings behind me.

Top: The Lone Ranger.

Bottom: Killers on tour.

Top: Me and Cliff Evans, a great guitarist and one of my best mates.

Bottom left: Last-minute adjustments before going on stage.

Bottom right: Looking pissed off about something – that usually means trouble for somebody...

Top left: A meeting of the Musicians' Union? Far left is Dennis Stratton, one of my Iron Maiden colleagues.

Top right: Would you buy a second-hand CD from this man?

Bottom: Pictured with a group of Japanese musicians in 1989. The blonde-haired geezer with his arm around me is Lea Hart, who's now my manager.

Top: Looking like an inmate at an American jail. (Funny, that!)

Bottom: A 'friend' backstage displays all her charms, Germany 1996.

Top: Toasting American beer and hair extensions!

Bottom: The day job – laying down a vocal track in the studio.

witnessed it at close quarters one time in Holland, when it almost ended in my death.

We were driving along the road in a car, just a few of the guys from the band, and this big black Mercedes has come right up behind us, flashing and honking.

I think Steve was driving, and he tried to get out of the way, but there's cars on both sides of the road, so there's nowhere to go. Anyway, I wasn't too worried about the finer details of the Highway Code. I just wanted to get out of the car and shove this bloke's fucking head up his arse.

So I'm yelling back at him, giving him the finger, making throat-cutting gestures and screaming blue murder, when they pull up alongside us as we're going along. We can see them properly for the first time, and these are big, nasty-looking motherfuckers.

I don't know if they have the Mafia in Holland, but if they do, these cunts must have been in charge of the branch office, believe me. So these mean-looking bastards are yelling back at me, but I don't give a shit; I'm yelling at Steve to pull over and let me out to have a go at them. I want to tear their arms off.

All the time this is happening, the two cars are hurtling along side by side on this main road, going towards Amsterdam. One of the guys in the front gestures to his mate in the back, and he produces this big ugly revolver from the back of the seat. Now it's obvious this geezer's used one of these before, because he's cocking it and starting to point it right at my head.

Steve sees this and almost shits himself, slamming on the brakes. The car goes into a skid, and we slew sideways towards a hedge, coming to rest on the grass verge. The Merc pulls up some way ahead of us, and for a minute it looks like they're going to get out and finish the job off.

As luck would have it, they obviously decide against it, and they drive off, slowly. There was this awful silence in our car, as we all let out a huge sigh of relief. I think we all knew how close I'd come to meeting my maker that day, as he was more than willing to blow my brains all over the upholstery. Another useful motto – when travelling in Holland, take the bus.

It's probably not too surprising that aggro does tend to follow us around, because some of our gigs have been mini-riots in themselves. When you've got a crowd of rabid heavy metal fans, psyched up to high heaven, and you give them a performance of real power and aggression, they're probably not going to all shake hands and wander off home, are they?

I've had a few rows with the security blokes at some shows, when I've thought they've been too heavy-handed in dealing with stage-divers and that. There was one gig in Brazil where they were just chucking the kids bodily over the barriers, not caring where they landed.

You've got a group of bloody great 20st geezers in these identical shirts, just laying into teenagers who are about half their weight, wringing wet. That particular night, I was really revved up with the whole atmosphere and everything, and the spark just ignited when I saw all this going on.

I dropped the microphone and dived off the stage, landing on top of one of the bouncers. He was a hell of a lot bigger and wider than me, but I think he was just stunned by the singer of the band he was supposed to be minding jumping on him. I punched him in the throat, and got in two or three more punches to his face before the other bouncers moved in on me and dragged me off. The guy was so shocked, he hadn't even raised his hands to defend himself.

The guys in the band couldn't believe what I'd done, they

thought I'd signed my death warrant, but fuck 'em. The fans who pay to see me play don't deserve to be treated like that.

On the other hand, a few people come along to cause trouble. One guy at a gig once was standing a few rows back from the front, and just kept giving me the finger all night. Finally, I lost it with him, and wrapped the bloody mike stand around his stupid head. He fell over backwards, disappearing down among the mass of feet and legs. The other guys have taken the piss out of me since, saying he was just trying to request a song or some such bollocks, but I know a fucking troublemaker when I see one. Well, I hope so, anyway.

Audiences can be a real hazard. At one show in Spain, I pointed the microphone out towards the audience, so they could sing along. When I drew my arm back, I saw some cunt had nicked my bloody watch! You're giving people your all on stage, and they're fucking robbing you. Now there's gratitude!

CHAPTER 12

When Battlezone finally split up, that was very nearly it for me. The end. I just went home and shut the fucking door on it all. I really couldn't be arsed with it any more. At that point, I could have turned my back on the whole business for good, and that's the truth.

I just lost interest in everything really, and I couldn't face the idea of starting all over again. I was still writing, still creating music for myself, but I'd totally gone off the idea of going out and playing again. What was once fresh and exciting had become tarnished and stale. There were too many bad memories now.

At this time, too, the drugs really took hold of me. Before, they'd provided a release from the madness of life on tour. But now, they did the exact opposite, virtually keeping me prisoner in my own home. They really affected how I thought, and I just became like a recluse, just slobbing around there in my apartment in LA, taking more and more drugs and writing songs by myself. Days went by without me speaking to anybody – I was retreating further and further into myself.

I was fed up with bands, managers and, most of all, musicians. I just didn't want to go through all the bullshit again. I'd been through the same experience before, after I'd left Iron Maiden, but while I'd still had the get-up-and-go to reinvent myself back then, this time I couldn't find the strength.

My priorities had changed completely – since I'd become a father, it had put everything into perspective, really, and I wanted to go back to England to spend time with my children. In the meantime, I just wanted to spend time with myself.

Battlezone had always had a self-destruct button, and I could see then how this had led to the group imploding like it did. It was like the group had been an extension of my own extreme personality. When you look at it like that, it was bound to end in tears, really, wasn't it?

Another problem was the people we had around us – promoters, managers and record companies; those people who are supposed to be helping you, often do more to fuck up your career than anybody else, and I think that was the case with us.

Thinking back on it now, I think they did this by giving us too much leeway, and letting us do what we wanted. Every band needs people around them, management who'll basically keep them in line.

The exceptions to this, I suppose, are muppets like those boy bands who obviously just shut up and do what they're told. They don't really count, as I don't class them as proper bands.

It's hard really, but when you've got a band with real

character, like we had, each individual has got his own ego, and they can get out of line. This is where you need someone to keep the whole thing together, before it implodes on itself.

We had a particular problem with our management; we were a bit upset with them, and it seemed the only thing we could do to get out of it was to break it up, split the band up, and just walk away. I think we still wanted to start again together, but we just didn't do it.

And, of course, there was the hard-living on tour, which really hadn't helped. We'd had groupies everywhere, mountains of cocaine everywhere – it doesn't really help clear thinking or long-term planning. Forget planning our world domination, most of us couldn't find our dicks for a piss, we were so out of it all the time.

I can remember so many times, when I'd be sitting in the dressing room before we went on stage, with a bottle of Jack Daniel's in front of me, and just polishing off the whole bottle before I went on. It was like, 'Fuck! Where am I? What am I doing?'

The only reason I was able to drink loads before I went on was that I'd usually snorted so much coke that it really didn't make much difference – they sort of cancel each other out if you do one straight after the other. And to think I used to wonder why my voice wasn't working that well!

If you do a show when you're out of your head on drink and drugs, you're always convinced that you sound all right; but, luckily, I've got great fans, who tell me when I sound rough. I've always had a great relationship with my fans; there's never been any of that stand-off rock star bullshit.

I'd do a gig, completely wankered, and then I used to come off stage and be chatting to them afterwards. I'd say, 'Was I all right?' And they'd say, 'Well, no, actually, you sounded like a cunt ...' Like I say, great fans ...

Come to think of it, they're probably one of the reasons that I decided to go back to touring and recording, just because they – above all else – make playing live such a pleasure. I can remember back in the Iron Maiden days thinking that audiences just went berserk at our music, and they still do.

I've got to know quite a few of them on a personal level over the years, I've been out with them after a show and that, when they've taken me to a club or something, and it's fantastic. I've got millions of fans like that round the world, and it's something I never take for granted.

I think the fans really got into Battlezone, and I think it was mostly because of our attitude. We had a good attitude – we were like a Heavy Metal version of the Sex Pistols. We just didn't give a fuck about anything.

I don't write songs to sell loads of records, I just write songs to please myself. I'm not answerable to anybody, apart from God (and my mum), and I just do what feels right. I think most people realise that, and respect me for it.

During this period of inactivity, I began to look at how this attitude had begun to change during the later days of the band, and I realised something that shocked me. I realised that I was starting to turn into the sort of rock dinosaur that I'd always loathed.

I'd come from a street background, that's where my musical roots were, and that's where my down-to-earth outlook came from. I wasn't about to kiss anybody's arse in the early days, just because they were rich and famous. Fuck them.

Bands like the Stones and Deep Purple were out-of-touch and irrelevant, as far as I was concerned, they were like a past generation living off its name. But now, fuck me, I began to realise that I'd started down the same path.

While our attitude was different to theirs, I was now drinking so much and taking so many drugs that I was living that whole excessive rock 'n' roll lifestyle, and I'd become a sort of parody of them, in a way.

Back when I was 16, if I'd have walked into a room with all of those clapped-out has-beens, I'd have machine-gunned the whole fucking lot of them; that's how strongly I felt about that scene, back then.

I think the best thing that ever happened to Jimi Hendrix was dying. He was a lot more successful dead than he would have been alive. I've just got no respect for that sort of shit. Those guys just thought the whole world owed them everything they had. To my mind, the world doesn't owe me fuck-all – what I want, I'll take for myself, and if I get caught out doing it, that's too bad.

While Battlezone had started out with the right philosophy, we'd always had this tendency to go a bit mad, and you could see the way it was going to go, what with all the groupies, drugs and stuff. It was just an accident waiting to happen.

We did a few last shows with a scratch band, just to honour some outstanding commitments we had (and so I didn't get my arse sued) but I knew it wasn't going anywhere. We were flogging a dead horse by then; they were adequate musicians, but the real spirit had gone. It would have been a joke if we'd carried it on, and I didn't want to fuck it up for the fans, more than anything. So I decided to call it quits and, if I'm honest, I was probably a bit relieved when the end finally came.

So, after all this, I'm back at home in Los Angeles, staring at the four walls. On the face of it, I've got everything going for me. I've got shit-loads of money in the bank, and fuck-all to do. And if you've got fuck-all to do, LA is just the place.

So I just went on this mad binge for a while. I'd sit around snorting coke, or embark on marathon boozing sessions, and get even more fucked-up. I used to look at my face in the mirror every morning, after yet another hard night of substance abuse, and see this puffy-faced, hollow-eyed monster staring evilly back at me. It was like coming face to face with the Devil.

Non-stop excess is OK for a while but, after a bit, you get more and more burned-out, you see your bank account going down and down, and you think, 'I'd better get myself together and go out and play again.'

I think it was boredom that did it in the end, because after all my thoughts of giving up on music altogether, there was never really any question of me doing something else. After all, what else could I do? Mercenary? Gun-runner? Pimp?

It's not the money, it's not the fanny, it's not the drugs. As I've said, the feeling you get when thousands of kids are screaming your name is not something you can ever turn your back on. Those who've done that out of choice can't have wanted it very much in the first place, and so they shouldn't ever have been up there.

The reason all these old-timers climb out of their bath-chairs and squeeze themselves into their leather trousers year after year has fuck-all to do with money. Most of those guys are so loaded, their dosh would sink the Isle of Wight, so it's not that. I'm sure they feel the same as I do, that they just can't imagine not doing it any more.

Amidst the haze of narcotics in my LA flat, I'd worked all this out for myself. I just woke up one morning, determined to get on with it again. It was like a lightbulb coming back on. Suddenly, it seemed like the most natural thing in the world, and memories of all the previous hassle seemed to evaporate overnight.

It took a little while, because I didn't really trust too many other musicians, and I'd had all these problems with record companies that I'd had to overcome. It would have cost me a load of money to sue everybody that I wanted to, so my attitude was that they could just go fuck themselves. And if I ever see any of them again, I'll just fucking shoot them. I'll get revenge one way or another. Simple as that.

Although I'd already been thinking about it, my actual return to the scene came about almost by coincidence, and it started with a phonecall. The phone rang in my apartment one day, and it was my mate Steve Hopgood, who'd been the drummer in Battlezone.

It was before noon, so I was still in bed. When I answered it, at first I didn't know who the hell it was, or what he was talking about, but he explained that he was trying to put a band together. Fucking hell, I'd heard that one before.

Steve said he'd had this idea, and he wanted to give it a go. So, all suspicious, I said to him, 'Who's involved?' If there were any wankers who'd piss me about, I wanted to know now, so I could tell him to go fuck himself. I listened hard as his voice came across the Atlantic, 'Well, there's me, and there's Cliff Evans, who used to be the guitar player in Tank, he's in New York at the moment putting a few things together, and we've got a lot of people looking at what we're doing – would you be interested?'

He went on to tell me that another old mate of mine would be the bass player, a guy called John Gallagher from the band

Raven. Apparently, John was in New York as well, waiting to get started on this new band. So I said to Steve, 'It looks like I'm going to have to get myself to New York then, doesn't it?'

And that was it – the beginnings of the new band. So I flew from LA to New York, and I sat down with them for a meeting. They were all there, along with this wild fucker who played guitar, and we just got chatting about the idea.

This new guy was called Ray, and he'd been in a successful American band called Drive She Said. He looked the part, like some rock god with all this hair and that, and he seemed absolutely fucking crazy, which was a definite bonus, as far as I was concerned.

It was as I was there chatting away with them that I first thought that this could actually work. Like the cup of tea with Steve Harris all those years before, something just sort of clicked. I even started to think that here was something which had the potential to be better than anything I'd done before.

So we sat there gassing on, and I discovered that there were a few commitments in the pipeline already. Apparently, some guys had offered us a deal to go out to South America, and record a live album. This album would only go on sale out there, and it would be priced at $5, because no fucker's got any money out there.

And we went for it. We went out to Colombia, and did a storming set of old Iron Maiden songs, along with some Battlezone numbers, and from those shows, the live album was born.

True to form, though, things didn't exactly pass without incident. For starters, the guys who'd been promoting these concerts over in South America ran into a slight spot of bother, shall we say.

Now these were two guys who never seemed to be short of a few bob. They treated us like royalty; first-class this, and first-class that, we wanted for nothing. If you're from a working-class East End background like I am, it's not that you think you deserve all that shit every day of your life, someone practically wiping your arse for you, but you just feel you'd better make the fucking most of it, because some cunt's bound to come along and take it all away from you. Make the most of it while you can, I say.

So we were having it large, going to the best clubs in New York, drinking champagne like it was going to be outlawed tomorrow, and getting as much Peruvian marching powder up my hooter as humanly possible. Night after night of getting pissed and causing uproar in clubs was probably the last thing I needed at the time, but it seemed a good way to christen this new band.

The other lads in the band were keeping me on a tight leash, as they didn't want me doing anything that was going to fuck up our chances of hitting the big time again. Needless to say, there were a few unfortunate episodes. I got a bit pissed in a club one night, and started chucking bottles over the bar, smashing all the glasses and mirrors and everything. There was a huge rumpus, and the cops got called, but I was smuggled out before I got any grief. I was escorted everywhere like Hannibal Lecter for a while after that.

The promoters seemed to know everybody, introducing me to this person and that, just giving me the red carpet treatment everywhere I went. Unfortunately, the wheels came off this particular gravy train one morning when I was watching CNN on telly.

It seems some offices had been raided by the FBI, who

claimed that someone somewhere had been smuggling up to $20 million of cocaine into the States every month. Fucking hell, I was impressed! Needless to say, the recording deal went tits up after that.

This left us in the brown stuff, as we didn't have a record deal. So, we figured that the best route would be to muster record company interest ourselves, having come this far in putting the band together.

So our new manager, Arnie Goodman, organised a showcase for us. To the uninitiated, this is a gig where bigwigs from record labels come to a specially organised show and have a a *really* good time. If they've got any time or energy left over after that, they look at a band for a couple of minutes and decide whether they want to sign them.

So we've organised this showcase in New York, and every cunt and his cousin from the music business is there. Big labels, competing against each other to sign this hot new band from England. Yeah, I didn't believe it either.

Now, we do have a slight problem, in that we haven't actually got round to writing any new material yet. So we solved this little marketing problem in the same way that a street trader on Oxford Street would, in other words, the stuff we supplied was knocked-off.

We did a whole showcase for the great and the good of the American music industry, doing early Iron Maiden songs, which were already years old. There wasn't one new song, not a note. And while I, of all people, was entitled to play those songs, it doesn't hide the fact that not one of those dozy fuckers recognised them.

Iron Maiden had been regularly in the charts over there, appearing on TV programmes and on hundreds of radio stations' playlists, both with myself and Bruce on vocals, and yet this little fact didn't seem to register with the people entrusted with the future of the international recording industry. If that doesn't speak volumes about the bullshit of the music business, I don't know what does.

In fact, once we'd finished, these twats actually started fighting over us, bidding against each other to sign us. In the end, we signed a $200,000 deal, and I reckon we had a result.

There was only one problem for me about this new group, and that was the name. Arnie suggested we call ourselves Killers. Straight away, I fucking hated the idea. I just thought it harked back to the Maiden days. It was looking backwards not forwards and, once again, it put too much of an onus on me and my history, rather than being a complete new band.

True to form, I went fucking berserk. Threw my toys out of the pram, and said I wasn't going to play any more. In a fit of pique, I just said, 'Fuck you lot, I ain't having none of that!'

The argument went on; they thought it was really good, but every time they brought it up, I just said, 'Bollocks!' I just fought tooth and nail against it, but there was one small weakness in my argument, namely that I couldn't think of a better one.

We had to give them a name before we did the album, so in the end, against my better judgement, we ended up going with that one after all. So there I was, going along with it under protest, when I saw the first flyers for the band, and they said, large as life, 'Paul Di'Anno's Killers'. 'Well, fuck me,' I thought, 'this is just going from bad to worse.' There I was trying to make a clean break from Maiden and start again, and there they were rubbing my fucking nose in it!

So, after a few more rows, we finally agreed that it would just be Killers. It wasn't anything against Maiden, and I could see plain as day why they were doing it, using my name like that, but in all honesty I just wanted it to be a band, a collective, where everyone plays an equal part. The last thing I wanted was some kind of 'vehicle' for me. If ever there was a vehicle for me, I'd have crashed the fucking thing long before that.

So, we recorded an album and shot a video, all that sort of bollocks. The video was shot on a rooftop in New York, and I managed to liven up proceedings by hanging over the edge and yelling at the druggies, pushers and pimps on the street below. Now, that really was my kind of place! I felt at home there from the off!

The video itself was a bit fucking weird, too. I don't know what the hell the director was on at the time, but I can remember the film featured loads of shots of llamas, intercut with the band playing. As if that wasn't fucked-up enough, a huge gunship appeared and starting blowing these llamas away! No, I couldn't work out what the hell it was all about, either.

After all that fucking about, we made a few more changes to the line-up, bringing in Nick Burr, who used to be in Persian Risk with Steve; and a bass player called Gary Cooper. I felt now, more than ever, that these guys made it come together. We'd been almost there, but now I thought it felt right. It's not always to do with musical ability or stage presence even, it's more to do with personalities and how the guys gel together as a band. You can have the best four musicians in the world, but if they don't fit together as one unit, you're fucked.

The more we wrote and rehearsed together, the more excited I got. I don't know if it was the fact that everyone in the band was British, but I can remember thinking that this was really something special. We'd really got it down good, and we just kept on writing and preparing songs all the time. Funnily enough, I didn't actually write any of the music at this time – I let the guys get on with it, while I wrote all the lyrics.

I was enjoying living in New York, the vibrant energy of the place made me feel right at home, while the bars and clubs were a major distraction. I took pleasure in finding the sleaziest, most down-at-heel places to hang out, and the same went for the people I hung out with. One of my best mates at the time was a guy called Kit. Now if you've ever seen the TV series *Starsky and Hutch*, you'll have seen Kit, 'cos he was exactly like the character Huggy Bear. He had the clothes, he had the streetwise attitude, he had the jive talk; it was him to a tee.

More to the point, like Huggy Bear, he was a pimp. He earned a living (and a very good living it was, too) putting girls on the streets to work as prostitutes. These brasses would be standing by every lamp-post, pouting at the cars going by, and old Kit would be strutting up and down the street like a king.

It was like a constant conveyor belt; girls would be getting in cars and climbing out of them, every minute of the day. You could be there at nine in the morning, and the scene would be the same. It's like the casinos at Las Vegas – you can't tell what time of day it is, because everybody just keeps gambling round the clock.

I reckon there must have been dozens of girls at any one time, scattered around New York City, doing the business for Kit. He'd be there preening himself in his fedora and fur coat, and they'd be on their backs on car seats or shoved up against walls, letting themselves be fucked for money.

If you looked in the windows of cars parked up along the main street there, you'd see – in broad daylight, mind you – a guy sitting in the driver's seat with a shit-eating grin on his face, while some girl's head would be bobbing up and down on his lap. Like I said, a colourful business.

Whatever you think of his chosen profession, Kit was truly a diamond geezer – he couldn't read or write, but he just seemed to shit money. He had a gold-plated Cadillac, and a wardrobe of the finest gear you've ever seen. He had these silk suits in purple and green, with colourful Hawaiian shirts and crocodile-skin shoes. He wore so much jewellery, it must have taken him an hour each day to unhook all the necklaces and bracelets. The man just shone.

He showed me some of his battle-scars one day, and I've never seen so many bullet holes and stab wounds on one person's body. However he came by those, it certainly wasn't collecting for the Salvation Army. In fact, some heavy geezers came into the club one night – luckily I wasn't there at the time – and filled him with a few more holes. There'd obviously been some sort of turf war or dispute or something, and these hoods came in and shot him up. He survived with a few flesh wounds, but it just showed the perils of his chosen profession.

He was quite cheerful about it when I saw him again, and we had a beer together. He talked about it like a bus driver talks about a minor shunt, or a gardener talks about backache. Just an occupational hazard.

You really can't piss about in New York – you've five Mafia families there, the Cosa Nostra, who control everything from drugs and prostitution to contract murder and extortion. It's a billion-dollar industry, and let's just say they get the right hump with people who piss them off.

During the time we were there, a guy called John Gotti, who was head of the Gambino crime family, got sent to the toughest jail in America, Marion Penitentiary in Illinois, to serve the rest of his natural life in solitary confinement. These are mean fuckers, and these were the guys who Kit seemed to be on first-name terms with. I suppose he had to have their permission to work that patch of turf.

The whole area where I used to hang out was a bit on the colourful side, to put it mildly. The sound of gunshots and/or police sirens were as regular as clockwork. The strange thing was, you sort of got used to them. It was a bit like living next to Liverpool Street Station, and being accustomed to the noise from the trains, I suppose.

Drugs were being peddled like candy. Whatever you wanted, you didn't have to walk 20 yards to get it. I think if you asked them for nuclear rocket fuel, they'd have been able to lay their hands on some, that lot. People who don't know me would ask why I hung around in this hellhole of sin when I had a plush uptown apartment at my disposal ... because I liked it there, is the answer.

Looking back though, all of this scene probably wasn't too healthy an influence on me, as I was getting through mountains of cocaine with Kit, who seemed as keen on the Peruvian national product as I was. The two of us would do so much coke that we wouldn't know who in the hell we were. In fact, lots of people actually thought I was his coke-dealer.

It was probably just as well to have some sort of pressure valve, as I felt like I had the weight of the world resting on my shoulders at that time, having just landed the biggest recording contract of my entire career. The record industry being what it is, they didn't waste any time trying to get their money back. Before we knew it, we were whisked off our feet, and despatched off to record an album for them.

I think they were obviously worried that I was going to run amok with their money if I wasn't supervised by adults, and I know they and the band took a conscious decision to try and keep me out of trouble while we were supposed to be working.

In order to do this, they sent us to a small town in upstate New York named Binghampton. It's an industrial town, which has obviously seen better days. The people were really friendly, and they actually made us very welcome, but they had to try and stay cheerful, really, because there was fuck-all else to celebrate in that town. It was an absolute shit-hole, stuck in the arse end of nowhere.

It's a four-hour drive from New York City, and I christened it Shitsville, USA, because it was such a fucking dump. If it isn't the arsehole of America, it certainly qualifies as its colostomy bag.

We had a laugh there, though; it was a case of doing anything to liven the bloody place up a bit. Even setting it on fire would have been an entertaining diversion. As I say, the people were great, but Christ knows how they got through the day.

We booked into the only half-decent motel for fucking miles, and that was perched on the edge of these railway sidings. There was only one bar in the neighbourhood, and we managed to get barred from that almost as soon as we'd arrived. I'm sure by now you don't need me to tell you who was responsible for that. Nice one, Paul.

I remember being in some shitty burger bar there, surrounded by people whose first cousins may well have been sheep. They were looking at us like some retards convention. I decided to lighten the mood by standing up and announcing that they were all a bunch of fucking inbreds. As you can imagine, that lightened the fucking mood no end.

We'd been there for a while, when we realised the album was coming together really well, and that it hadn't taken as long as we'd thought to get it into shape. Now, if you're some dinosaur rock band from the Seventies, you'd probably find something else to do on it, re-recording it with harpsichords or putting an extra kazoo in the mix, or some such bollocks.

Not us. We decamped to the best club in the area – yeah, OK, it was the only club in the area – and we went on a fucking great bender to celebrate.

So we're there in this club, and we're pouring booze down our necks like there's no tomorrow, and we've got women hanging all over us. The guys have since admitted to me that the main reason we were sent to this place was to prevent me from getting my hands on any drugs. This was for the benefit of myself and everybody else within a mile radius, and also because drugs really fuck your voice up. Besides, there weren't very many dealers to be found in the middle of Binghampton, so I was left to drink myself stupid to get my kicks.

Now, our guitarist didn't actually drink, so in the spirit of friendship, we decide to help him get started. But once we've poured a few pints down his neck, he just disappears, we can't find him anywhere.

After about three hours, we meet up and discover he's still not back. I'm in a right state – as well as having a skinful of booze, I've fucked some bitch round the back of the club, so I'm already in the party mood. We stagger back to our hotel to see if he's there and, sure enough, we find him with his head down the bog, heaving his guts up. All you could see when you walked into the room was this arse stuck up in the air, with all these retching noises echoing in the bowl.

So we agree he's all right, and we go back down to the club, and carry on where we left off with these women. There's concern for you.

I managed to crown the evening by pulling the waitress's top down to reveal two outsized and bra-less tits (much to her annoyance) and then fighting a pitched battle outside with bouncers, locals and anybody else who wanted to get involved.

I staggered back to the safety of my hotel room with one earring ripped out, half my shirt torn off and blood streaked across my hands, arms and face. (Most of it wasn't mine.) I've got a vague feeling that one of the blokes involved was the boyfriend of the waitress whose tits I'd displayed to the world, so that would sort of explain the animosity, really. Still, she had a nice pair.

After we'd finished the last recording session, and once we'd torn ourselves away from the delights of Shitsville, USA, we travelled to Vermont, to finish off the drum tracks.

Now, Vermont is a beautiful place for skiing, with beautiful towns and landscapes wherever you look. There are loads of upmarket shops and restaurants everywhere, it's just so bloody civilised. It's certainly not the place to send a bunch of long-haired rock musicians – even the local bands who play there are like bloody missionaries, they're so well-behaved.

So, our bloody shower turns up in Vermont, in the town of Burlington, and we've got two days to finish off the drum tracks. As it turns out, we get them done in half a day. Lovely studio, all the gear – we knew what we were doing; there you go, job done.

So, we have to try to amuse ourselves in this Vermont town; and, once again, there must have been some raised eyebrows at us being there, so we'd have done well to keep a low profile.

But, of course, we go straight to a club and set about the business of getting absolutely wankered. I'd snorted some coke I'd managed to blag, while drinking enough booze to float a small ship, so I'm absolutely fucked. Now, in the club where we're misbehaving, there's one of these bands I mentioned, all Perry Como haircuts and co-ordinating sweaters.

So, we storm the bloody stage and throw them off, taking over their instruments. The place just descended into chaos. The club's management were trying to throw us out, the band were trying to get their instruments back, and the punters just didn't have the faintest what the hell was going on.

I think we managed to do most of one song, which was some achievement considering the state we were in. I was too drunk to stand up, let alone sing, and the others weren't much better. I fell face-first off the stage, and landed in the middle of a table, scattering glasses everywhere. Christ, we must have looked a bloody sight, crashing all over the place and making complete cunts of ourselves.

In between all these wild nights, we somehow managed to finish that part of the album, and we then went on to the final mixes at the Powerstation Studios in New York, which must have been an immense bloody relief to the residents of Vermont and all the local bands there.

It was certainly a fucking relief to me, as it goes without saying that drugs are far more readily available on the mean streets of New York than they are in the 'hood' of Burlington, Vermont.

When we returned to New York, I went back to my apartment on West Fifty-Seventh Street and Broadway, which is about the best location in New York, smack in the middle of everything.

This place was the dog's bollocks, very posh, with an immaculately-uniformed concierge on the door. There's a bit of a story attached to that, as it happens, because this concierge was a massive guy, just huge. I used to speak to him when I was going in and out every day, and I said to him one day, all cocky like, 'You're a big guy, ain't ya?'

He looks at me, a bit puzzled. 'Well, yeah,' he says.

'Well,' I said, 'I reckon I could take ya!'

He obviously didn't reckon I could, so we went for it, there and then, in the plush foyer of this luxury apartment block. Gawd knows what the hoity-toity residents of the other apartments must have thought, when they walked in to see their concierge fighting with this lunatic in the lobby. (I have to tell you in all modesty, I had him on his arse twice, the soft cunt.)

We were actually thinking of giving him a job as my bodyguard, but he blew it then, really. To be my minder, you've got to be able to put me on my arse!

Mind you, his co-operation came in handy when I had a little 'mishap' in my apartment. Somehow, and I can't really say why, a gun went off by accident, and destroyed the luxury bath in my suite. It cost $500 to put right, so whoever I was aiming at (and I can't honestly remember) next time I'll do better.

When I wasn't fighting with doormen or shooting up bathrooms, I was recording the vocals for the album, and working really hard at it. In case you didn't know, Powerstation is the place to record in the USA, and is frequented by all the top stars. It's actually owned by Jon Bon Jovi's uncle, funnily enough.

While we were laying our tracks down, me and Steve Hopgood got chatting, and we started thinking that the producer we were working with didn't really have the same ideas as us, that we weren't working towards the same thing.

So this was all costing us a shitload of money, because as well as his fees, we were paying something like $15,000 every two days for the studio. So me and Steve would go out for a drink and start bitching about this, because it was costing us money. He was a good producer, and he was getting there with the songs, but we just felt we could do better.

So, in the end, we just let him get on with it, but when he nipped out for a piss or something, we just sneaked over and twiddled all the knobs ourselves, just tweaking it here and there, and he never noticed the fucking difference! The studio engineer was in on it, of course, but he kept his gob shut, and just smiled.

So this producer would be there, all loud and American, saying, 'What do you think of that, guys?' And me and Steve would be, like, 'Yeah, it sounds good that, man!' And all the time, we'd be giggling like bloody schoolboys.

Don't forget, I'd been in the business quite a while by this time, so I knew a good track from a fucking duff one. No one knows better than me what makes a heavy metal song sound good!

One of the stars I met at Powerstation was Chaka Khan, who turned out to be a bloody great laugh. Me and her got on like a house on fire, and we were going to have her doing a guest vocal on the album, but her record label wouldn't wear it. Paul Di'Anno and Chaka Khan – who'd have thought it?

Anyway, between recording sessions, once again I was busy finding other ways to amuse myself. I found a nightclub called the China Club, which sort of became a kind of spiritual home for me. While other people make pilgrimages to Jerusalem or wherever, I really felt I was coming home when I walked into that place.

It was a great club, packed out with rock stars, wannabe rock stars and never-will-be rock stars. Added to this mix were some of the most stunningly beautiful women you'd ever seen in your life, so you could imagine it was like a kind of heaven on earth in there.

I was treated like a celebrity from the minute I showed up on the door, to the minute I was carried feet-first back out again. They were practically straining to kiss my arse as often as possible in between. I'm not really into all that rockstar bollocks as a rule, but there was a definite atmosphere about the place, a buzz generated by the rock crowd who hung out there.

It wasn't uncommon to see movie stars like Bruce Willis or someone turn up there at night, it was a really glitzy sort of hangout. I'll give you another idea as to the kind of clientèle it attracted – someone I used to drink with there was Ace Frehley, the guitarist from Kiss who I'd first met all those years before during that early tour with Iron Maiden.

Ace, like myself, likes to walk on the wild side, and if a club's good enough for one of the rock world's most legendary party animals, it's certainly good enough for me.

The manager was good as gold to me as well, always laying on the five-star treatment when he saw me. We had some bloody explosive nights, as you can imagine. I used to go absolutely crazy, putting a thick wad of notes behind the bar and standing drinks for everybody. I was going through booze there as if they were going out of fashion. As I've said, the lads in the band had been under strict instructions to keep me clear of any trouble while we were recording, which meant keeping me away from any hazardous chemical substances. In

Shitsville, USA, they'd be too fucking stupid to recognise a gramme of coke, let alone snort it. They'd probably try to stick it up their arse, or something.

So, all in all, things are going pretty well. I've got a recording contract with a major record label, I've got so much money I don't know what to do with it, and I've got access to an entire pharmaceutical industry.

Now, 'normal' people are happy to just let things wash over them if they're pretty contented about a situation, just enjoy the moment and all that. Not me. The minute things are anywhere near settling down, I have to do my best to shake them all up again. Maybe it's that chemical imbalance thing in my head, making me a bit nuts.

So what do I do to complicate my life at this point? Yes, that's right, I decide to get married again.

Now this whole episode is pretty painful to talk about, even now, especially as the person who suffered the most really didn't deserve to. The victim of it all was a pretty, fresh-faced girl from England, who used to work behind the bar of my local pub.

She was a lovely girl, about 18 or 19 at the time, and we'd got to know each other back in London. I think she'd been an Iron Maiden fan, so it was probably a novelty at first to be going out with Paul Di'Anno.

While me and the band were rehearsing and recording over in the Big Apple, I asked her to come over and join me. It must a been a thrill for her, coming over to New York and hanging out with us, going to all these glamorous clubs and that, and we had a real laugh.

I think she'd been out there for about two weeks or so, when I hit on the idea of getting married. When I think of something like that, I just jump in feet first, without worrying about the details. I leave the worrying to other people.

The whole thing was like a real spur-of-the-moment thing, but I just felt like we ought to get married straight away. It just seemed like the natural thing to do.

We tracked down a minister, and once he'd had time to iron his frock, we had the wedding ceremony up on the Brooklyn Bridge, with the lights of New York twinkling away underneath us.

We went to City Hall for the marriage certificate and all that, just to complete the formalities. We came back to my apartment for a bit of a fiddle about, just to consummate the marriage sort of thing (actually, we'd been doing it for about a year before that, but never mind) and we got ready for our wedding reception.

Then it hit us. What should we wear to the reception. She said I should wear a suit, but I just laughed. 'What? With all those wankers there in their leathers? No fucking way!'

So I'm on with the Doc Martens boots and combat trousers, stuff like that, and I'm like, 'Right, let's go!' She was much the same, 'cos she had all her hair sticking up in a sort of Mohican do, which made her look a bit like a chicken. She's put on her Doc Martens as well, along with a tartan kilt and tights, so we're ready to roll.

We took over a whole floor of the China Club for the event, which cost a fucking fortune, and anybody who was anybody in the rock world was there. Our wedding present from the club's owner was a $250 bottle of champagne. With all the rock stars there, the place was just swimming in champagne and coke. And that, in a nutshell, was the problem, or at least the start of it.

My young bride had never seen cocaine before, let alone tried it, so she had a baptism of fire that night, with all the excess going on around her. Everybody came back to our apartment, and we stayed up all night, doing line after line of cocaine. The valuable champagne was polished off by my good self, poured down my throat without even touching the sides. While my wife was really out of her depth in all this, I was like a fucking pig in shit with it all, as you can probably imagine, lapping it up all night.

So my new bride got pretty fucked up, and she just couldn't handle it, really. She was a sweet girl, and this was a world which she had absolutely no knowledge of. When everybody had gone, we were just left there in the apartment alone together, both too high in our different ways to sleep.

We started talking, and we ended up having this fantastic chat, with both of us being totally honest with each other about who we were and how we felt, for perhaps the first time since we'd met.

I know some people might think it's a bit late to start getting to know your wife on your wedding night, but I honestly believe we found out more about each other that night than we ever had in the year we'd known each other before that. I think because she was so drunk, she was really straight with me, and in a strange way it was quite cool, actually.

That night took its toll on her straight away, though. When the guys saw her the next morning, they were really shocked, it was as if she'd aged overnight. Having done that shit night after night for 20-odd years, I forget what a heavy session can do to people who aren't used to it, and it did hit her hard.

I think that night was the turning point for her, when she went from being a pretty young barmaid to a rock star's wife.

And there's no prizes for guessing which is the shittier job of the two.

Later, when we got back to England, various personal problems were making my life hell, and she ended up getting the brunt of it, the poor cow. There had been a few delays in getting the record out, and I was having trouble transferring money from the USA to Britain, so I was absolutely skint – we had no money. These aren't excuses, just things which affected the way I behaved at the time.

I'm ashamed to say that when I lost it, I really lost it, and in the middle of my schizoid moods and general paranoia, I must have turned into a demon in front of her eyes. After trying to give it up for a while, I was back on the cocaine in a big way, and if you have a disposition like mine anyway, it just makes you fucking insane. I had these huge mood swings, where I'd be OK one minute, and a ranting, raging psychopath the next. Anybody who got in my way got battered.

I wasn't sleeping at all, and the days just blurred into each other, as I lost all grip on reality.

I was violent to her, and that's all I'm going to say. I wish there was something I can do to change that, but I can't. If I could turn back the clock to make those things go away, to erase them from a young woman's life, then I would, 1,000 times over. But we can't do that, so we all have to live with what's left. It would have been the best thing for her if she'd never laid eyes on Paul Di'Anno, but I suppose she'd already worked that out for herself by then.

Of course, we split up, but not before I had some really ugly scenes with her family. They were trying to protect her from me, of course, which was right and proper in the circumstances

– I'd do the same – but by coming round for a row, it just made it all even worse.

I've said it before, but I would say again to my ex-wife, if she was in front of me now – I'm really very sorry.

*   *   *

For a while after that, I really tried to clean my act up. Not only because I was in danger of becoming a monster, but also because I felt I owed it to the guys to give the Killers thing my best shot.

We'd been given this massive fucking deal, which would put us among the top heavy metal bands in the world, and I was anxious not to fuck it up. Maybe I was getting a bit more responsible in my old age, but even I could see how important this was. We were being treated like superstars, with the red carpet rolled out for us wherever we went; now it was time to deliver the goods.

So, on the first tours to support the first Killers album, we made a pact that the bad old days of drinking and drugging were behind us. There was an unofficial rule that you'd only have two bottles of beer before a show, and coke was off the menu altogether.

People didn't believe us – come to think of it, they still don't – but that's how it was. For a while, we were the most sober band out on the road, and I was so straight, I was like a fucking ruler.

No snorting up piles of coke, no smashing up hotel rooms; I wasn't even taking out my sexual perversions on unsuspecting groupies any more. After the show, I'd leave the arena, go straight back to the hotel, and go straight to bed. For the first time in my professional career, I was living like a fucking librarian. Paul Di'Anno – the heavy metal monk.

It's fair to say that all the boys in the band were pretty much the same. I think they wanted Killers to be a success just as much as I did, perhaps even a little bit more. After all, none of us were getting any younger. We may have been thinking that this could be our last ever chance to make our mark in rock history.

It was slightly different for me, as I was the old hand – I'd already been there and done it with Iron Maiden, but some of these lads hadn't known success on that scale, and they were hungry for it, just itching to grab it with both hands.

It pains me to say it, but perhaps that's what I should have been doing all along. If you needed any proof of this, the shows we were doing at that time were without a shadow of doubt the best I'd ever done. We kicked arse from the time we burst on to the stage to the point where the last chord faded away. They were fucking fantastic. Audiences were going berserk, and it must have seemed to the record company that they'd made a good investment. We were well on the way.

Of course, things didn't always run like clockwork – there was still the Di'Anno factor to liven things up a bit. People say I'm my own worst enemy, that I have this self-destruct device which makes me say or do things which are likely to fuck things up around me. It's ironic that the person who gets the most grief as a result is always me. Perhaps they've got a point ... I don't know.

Certainly, when you look back at most of the calamities that have happened, they can be traced directly or indirectly back to me. This one was a case in point. We were touring in Holland and, again, we were doing some really good shows. Everyone was on top form, and we were sounding great.

I don't know where they came from, or who they were, but there was a load of skinheads at one of the gigs, all pogo-ing up and down and yelling and that. It may have been a coincidence (then again, maybe not) but I'd been wearing this long leather coat for the last few dates, a really flash number that cost about 500 quid.

The only problem with it was this huge swastika emblazoned on it. So there I am, on stage with this Nazi insignia on show. Well, Lemmy's worn them over the years, and Zodiac Mindwarp had a version of it, so I thought I could get away with it, too!

As luck would have it, one of our road crew was Jewish, and he's already made his feelings clear about my coat, going on about death camps and that. There was another slight problem as well – the large swastika tattoo I'd had done all up my arm a while before. Admittedly, the two things together may have given something of a wrong impression, shall we say.

Can I state here, for the record, that I am not a racist. If anybody is fully aware of the damage done by bigots, it's me. I have an ethnic background – my family is part-Italian, and I fucking hate all that racism shit. It stinks.

Yes, I was a skinhead when I was a teenager, and so, yes, I shaved my head. But my reason for doing this was just an excuse to go up to West Ham on a Saturday, and have a fight. Not the most noble of reasons perhaps, but better than some.

I never joined the National Front or the British National Party like some of the others did, and I never would. I think people should just get along with each other, whatever colour their skin is, or whoever they want to worship. My brothers around the world have suffered for generations because of all that bigotry crap.

So the reason for the insignias was just to take the piss. If you look up the swastika symbol in ancient Indian readings, it means the reverse of what it's come to represent. It means 'love'.

But anyway, it seemed like I had drawn a following which I hadn't intended, but there you go. The guys say I goose-stepped on to the stage at one point, but I can't remember doing that.

My memory of the rest of that particular night is a bit hazy, because it was one of the few nights on that tour that I fell off the wagon. I went on a bender after the show with some fans, and got as pissed as a cunt. I was so out of control that they threw me in the back of a flatbed truck and took me back to the hotel in the early hours of the morning. They dragged my lifeless body out of the truck and dumped me on the front steps. So you could say I really did fall off the wagon that night.

To appease the Jewish element in the crew, and to avoid any more neo-Nazi accusations, I chucked my 500 quid coat in the bin the very next day.

Around that time, I was changing my hairstyle. My hair has always been an issue with people – you wouldn't believe how important having the right hairstyle is in our business, it's a major political thing. Personally, I couldn't give a fuck, but there you go.

I've said before that there's no particular reason why I've always had fairly short hair compared to the other guys in Iron Maiden – it's just that my hair's naturally curly, and it grows outwards like an Afro.

Just before we went to New York, I had these hair extensions done, like dreadlocks, which went all the way down my back. Now I thought they looked pretty cool, but one problem was that the fucking things kept falling out. I was losing my own hair at that time anyway, and these bloody things just seemed to make it worse.

Everywhere we went, people would be picking these things up after me, like long black snakes. If I went to my local bar, chances are the barman would hand me a bunch of these things, which had dropped out the previous night. Of course, the guys just took the piss, non-stop.

So I took some pretty drastic action as a result, which led indirectly to my current shaven-headed look. I had all the hair on the top of my head shaved completely off, and I had this long plaited ponytail at the back, which went down to my waist.

I have to say, it made me look pretty fucking fierce. In a city which is practically full of crazies and hard-men, people used to step off the sidewalk and cross over to the other side of the street when they saw me coming. I looked like a cross between an Apache brave and a Japanese martial arts master.

I realised the effect of this when I went to meet my wife at the airport, and we were travelling back into New York in this yellow cab. The driver's Russian or something, and he's clocking me in his rear-view mirror, just having a good look as we're driving through the suburbs.

Finally he plucks up the courage, and he says to me, in broken English, 'I see you on TV the other night!'

So, all polite, I say, 'Really? Is that right?' I didn't pay much attention to it, I just thought he'd been watching MTV or something.

Pleased, he pipes up again, 'Yes, you were very good fighter! Very good!' I'm a bit puzzled now, because I think he's seen some footage of me kicking the shit out of someone, which, let's face it, wouldn't be beyond possibility.

It turns out the dickhead's seen the film *Kickboxer* with Jean-Claude Van Damme, where he fights this really evil Japanese guy with a hairstyle like mine. This cab-driver had thought I was this martial-arts expert, the cheeky fucker.

After that embarrassment, I cut the pony tail off as well, and I've had a bald bonce ever since.

*   *   *

I was happy with the music we were producing. I felt it was gradually getting darker and heavier, showing the aggressive side of my personality. I can't stand there and sing a song that goes, 'Ooh, baby, I love you, your eyes are lovely and I want to hold you for ever ...' That's not me. That's not what I'm about, and it's certainly not what my life's been like. My life's been about violence, drinking, drugs, people getting shot and stabbed, that sort of stuff. It's unfortunate, but that's the way it is, and I can't pretend any different.

That darker side of me comes out through my music – I can't help it, it's not a conscious thing. I've always been drawn to the bad side of life, I don't know why, it's just the way I am. Anyway, the newer songs were a lot harder-edged, they had more of a real heavy metal feel to them. I really felt that at last we were getting where I wanted to be, musically. For once, my career – and my life – seemed to be on the straight and narrow.

For a while during this particular period, as well, I seemed to be keeping my self-destruct mode in check. I've said that when things are going well, my natural instinct is to throw a hand-grenade into the machine, as I had in Iron Maiden, but I think the guys were keeping tabs on me as well, sort of keeping me in line.

Me and Steve Hopgood would still go out for a few beers, shaft a couple of birds, but nothing serious, you know. Steve's one of my best mates, and we go back years together. They used to call us the Toxic Twins out in LA, when we were really up to bad stuff together.

It's funny, really, because me and him are like chalk and cheese, the rough and the smooth. Steve's still got the long hair and all that, and he's a real ladykiller. He puts on this really posh voice when he goes up to women in clubs, you know, 'Hello, girls ...' and all that.

Then there's me, rough as a badger's arse, but that seems to work just as well. During our time off, me and Steve hung out together in LA, going to the Rainbow and that, and the two of us used to go through women like you wouldn't believe. There weren't that many tarts in that town that hadn't been shagged by at least one of us, believe me.

I really hate the airheads you see hanging around there, with their peroxide perms and plastic tits. Stupid fucking whiny bitches, all of them. All right to look at, but thick as pig shit underneath.

When I found a British girl amongst this shower of shit, I thought I'd hit the jackpot. She was from up north, dead smart, with a body to die for. This was one of many liaisons I went through at that time, but I thought she was a bit different, and we seemed to have plenty in common.

It turned out that this fragile English rose wasn't all she was cracked up to be. She was dead smart all right, with a good business brain – she happened to be one of the biggest drug-dealers in California!

I went out with her for a while before I discovered her secret – I was living in Van Nuys at the time, just outside LA, and we used to go out on the town and have wild times together.

As so often happened, Steve was shagging her mate, so we used to meet up as a foursome sometimes. We'd got chatting, she and I, while watching some English TV on PBS in a bar, and we immediately hit it off – it was one of those situations where you immediately feel at ease with someone, you know? Like you've known them for ages, when you've actually only just met.

We even moved in together for a while, and it was only then that her somewhat unusual occupation became obvious. You'd find bloody great guns in every drawer, there'd be little bags of coke all over the house, and she'd disappear off for about seven hours at a time most nights, going round bars and clubs to make deliveries and pick up payments. I'm all for women having a career, don't get me wrong, but this was not quite what I had in mind.

CHAPTER 13

Of course, the monastic lifestyle didn't last long. Because I had people practically sticking their head up my arse wherever I went in the States, and the cash to fund my dirty habits, there were some 'memorable' incidents, shall we say.

Despite its image, the music business is actually quite a conservative business. Men in suits, looking to make money, mostly. There are some exceptions, some people are in the industry for absolutely the right reasons, but others don't really give a flying fuck about music. They just want to turn up to work, sign a few contracts, and then sit around on their soft flabby arses and wait for the money to come rolling in. If they can shag the secretary over the desk while they're doing it, so much the better.

Most of them wouldn't know how to handle a rock band if you stuck a drumstick up their arse. So it comes as a bit of a shock when people like me crash into their safe little world, smash the place up, snort coke while swinging from the chandelier, leave a trail of destruction like a fucking cyclone has just breezed through, and then shag the secretary on the desk. Only I'd do it better.

There's a well-known event held in Los Angeles called the Foundation Forum. It's like a convention of rock bands; they're all there doing loads of showcase gigs, loads of interviews and, in my case, loads of cocaine.

So our band, Killers, has been invited to this prestigious event – I'm not quite sure why – and we're there, hanging out and having a pretty good time. Me, Steve and Cliff had flown out from New York, and we've checked into the Marriott Hotel, where it's all going on. I saw Ozzy there as we arrived, and Kiss were around, too, doing press interviews and that.

Now, it's at this point that I've got a confession to make. I get easily bored, and just sitting around and yapping all day frankly bores me to buggery. I'd rather chew my own leg off.

So I've slipped off, like I used to hop off school when I was a kid. So I'm playing truant, if you like, but whereas most truants go nicking sweets from Woolworths or drinking cider in the park, I had the whole of LA at my disposal. Fatal.

I'd bunked off at about noon, and just headed for the nearest bar. The rest of the day is a bit of a haze, but the simple truth is that I managed to get absolutely shit-faced, to the point where walking and talking were virtually impossible, especially at the same time.

I think the band must have missed me, and they managed to track me down. When they find me, I'm in some bar, pissed as a cunt. They have to overpower me, carry me out and, after a bit of a struggle, they get me into a cab. So we're heading back to the hotel, and I'm on the point of going into a coma, laid out on the back seat. I think I must have drunk my own bodyweight in Jack Daniel's that day, and if you add coke into that mix, well, you'd better stand well back, believe me.

So the cab pulls up at this posh hotel where all the rock stars are staying, and I'm dragged out on to the tarmac by my band members. They each grab a leg or an arm, and proceed to drag me through the lobby like a corpse.

Kiss were being interviewed by a crew from MTV at the time, and apparently there were looks of amazement on all their faces as Paul Di'Anno was carted through the lobby, his head lolling like a dummy. Fuck me, what an entrance.

One partner in crime from those days was Zodiac Mindwarp, who had several big hits in the late Eighties with his band The Love Reaction. Zodiac and I were pretty much on the same wavelength, shall we say.

I can remember we were travelling on a ferry going to this gig in Greece, and there's a band with us called Metal Church. They've got a new band member, who's young and inexperienced in the ways of touring, and therefore easy prey for old hands like us.

This young kid was all excited because it was his first tour; I think it was probably the first time he'd been abroad. He's in the swimming pool on this ferry, splashing about, and he comes over to me and Zodiac, who're sitting nearby.

He hands us his camera, and asks us to take a few pictures of him in the pool, so he can send them to his mum, or something. So off he trots, and he's jumping in the pool, waving and mugging for the camera.

What he doesn't know is that Zodiac, the evil bastard, has proceeded to take his dick out right there on the deck, and quickly take 20 pictures of it. When he comes to give the camera back, the kid's all grateful for what he's done. I bet he wasn't so fucking grateful when he went to pick his snaps up from the chemist's.

It's those sort of things which really make life on the road worthwhile for me; I've always said that a day on tour is two hours of fun on stage, with another 22 hours of boredom in between.

When we stop at shops, service stations, roadhouses or whatever, I just go in and buy loads of stuff that I don't really need, just for something to do. Clothes, toys, anything just to pass the fucking time, really — I've spent hundreds and hundreds of dollars in one go on complete crap that I've got bored with inside of 20 minutes.

It's the same on planes. I'm ordering up stuff from the duty-free catalogue, just because it's there, really. God knows how much money has flowed through my hands through the years; I've earnt several fucking fortunes through music, but when I've got money I'll piss it up the wall, it's as simple as that.

I've hired out entire nightclubs for my birthday parties, places like that China Club in New York and the Rainbow in Los Angeles. I've kept the champagne flowing all night, for anyone who wanted it. No one could accuse me of being a tight-arse when there's good times to be had.

One of my mates from the China Club turned up at a show we did in Staten Island, and we headed off to a bar together beforehand. He liked a drink, and he was almost as partial to the old charlie as me, so we had a pretty good time.

In fact, we got completely off our heads together, so much so that I forgot all about the show. So when we get back, everyone's been looking for me and carrying on, so they just bundle me on to the stage, like some sort of naughty schoolboy. The problem is, I've snorted so much coke that I can't sing a note.

I'm ashamed to admit I tried to blame the monitors, and even the sound-man at one point; I can vaguely remember screaming at him, 'You fucking cunt, I hope you fucking die of AIDS!' Yeah, charming, I know. I think that was the last time he worked with us, funnily enough.

So I'm up there on stage, making a complete cunt of myself, when I saw this big guy gesturing at me. I jumped down into the crowd to get into his face, and we ended up toe to toe. He was a big, nasty-looking fucker, with even more tattoos than me. Luckily, the situation calmed down before a riot started. I was in enough trouble already, after all.

So the good news was that I bought this bloke a beer and we immediately became mates, instead of knocking lumps out of each other. The bad news was that the tour promoter had been at the venue that night, had witnessed the carnage I'd caused, and wasn't too impressed. He sacked us the next day.

Not content with causing mayhem in America (this was before they kicked me out and banned me), Killers also did a tour of Japan. This was an interesting one, because none of the other guys had actually been there before, although I'd done shows there with Iron Maiden.

Now, our tours are not usually what you could call diplomatic missions; in fact they usually do very little to foster international relations. Usually, it's just the opposite. This particular one started off on the wrong foot within a few minutes of landing in Tokyo, as there's a geezer standing there at Customs, holding up a copy of the book Madonna had just written. (You remember, the dirty one.)

Anyway, it turns out this book was banned over there, as it

was considered too strong for the Japanese psyche to deal with. So this bloke's asking us if any of us have got a copy, as we're not allowed to bring them in. I suppose he saw a group of long-haired hooligans, and put two and two together.

So I've cracked a gag as I've walked up to him, saying something like, 'How much for the book, mate?' Well, OK, it wasn't side-splittingly funny, but honestly, you could have heard a fly fart at that moment.

Once we'd got that particular diplomatic gaffe out of the way, I swiftly committed another one. For our backstage rider, I'd specifically requested loads of sake and sushi. Well, when in Rome and all that – I was getting into the spirit of the place, and doing my best to broaden the band's cultural horizons.

When I actually got round to trying it after a show, all that culture bollocks went out of the window. Fuck me, it tasted like dog shit. I spat it out, and ordered a KFC instead. Despite this insult to their national cuisine, they sent someone out to get some of Colonel Sanders' finest for me. Stick to what you know, that's what I say.

You may think it couldn't get much worse after that, but you'd be wrong. We were in the bar of the Lexington Queen in Tokyo, which is one of the top clubs in the world. Five-star silver service and all that shit.

Anyway, we're there in the bar, and I've had a few to drink, so I'm getting a bit loud. I couldn't get hold of any drugs over in Japan, and I've had to make do with the booze, so I'm pissed as a cunt again.

Earlier that day, I'd been lecturing the band about the importance of etiquette to the Japanese. I was explaining that a lapse in decorum can represent a real insult to a Japanese person, so they'd better fucking behave themselves.

It was a case of 'Do as I say, not as I do,' though, because that night my whisky-addled mind decides that the waiter wasn't lively enough in bringing me some more drinks. I'm embarrassed to admit offending every English-speaking person in that bar, when I lost my rag, and called the poor waiter a 'fish-eyed yellow cunt'.

Apparently, everybody around me was so embarrassed, they were praying their appendix would burst. Sorry mate ... nothing personal.

The footnote to the Japanese tour happened when we were safely back home in America, when our guitarist, Graham (he of the kicked-in face) was going through the pockets of a leather jacket I'd given him before we'd gone over there. He'd worn this jacket throughout the tour, and on both flights.

It turns out there was a little plastic bag in one of the zip pockets, with a bit of coke in it. Seems I'd forgotten it was there, and he'd gone through US and Japanese Customs with enough Class A drugs to see him put away for a very long time.

So he was highly fucked off with me – with good reason, you might say – and I was equally fucked off with him, as the silly fucker went and flushed them down the bog in anger. What a waste.

As Killers got heavily involved in more touring, I lapsed deeper and deeper into my bad old ways. Once again, I started doing all the crazy stuff that I'd done on previous tours. You'd have thought I'd have got it out of my system after all these years, but I think I was getting worse, if anything. I had developed the skill of finding local drug-dealers down to a fine art. We could arrive in pretty much any town for a gig, especially in America, and within a few hours I'd have got our cocaine supply sorted, having sniffed out the local dealer.

In truth, it was often quite easy, as they came to find us. You'd see them hanging around backstage with a load of gear, ready to set up a deal. I suppose I must have represented quite a reasonable pension scheme for coke-dealers the world over – when I was in town, they knew they were going to do good business.

Quite often I'd hang out with them after the show, and they'd come with us on the tour for a few dates, just another part of the entourage. We were incredibly lucky in avoiding getting busted ourselves – if the cops had found any coke on me, they'd have thrown the fucking key away, but other people were always getting picked up. This used to happen a lot in New York, where the NYPD would kick the door in if they thought anybody was dealing coke.

Just as I had in Battlezone, I was getting through vast amounts of the old white powder. I'd often wake up with my nostrils caked in blood, just numb from the pounding they'd taken the night before. These would usually be all-night sessions, until six or seven in the morning, just constant abuse, night after night. How I survived it is a fucking miracle. I stashed it on roofs, down toilets, under seats ... you name it.

The management and the rest of the band used to keep me away from the support acts as much as possible, as they were convinced I'd lead them astray. The combination of a young, inexperienced bunch of party animals and a seasoned old stager was just like a ticking bomb.

If I wanted a bit of charlie, I'd move heaven and earth to get it, no matter what time of day it was. If I didn't have any currency on me, I'd sell something, just to quench the thirst. Once again, I wasn't alone in these sessions and, once again, I was usually the last one standing.

The other temptations were still there, as well. If there were girls around, I'd be up their tubes like a fucking ferret. On one visit to Denver, Colorado, we were met at the airport by these two huge limos, one black and one white. They took us to our hotel, the Holiday Inn I think, and the promoters had laid on this huge party for us there. We ended up around the pool, and you've never seen so much fanny in one place in your life.

The funniest thing was, a load of them came from the same family, they were all sisters or something. I've a feeling their mother may have been there amongst them as well, but I couldn't swear to it.

Anyway, there's this massive orgy, and all these sisters are lying side by side on a bed with their legs in the air, getting fucked by all the guys in the band, one after another. We're swapping over, taking turns, watching each other, you name it. Everybody's running in and out of the bedrooms, it's just total chaos, like a scene from some porno movie.

At one point, I saw our bass player walking through the hotel corridors with this naked bird perched on his shoulders, facing him. She had her legs wrapped around his back, with his face pressed into her bush as they walked around. There were all these cheers as we saw them, and he thought it was just the coolest thing to do.

Later, the sisters are wandering around completely naked, with spunk all over their pussies and dripping down their legs, it was just unbelievable. The evening ended with me giving Steve Hopgood (drunken) swimming lessons in this big indoor pool. He's not a strong swimmer, but I convinced him I was Olympic standard, so we're both floundering around like a pair of pissed jellyfish. How the hell we didn't drown is anyone's guess.

It got worse, though. There was another similar episode, which happened in Philadelphia. We're staying at one of the big hotels in the town, I think it was the Marriott, and we've all got rooms up on the top floor.

There was this girl who'd come along to meet us, I don't know how old she was, but she didn't look much older than 14 or 15, although she was clearly older – about seventeen or eighteen.

She ended up in a bathroom, and the whole crew – about 30-odd blokes – took turns with her. She was there of her own free will – she seemed to get a huge kick out of it, but she was just being fucked rigid by one guy after another.

What made it worse was the fact that her mother was downstairs in the lobby waiting for her, I suppose she thought she'd gone up for autographs or something like that, and she kept ringing up. The mother would be like, 'Where's my daughter? Is she coming down yet?' And these blokes would be saying, 'Yes, she'll be down in a minute!'

And there she was all the time, kneeling on all fours on the bathroom floor, with some hairy-arsed roadie giving it to her up the arse, and the others forming an orderly queue behind him.

*　　　　*　　　　*

As my new band was giving me fresh credibility in the world of heavy metal, it seemed for a while as if I would actually be more famous for being the singer of a successful band, than for my wilder exploits with booze, drugs and women. (Some hope!)

Then, of course, I go and fuck it all up, by getting sent to prison. I've described this particular episode in an earlier chapter, where I've recounted the fight with me and my common-law wife, which ended in a charge of assault with a deadly weapon. But just let me fill you in on some of the background to that story, just so you know about the events leading up to it.

I'd met this woman (who shall remain nameless, for legal reasons) at the Rainbow in LA. After recording the album in New York, and splitting up with my second wife back in England, I'd come over to California to keep out of harm's way, basically.

Of course, in trying to avoid trouble at home, I was about to run into more fucking trouble than I'd ever thought possible; but if my guardian angel told me that at the time, I wasn't fucking listening.

It was the same old story; we started off getting on with each other really well and, pretty soon, we fell in love. She was a smart, sexy lady, with a good job in the record industry, so she knew all about me and my notoriety. It's a bit of a shock that she agreed to set up home with me, knowing all about my past, but there you go.

We shared a lot of the same friends in the record industry, the 5 per cent of people in LA who are just the greatest people on earth. Ninety-five per cent of people in LA are cunts, but the rest are just the best, OK?

Those 5 per cent are just like me – they're musicians, or into music; just normal people who like having a good time. Why they choose to live among some of the most obnoxious, arrogant wankers on God's earth is another story, but that's just the way it is.

These guys with the fake tans and the hairspray – you've just got to laugh at them, because they've been in all the papers and magazines, they've got the look down to a tee. You can see them on any day of the week, walking around Hollywood Boulevard sweating their arses off in leather jackets and cowboy boots, really thinking they're God's gift. When I'm walking by in my shorts and vest, it's as much as I can do to stop myself from smacking their mascara'd faces in.

Give them a guitar, and they'll look at you as if you've just put a turd into their hands. They're fake – it's as simple as that. The tragedy is that as some of the old shit ones either snuff it or fuck off back to Dogshit, Ohio, more fuckers come in on the next bus.

It's like they picked up the United States and tipped it up, and all these losers just came tumbling over to the West Coast. Mind you, they say that's the first rule of plumbing – shit rolls downhill.

Anyway, me and this classy bird are shacked up together and, before very long, it's like War of the Worlds at our place. She's got the same volcanic temperament as me, and it soon becomes clear to anybody that if there are two people on this earth who shouldn't be let loose on the same continent, it's us. It was a bit like Maggie Thatcher and Saddam Hussein going on a blind date, you know?

The band hate her. They see it as a real John and Yoko thing, that she's turning me against them. But it was me who brought out the worst in her. We couldn't spend five minutes in each other's company without trying to claw each other's eyes out.

I'll give you an example: we were doing a show somewhere in Europe, and I'd done so much cocaine the night before that I'm sounding like Kermit the Frog. I can barely raise a croak, and I didn't help matters by drinking one-and-a-half bottles of

Jack Daniel's before going on stage, so yet again I'm barely able to stand.

I'm totally out of control, crashing from one side of the stage to another, knocking amps over, abusing people and generally making a cunt of myself, when my bird pokes her head around the curtain from backstage and shouts across at me in this loud American drawl, 'God! You suck! You're shit!' Of course, she was right.

Well, I just went fucking berserk. I chased her off the stage and into the audience, who were just standing about with their jaws dropping. It's not every day you see the singer of your favourite band chase his live-in lover through a packed concert hall, trying to kill her, but I was just spitting with rage, screaming obscenities and hurling death threats at her.

I think I picked up a weapon of some kind, a mike stand or something, and chased her all down the side of the auditorium, as she took off in fright. It's lucky I never caught her, 'cos I would have wrapped that mike stand around her fucking head if I'd got close enough. She's lucky that I've got a bad leg (old bullet wound) so I can't really run properly.

Meanwhile, the looks on the band's faces are a picture. They're just left standing up there, playing away, while their singer's gone AWOL. They said afterwards that they just couldn't believe what was happening, it was like, 'What the fucking hell's he doing now?'

As I said, they hated her guts. I think they'd have been privately pleased if I had brained her, to be honest. The feeling was mutual, as well. She insisted that when she came with me on tour, we'd travel separately from them. They didn't like it, and they made their feelings clear. It was like the band felt she was driving a huge wedge between me and the guys, but I just couldn't see it at the time, though I don't think it was her intention to cause a rift or trouble.

This situation wasn't going to go on for ever; it was obvious that there would be real trouble before long, but I don't think any of us expected it to blow up with the intensity that it did, or for the consequences to be quite so devastating.

We loved each other with a passion; we'd just tear each other's clothes off and shag like wild animals at the drop of a hat, but when we fought, it was like hell on earth, it really was.

Furniture would get destroyed, glassware smashed, doors kicked down, you name it. These white-hot rages were always fuelled by my taking cocaine, and they always left our luxurious LA apartment looking like a Tomahawk missile had come in through the window. We were the neighbours from hell; even on a good day, our apartment building must have sounded like the Battle of the Somme.

We'd throw stuff, we'd batter each other with stuff, we'd just try to rip each other's fucking heads off. She'd drag her nails down my face, I'd smack her in the mouth. She'd scream in my face, I'd batter her to the floor.

Of course, when it came down to the bare-knuckle stuff, she always came off worst. At least three times she was admitted to the hospital Emergency Room with broken ribs, a broken nose, black eyes; and yet she always came back for more.

It's not an excuse, but I was just out of my head all the time, both with all the coke I was doing, and with the white-hot rage she used to inspire in me. At its worst, I just wanted to fucking kill her, I really did.

Then there was the fight of all fights, which I've talked about, and the aftermath of that. She was determined to get me put away, there was no doubt about that. You couldn't blame her, she was shaken up and frightened, and the whole thing was just a huge trauma for everyone involved.

I was being led in and out of LA court rooms in my orange boiler suit, handcuffed to giant LAPD officers. I thought they were going to throw the bloody key away, and charge me with attempted murder. Then there was the matter of all the coke they'd found, and the Uzi which I'd had, in case of emergencies.

It was like a movie – the only difference being that I was in the middle of it, rather than watching it. I can remember thinking to myself, 'Fucking hell, Paul, you've really done it this time ...'

In the end, I suppose I escaped fairly lightly. Four months isn't a great deal for what I'd done, and it could have been a damn sight worse. As I mentioned earlier in the book, LA County Jail's no picnic, but it's not as bad as everybody said, either.

I had to sleep on the floor for the first four nights, with no blankets or anything. I was sharing a cell with a 7ft black geezer, and he nabbed the bed. Fair enough, I thought.

The one big knock-on effect of all this – and this didn't really hit home straight away, for obvious reasons – was that it fucked Killers up, big style. No matter how cool and tough they pretend to be, music industry people do not like their highly-paid recording artists to be sent to the slammer.

It's OK to sing about it, it's OK to brag and pose like it's the coolest thing ever, but when the shit hits the fan, most music executives revert back to the frightened little schoolboys they actually are, and throw up their hands in horror. You become the anti-Christ, the demon who got out of control.

It goes without saying that while I was a guest of the US

Government, our writing, recording and touring schedule was bollocksed, to put it mildly. You're gonna have a job to keep your band in the public eye when your singer's in prison, after all.

I managed to write some lyrics for new stuff which the guys were working on, and these were mailed over to them, once they'd been checked and censored by the Federal authorities. There's me, sitting in my cell in leg-irons, composing vocals with pen and paper, as if it was the most natural thing in the world.

If Killers was on its way to becoming one of the biggest heavy metal bands in the world, my little escapade had pissed on that particular bonfire for now, well and truly. Even after my release, I was virtually deported under armed guard, like some major-league criminal.

It was made obvious to me that I would be about as welcome as a turd in the bath if I tried to get back into the States from then on, even for a recording session or tour. When I tried it a while later, I was arrested the minute I set foot on American soil, clapped in handcuffs, thrown into a holding cell, and put on the first fucking plane to Heathrow.

I think perhaps the guys in the band blamed me for this major obstacle in their way, and I couldn't deny it was certainly my fault – I had no one else to blame but myself for this mess.

But this was a major fucking problem. To be on the international rock scene, you have to break America, no question. But it seemed the only thing I'd be breaking in America for a while was fucking rocks on a chain-gang.

Yet another bizarre attempt ended in failure. This one involved smuggling me across the Canadian border near Niagara Falls. I tried to get across on foot, disguised as a Hell's

Angel, but once again they threw a fucking fit when they checked my ID, and once again Di'Anno was clapped in irons and led to jail, before being kicked out of the country on his arse again. The message was: 'Fuck off and don't darken our door again.'

They even told my manager as much when he tried to sort it all out. The US immigration authorities just didn't want to know. They told him that they never wanted to hear my name mentioned to them again. Charming.

Another idea somebody came up with was to smuggle me on to the American coast on a fishing boat from Vancouver. Well, fuck that. Can you really see me in a woolly jumper and oilskins?

It's not like I'm a fucking terrorist or subversive or something, I'm a rock musician with an admittedly colourful past, who got into an almighty row with his common-law wife. There's far worse than me in their bloody country, believe me.

Actually, being kicked out of America wasn't as straightforward as you'd think. Before I could get on a plane home, I had to get all my clothes back from the apartment me and my missus had shared together, where the famous attack had taken place.

Now, in terms of missions, this one would make the SAS shit their pants. You've got one seriously pissed-off American woman (and you should never piss off American women) who'd got me nicked in the first place and is still hell-bent on having me put away for life. Would you have gone back there to ask for your pants and socks? No, I thought not.

Some of you reading this may already be aware of this fact, I don't know, but when you're released from jail in the States, they actually open the gates for you at around 3.00 in the morning. I don't know why – perhaps they think if you're going to run wild immediately and cause mayhem in the streets, you can at least do it when no fucker's about. Fair enough.

So, when I'd been released from my cell, escorted from the jail complex to the perimeter gate, and finally released once more back into the world, I went straight across the road from the jail to a Denny's restaurant, where I made up for months of prison food. I stuffed myself silly – it was fantastic. I was like a great hog, with its snout in the trough. Once I felt more human, I started to summon the courage to contact my (ex-) missus and ask her for my gear.

Me and a few mates who'd come to greet me were all there sitting in this restaurant, and I got my mate Eddie to ring her and ask. (Well, you didn't think I was going to do it myself, did you?)

Surprisingly, considering the circumstances, she actually offered to bring them over to me. Was it a trap? Would she pull out a .33 when she saw me and blow my brains out? Well, there was a good chance, but I decided to take the risk.

Now, she's got me in a bit of a fucking bind, really. Everything I had was at her place. American Express cards, cash, clothes, personal belongings; you name it, she had it. More importantly than that, there was a sizeable stash of drugs (which I'd hidden away and which she wouldn't approve of) which the cops hadn't found in the raid, which I was more than a bit anxious to lay my hands on again, to sell on for cash.

So on the one hand, I needed to get back in her good books before my repatriation, otherwise I'm about 20 grand out of pocket. That's no mean feat with someone you've recently been jailed for trying to murder, but I was hopeful the old charm would work its magic one last time.

On the other hand – and this is a small detail – I wanted to decapitate the fucking bitch for what she'd done to me. She'd been hell-bent on getting the LAPD to lock me up and throw the fucking key away and it was understandable. OK, I shouldn't have tried to kill her, fair enough, but she'd gone way over the top in getting me banged up and, at that time, I'd have liked nothing better than to finish the job off.

But that sort of talk wasn't going to help, so I had to swallow it for the time being. We arranged a meeting and left it at that for now. If I'd gone around to the apartment, the cops would have been all over me like crabs and, even if they didn't, World War III was likely to erupt again between the two of us anyway.

I checked into a plush hotel in Hollywood with some cash I'd borrowed from a mate, and enjoyed my first night of freedom, sprawled out on this kingsize bed in the hotel suite. After my small, hard bed in the cell, it felt like I was floating on air, it was just luxury.

Anyway, in the morning, there was the tricky matter of the meeting to sort out. To say this would be a bit tense would be a bit like saying the captain of the Titanic should've looked where the fuck he was going.

But what do you know ... first thing, she shows up at the hotel. It's always going to be a bit awkward coming face to face in the cold light of day with someone you've recently tried to kill, but our turbulent past made it even worse.

There's not really much call for small-talk, know what I mean? 'Hmm, how have you been recently? Are your wounds healing well? ...'

So the atmosphere's a little bit strained, to say the least. Anyway, we managed to avoid starting where we left off, and the upshot of the meeting was that I would be allowed to go round and pick up my things. Her exact words were that I had to come and 'pick up all my shit', which was quite a warm welcome really, considering.

Strange as it may seem now, after that we got chatting a little bit about the things that had happened, and how stupid we were for letting things get that out of control. Perhaps my guard was down, but I actually showed her a copy of a song I'd written while I was in jail, which was about that very thing.

It's working title was 'Three Little Words', and it basically looked at the fact that if people said these three words – I love you – a bit more often to each other, the world would be a different place to live in. You might think this is a bit strange coming from a man who's just done time for almost murdering someone, but who's better placed to judge?

If everybody in the world told each other honeestly how they felt, there'd be no need to kick the shit out of each other, and there'd be more understanding. We could avoid all these fucking wars just by communicating better.

And that's just what we were doing. We ended up having a real heart-to-heart, talking over old things about me and her which had gone unsaid until then. I think things had been simmering so long that the tension between us had finally reached breaking point, which is when the big explosion happened, and almost took everyone down with it.

So we're sitting there chatting away, and it's like the floodgates have opened. If only we'd have done that before, the nightmare of the last few months could have been so easily avoided. She got a bit emotional, and she's crying a little bit, and saying she's sorry, and I'm like, 'Fucking hell, here we go again ...'

She'd brought me a load of stuff – cigarettes and things like that – as a sort of coming out present, I suppose. It was a small gesture, but it meant a lot to me, as it seemed to show that she was trying to put everything behind us.

When I went round to pick up my 'shit', she'd laid this massive meal on for me that she'd made herself, a massive pot roast with all the trimmings. When we'd finished the meal, we just lay there together on the sofa, talking about the songs I'd written while I was in prison, and whether what I'd been through had had any effect on me.

I think it probably had, because I was able to lie there with this woman – nothing sexual, just side by side – and discuss things which a few months before had led me to try and kill her.

One of the songs from the new album – 'A Song for You' – was inspired by that whole episode, and it sort of draws the line under our relationship, really. If it sounds like something out of Love Story, well, don't reach for the sick bag just yet, because it wasn't quite like that.

Yes, I was still attracted to her; and yes, I would have shagged her that night; but, really, I think we both decided that if we ever got back together, it would be just as bad as before, with both of us spending all our time trying to beat the piss out of the other.

I loved her, despite all our ups and downs – it was as if she'd taken the wind out of my sails. In a strange way, that partly explains my behaviour – because I loved her so much, she was able to incite the worst rages in me that I'd ever known. The same passion that makes you want to sweep someone off their feet can also make you want to hurt them as deeply as you can.

It was a bizarre scene – the two of us there in that LA apartment, talking about our wild fights as if we were discussing two strangers. Was I maturing? Well no, not really. I can't say that I found the guiding light at that point, and followed the path of righteousness from then on. Just the opposite, in fact; I went back to fucking around just as I had before, but hopefully the whole sorry affair taught me something – I'm just not sure what.

We ended up falling asleep together on the bed, having sat around talking intently into the early hours. I have to be honest at this point, and say that I probably would have ended up giving her one (well, I'd been in jail for fucking months, come on!) but it was then that God took a hand.

We both woke up very early in the morning, and I think we'd probably have gone for it there and then, but at that precise moment, Los Angeles was hit by one of the biggest earthquakes in years. It was the news event of the year – a load of homes were destroyed, our apartment felt as if it was going to collapse like a house of cards at any minute, and the moment was lost for ever. We scrambled to safety, and that was the end of our relationship.

It was as if God had seen us, and boomed from the skies, 'Oi! Di'Anno! Don't you fucking touch her! All that shit will start all over again, and I'm not fucking having it!' OK, God. Message received and understood.

With the LAPD, the US Federal Authorities and now God all trying to get rid of me, I had to catch the first available flight back to England. It's quite an achievement when you think about it, getting kicked out of an entire country.

I've been kicked out of pubs, clubs, venues (even bands, come to think of it ...) but I'd never actually been deported before. When you're arrested in a foreign country, they normally just turf you out and tell you to behave yourself. It's a bit fucking serious when an entire nation turns round and says, 'Fuck off, Di'Anno ... and don't come back!'

Besides my prison sentence, it was all tied up with my visa, working permits and all that. I was now an illegal alien, a bit like ET with an attitude. As luck would have it, they couldn't get rid of me as quickly as they wanted. The earthquakes had caused such havoc in LA that flights were being cancelled, delayed ... it was chaos.

In the end, it took me two or three days to get a flight back to Heathrow. And as I settled back into my seat, and watched the sun-bleached suburbs of Los Angeles disappear under the wings, I looked forward to grey skies, endless drizzle, and soggy fish and chips. Look out Britain – I was coming home.

CHAPTER 14

Now, I'm not deaf, or stupid. I've heard all the things people are saying about me. There's been a series of vicious rumours going around the music business for a few years now, namely, that I'm a cocaine addict, a desperate junkie who'd sell his granny to get his next fix.

It is true that I've taken cocaine and other drugs throughout my adult life, that I've abused drugs in ever-increasing amounts through the years, and even experimented with heroin. But if you think I'm a sad addict who'd rob and steal to feed his habit, you're wrong.

I've said already that I don't have a drugs problem as such – I can go for months without taking them. On the other hand, if there was a pile in front of me, I wouldn't be happy until I'd taken the whole lot. It's not the drugs that are the problem – it's just what happens when I take them that causes a problem – both for me and everyone else around me, just because of the bloody stupid things I do.

I've certainly taken a lot of drugs in my time, mountains of them in fact, but it's usually just when I get bored. I can party with the best of them, but I do tend to get a bit cross-eyed when I've been putting some of the old stuff up my nose, and this does often end in disaster. I've destroyed stuff, gotten into fights, just generally misbehaved – but I think that's just me, rather than the effect of any drug.

In fact, I'm probably past the addict stage – having stuck half of Peru up my nose over the past 20 years or so, I've developed what the doctors call a deviated septum. That's a bit like that bird from *EastEnders* had; when you've snorted so much charlie, it's just blown your fucking nostrils to shit.

Although I've still got my nose, it does cause a few problems with my sinuses, which means I make this funny noise as I breathe, which sounds like I'm snoring. I can be wide awake in a hotel room or at home, and people think I'm fast asleep because they can hear this snoring noise. Of course, when I am asleep, I snore like a fucking stuck pig, which means that band members would rather sleep on top of the tour-bus than share a room with me.

In fairness, this is partly because when I've been drinking, I tend to wake up and take a piss wherever it suits me, whether it's in the wardrobe, over the dressing table, on the floor, you name it. This – coupled with my heavy smoking, not to mention the rest of my antisocial behaviour – can lead to a bad night all round for someone, so they let me have a room on my own now.

I've tried, over the years, to stop taking drugs, but it's a bit like slimming; you never quite manage it. On average, I've probably taken between three and five grammes of cocaine a day, every day. When you've got the money, it's really not a problem getting hold of it.

I remember doing a *Top of the Pops*-type TV show in Europe, and when I'd finished, someone in the hospitality suite asked me if there was anything I wanted. I said I'd like some coke. Talk about the five-star treatment – a few minutes later they brought through this huge trolley, all silver and glass, with a massive tray on top, which was covered with lines of cocaine. Now that's what I call service.

I started, like most kids do, just experimenting a bit when I was a kid, taking French Blue pills when I was going out. I'd give them to girls and that, you know, just to look a bit flash. It wasn't anything serious, and was certainly no more than hundreds and thousands of kids are doing right now across the country, as you're reading this.

I was taking speed throughout my teens, just to get an extra buzz during a night on the town. I'd walk back from Camden all the way to East London, still 'high' on the effects of a heavy night. The pills, which I used to buy off a local dealer, cost a fiver for ten, so it was a cheap trip, really. Sure, they smelt like cats' piss, but you couldn't afford to be fussy.

The first time I ever took cocaine was at a party in Dagenham, when I was about 17 or so. I remember just feeling numb, I couldn't swallow or anything at first. At it began to take effect, I can remember this huge rush coming over my whole body, just feeling high as a kite. It was like the drug had turned me into someone else, that I'd left my own persona behind.

I can distinctly remember feeling like Superman, and wanting to fuck every woman in the room. That's a feeling

I've experienced on more than one occasion over the years, and I've even tried to carry it out from time to time.

I was offered cocaine regularly by various people I met on my first tours with Iron Maiden, especially in America, where it seemed to be the drug of choice. There was the party I mentioned before at a film director's house in Los Angeles, where it was neatly laid out in little silver bowls, so the guests could help themselves. There was also a radio interview I did with a couple of DJs in Florida, where we all snorted coke together after the show. They had ideas about continuing the party back at their place, when I realised in time it was my arse they were interested in, rather than my witty conversation, but that's another story.

In rehearsal rooms, recording studios and hotels over the years, cocaine has been pretty much on tap for someone like me – it's just like ordering a club sandwich from room service. There was this one posh New York hotel where they brought it in in a special little egg-shaped container, with your own little popper to snort it from.

Cocaine has become an integral part of touring for me – I remember catching a flight from LA to Heathrow once, and I'd been indulging from this huge bag of coke a dealer had given me in Beverly Hills. I'd done so much of it that even on the morning of departure I was out of my fucking skull. I didn't know what to do with the rest of it, so I just stuffed it down the back of the seat in the airport shuttle.

It wasn't worth the risk getting caught with it at Customs, so although it was a criminal waste, it was the only thing I could think of. I could hardly pop up to a litter bin and just lob it in in front of cops and airport security now, could I?

I just hope some poor fucker didn't find it, open it up to see what's in it, get jumped on by 20 LAPD officers and end up with a 20-stretch in the Penitentiary.

On other occasions, I've posted it to myself in the UK, using somebody else's handwriting. (If anyone from HM Customs is reading this – yes, it's a very bad thing to do, and I'm very sorry ... honest!) My drug habits have led to countless nights on tour when I've gone for five or six days without sleeping, just taking drugs and more drugs. If I feel like shit, I'll eat something quick, like a tuna sandwich or chicken soup or something. These are like instant protein, like an adrenalin shot to the heart, which is probably a good thing when the only other things you've ingested that day are six lines of coke and a bottle of Jack.

When I really need to sleep, I use more drugs to do it, ironically. I take a sleeping tablet, washed down with a large brandy, and I'm away. It's perhaps not a diet that a health guru would advise, but it seems to work for me. I'm still around, anyway.

But it's when drugs take you over that you realise you're in trouble, rather than if you're just taking them to get high. When I wasn't working, I'd just sit around all day in my LA apartment, doing coke and staring at the fucking walls. It was like a scene from a movie, Trainspotting or something; I'd have a couple of grammes beside me all the time on the couch, along with a gun nearby.

My dealer used to come round most days, and we'd snort it there together. The day just revolved around drug-taking. Often, I used to wash it down with tequila or whiskey, so that my brain would get even more addled than before.

On average, I suppose I was taking about three grammes of cocaine every day, washed down with two bottles of Jack Daniel's and another half-bottle of tequila in the evening.

Getting up to take a shit was a major effort. The three flights of steps which led out on to the boulevard seemed like fucking Everest. I'd watch TV, play Scrabble, scratch my arse, and that was about it, really. It's perhaps not the most constructive way to spend your time, but I was happy enough.

I know other people who've become casualties of drugs – one of them was an ex-girlfriend of mine, who was this absolutely stunning model. She started taking drugs, and she hit them in a big way after we broke up. She was later involved in a serious car crash, which fucked her face up completely, and ruined any future modelling career she may have had. I got the blame for all this, naturally.

Usually, though, whenever the subject of drugs comes up, you'll hear from some puffed-up twat with an Oxbridge accent who'll say that drugs are a menace to society. He'll go on to say (regardless of whether anybody's listening) that possession of any drug should carry a prison sentence, and add that cannabis will never be legal while he's got a hole in his arse, and so on.

Probably that same evening, this fat, over-privileged arsehole will stop off at the golf club or wine bar, and get as pissed as a cunt, before driving home to give the wife one, assuming he can do so without shitting in his pants. D'you get the hypocrisy here? The dickhead who'll puff on 20 cigars a day will lecture the poor guy who wants to have a spliff in his own home, without bothering anybody. Fucking arseholes.

I honestly believe that cannabis – God's natural gift – should be legalised, not only due to the fact that it's less harmful than cigarettes or alcohol, but also for the reason that it can help people who're in physical pain.

A guy I know who's got a high-pressure job in the City just gets mellowed out on marijuana every weekend, because that's the only way he can really switch off and relax. That's up to him – it's his body, for God's sake.

Ecstasy could also be legalised – as long as it's pure, I don't believe it's any more harmful to you than drinking. I still take some every now and again, it just gives you a nice buzz.

As for Class A drugs, the real hard stuff, well, I would be firmly against legalising any of them. The reason? Well, it wouldn't be half as much fun taking something that's fucking legal, would it? Can you remember the disappointment when you had your first legal pint at 18? Never quite tasted the same, did it?

While we're on the subject of drugs, one of the weirdest drug-related stories I can remember happened to me after a visit to the Oregon State Prison. I wasn't there as an inmate, I was actually playing a show with the band for the guys there, which was quite an experience really, playing to a crowd of murderers, thieves and rapists.

So after the gig, I got chatting to some of the lifers, and I met this one bloke who told me he was serving a maximum life sentence for killing his wife. I asked him what had happened, and he told me that he'd come home one day to find her fucking the neighbour. So, they'd had this massive fucking row, as you might expect in the circumstances, and he'd stormed off with the right hump.

Now that would have been all right if he'd just gone off for a sulk, like we all do, but this geezer has come back with a fucking great bazooka – God knows where he'd got it from – and he's blown the absolute shit out of his house, snuffing his wife out in the process. A pretty bad day, all things considered.

But that's not the weird bit – that came later back at the hotel, when I was pretty fucked-up. We'd been thrown out of a local bar, and stopped by some cops, due to the fact that I'd fallen – pissed – on some razor-wire, and done a pretty good job of cutting myself to ribbons. So I'm going back to the hotel, clothes all torn, covered in blood, looking like something out of Mad Max.

Anyway, later, when I'd cleaned myself up and generally chilled out, another set of cops, this time local sheriffs, came charging in. In my addled state, I thought it was some kind of raid.

Just as it was looking as if I might be joining my new friend in the Oregon State Prison, I managed to hide the coke I had on me and tried to look innocent, which isn't something which comes easily to me.

It turns out I was a bit previous in hiding the gear. They were not only looking to do some coke with us, they even had some on them, which they very kindly cut up and passed around, so we had quite a party. Like I say, strange evening.

Another strange evening was one spent in Paris after a show we'd done there, when I discovered the coke I'd snorted was actually heroin, which fucked my mind up big time. If you've ever seen the scene in Pulp Fiction where the girl snorts H by mistake, it was a bit like that – just fucking horrible.

I felt really sick, and imagined some demon had been unlocked from inside me. Everything just seemed really black, and I was suspicious or everything and everybody. I lost all sense of my surroundings, and the world seemed like a dark, scary place, with monsters and devils waiting in the shadows that surrounded me. I imagined I was one of them, living out a wretched existence for eternity.

When I woke up the next morning, I'd sprayed my entire hotel room with dark, bloody vomit. I think I'd torn my stomach lining, and bled heavily as I was being sick. My room looked like a vision of hell.

I tried heroin again a while later but, again, it just made me feel so bad, I decided it wasn't for me. Me and a few mates went to some clubs, but no matter how much I drank, I had this strange, detached feeling, like I was completely detached from everything that was going on around me. I can just remember feeling really freaked-out, and then I crashed out for about 14 hours.

There's so many people I've known who've died from the stuff since then, and it makes me think I was probably right to knock it on the head when I did.

Drugs are so much a part of our modern culture, especially in the music business, where they're often a form of currency, that a couple of my relationships with women have been pretty much based on our mutual drug habits.

There was this one girlfriend I had in America, who I used to live with, and we just used to get off our heads all the time together. She had a really good nine-to-five job, so she'd go off to work in the morning, and leave me lying around the apartment.

In the evenings, we often used to go down to a club in LA, and do some coke together to get the party started. And we'd be there all night, just partying like there was no tomorrow.

Usually, we'd sneak into a cubicle together in the toilets, and while she squatted down to have a piss, I'd be separating out the lines of coke for us.

It used to really affect this girl's behaviour — as she took more and more of the stuff, she'd start to act oddly, and do strange things. We were Christmas shopping one day at this mall in California, and we'd just parked the car up in the parking lot.

We did a couple of lines to get us going, right there in the car in broad daylight, with shoppers walking by us loaded down with Christmas presents. As if that wasn't bad enough in the middle of the day, this girl then decides she's up for a bit of the old chap, and she starts stroking my thigh and squeezing my crotch as I'm sitting there beside her.

Before you know it, she's undone my flies, opened my trousers and unleashed the beast. She starts giving me the most fantastic blow-job, and as the shoppers continue to walk by the car, they're all looking in, watching her head slowly going up and down on my lap. So you see, there is something to be said for drugs.

There have been a few times, though, when I've gone too far. I've never been one for doing things in moderation; I'll do something until it nearly kills me, and only then will I think about stopping.

Through years of substance abuse, I think I've built up an immune system which is all but invincible. When I'm really in the mood for having it large, I just leave the casualties strewn by the wayside. When we're running amok through hotels, banging on sleeping band members' doors, seeing if they've got any drugs, I'll be the one leading the charge, like the geezer from *Braveheart*.

And yet, even when I'm the last one standing in the pre-dawn hours, when there are bodies littered all around me, I'll still be the first one up in the morning, hammering on everyone's doors to wind them up. After a while, you just learn to soak it up, your body reacts differently to most people's, I suppose.

It's the same with alcohol or sleeping tablets. If you give me four times the recommended dose, an amount which they'd expect to kill a horse, it would probably just about touch the sides with me. This talent didn't happen overnight – it's taken years and years of practice.

We were in Los Angeles once, playing a gig at the Country Club there, and I think I must have taken so much coke before I got on stage that it's a miracle I was still conscious, let alone able to sing. This was at the height of the LA rock scene, and all these bands are there, passing around drugs like candy.

We're staying at a swish hotel, which was a really popular place to hang out at that time; you'd see members of Motley Crue, Guns 'n' Roses, Poison, everybody. One wild fucker of a rock star took a heroin-and-cocaine overdose there, and almost died. I think his heart stopped for a few minutes until they got him going again.

Anyway, this particular evening, every cunt and his cousin is there. Every LA rocker you've ever heard of was in attendance that night – it was a fucking major league party.

And, of course, like flies round a pile of shit, the LA slags are just hanging off them. There's tarts everywhere – the real hardcore ones, who've fucked every musician in town.

As this party starts to break up, the boys in my band pair up with girls and disappear, and I'm left to escort these two birds back to my room. Tammy and Anne they were called, and I remember Anne especially, as she had what was probably the best cunt in LA, but I'm getting off the point a bit.

Anyway, so we've gone back to my room, and we're just standing about, chatting and doing yet more charlie. That's all I can remember really, just going on about some old bullshit, and snorting up line after line.

I only realise how long we've been there when one of the guys comes back and says, 'It's two o'clock in the afternoon!' We'd been there all night and all morning, without even moving from our positions. I think I passed out then and there on the floor, but after a couple of hours kip, I was up and about again and, sure enough, we went out again that night and did the whole thing all over again. Some of the guys were fucking whining about how they were feeling ill and dying and all that, but I was right as rain, and raring to go. Fucking wimps, all of them!

When things have gone a bit pear-shaped, it's been all the more scary for people around me. We were on tour in Brazil not that long ago, and we'd gone to this club. It was a fantastic place, with all these knockout birds walking around. Dark-skinned, legs that go up to their necks, dazzling smiles – you know the type. You wouldn't see a bunch of fat slappers dancing around their handbags in this sort of joint, that's for sure.

Anyway, I'm there with the guys from the band, and we're all having a few drinks and generally getting a bit lairy. As usual, I'm holding court, knocking back the free booze and ogling these stunners as they stalk past.

I know that the management have given orders to the other guys to keep me under control. I also know that the band have deliberately tried to keep me out of harm's way as far as drugs are concerned. But I also know a few dealers in Brazil, and what they don't know is that I've already cut a deal for some of the infamous powder, which was nestling in my jacket pocket.

It was a bit like being on a fucking Sunday school outing sometimes, everything I did, or tried to do, there were all these eyes watching me, frightened of what I might get up to next. There are times when it's a real pisser having your reputation go before you.

So, when they weren't looking, I sneaked off into the bogs and laid out the coke into a line on the toilet seat, about a foot long. I took a good old snort, because it had been a while. Because you can't really take coke with you from country to country, you have to look it out wherever you are. It's a bitch, but there you go. I think sometimes people don't realise the everyday stresses and strains of your average rock musician, and the problems we face.

Now, this coke is a bit on the strong side. Dealers usually mix in other powders with the genuine stuff to make it last longer and increase profit margins. So the strength of stashes can vary wildly. But this one was a lot purer than most. Either that, or I'd simply overdone it on the amount. Either way, my body reacted violently.

It was like my engine seized up – within minutes, it seemed as if every nerve, muscle and sinew in my entire body had tensed like a bloody tuning fork. My face was frozen solid in a bizarre mask – I couldn't move my jaw to speak, even. As I stood up, my legs straightened, and wouldn't relax. I was standing like a bloke with something stuck up his arse that he wasn't expecting – that's the best way I can find to describe it.

I was a bit freaked out, to be honest. It just felt so weird, as if someone else was in control of my body. It was like I was some sort of wooden puppet, like a Punch and Judy doll, with someone else pulling the strings.

Paulo, our guitarist, was out in the washroom area, and he looked shocked when he saw me, stumbling over towards him like Boris Karloff. I know he heard me snorting the coke, so he must have instantly realised what had happened.

He looked really worried, and he said something like, 'Are you all right, Paul?' I tried to smile and say that I was, but I found I couldn't do either. The muscles in my face were so taut, I couldn't open my mouth. It was like some severe case of lockjaw. So, I just gurgled, 'Gggggg ... gggggg!' through tightly-gritted teeth.

Of course, everyone freaked out – I think they were worried I was going to kick the bucket in the middle of the tour. They could probably see the headlines: DI'ANNO OD'S IN NIGHTCLUB. So they helped me out of the club, and into a waiting car. Trouble was, I couldn't bend my legs to get in the car, so I end up getting bundled in sideways like some sort of fucking mannequin.

I think the worst of it actually started to wear off by the time we got back to the hotel – my gob was working again anyway. Everyone still looked a bit pale, so I ordered a round of drinks at the bar, and we had a full-on boozing session, which lasted until the early hours. Well, I was still alive, so I was celebrating, wasn't I?

*   *   *

In case you've read this chapter and think drugs are all fun and frolics, I've got a very serious warning as to the terrible consequences that can result from a good snort or two. Let this be a lesson to you, and if you've got a weak stomach, I'd think about skipping this bit, if I were you.

I'd been to a club in the West End of London. It was run by some mates of mine, and I was a regular there – it was one of the few rock clubs in London, and it was a pretty wild place. It was said to be noticeably wilder when I was there, it has to be said, but I assume you guessed that.

Anyway, another regular at this club was a pal of mine named Dave. Now Dave, among his other attributes, was that rare beast – a generous drug-dealer. He used to carry good stuff and bad stuff, and he'd sell the bad stuff to his clients, while keeping the good stuff for his mates.

There were two minor flaws in his business plan – one, that he was a fucking cokehead himself, so he snorted as much as he sold; and two, that he used to let his mates loose on the stuff for free, as if it was bloody sherbet.

On one particular occasion, Dave had obviously taken more than was good for him, and had somehow – the silly cunt – mixed some white laxative into the cocaine. Now anybody who's ever had troubles in the arse area will tell you that white laxative is the dog's bollocks of laxatives. This stuff could make you shit a bowling ball.

So loads of us have taken this coke, and all the others have immediately started clutching their guts and running downstairs to the bogs. There's a queue stretching out of the front door for the Gents, as all these guys are dying for a crap. Due to my iron constitution, I wasn't affected at all, and I had a bloody good laugh at them.

That would all have been very well, but – like the twat I am – I only went and helped myself to a few more man-sized lines, because it seemed as if nobody else was having any. I was happy as Larry, laughing at that lot and doing more and more lines of the stuff.

Well, that did it. It finally hit me later that night, when we'd gone back to the flat of a very famous rock star (who shall remain nameless). He shared the flat with his Japanese girlfriend, who was obsessively houseproud, and the place looked like something out of the Ideal Home Exhibition. Not for long ...

I felt my guts starting to gurgle and turn over, and I realised what was happening. I dashed downstairs to the bog like Linford Christie, desperate to avoid the dreaded 'follow-through'. That's when I realised I had a problem. I was wearing a pair of leather trousers, which didn't have a zipper. Instead, they had an intricate series of laces, which tied up across the front. You couldn't get out of those bastards in a hurry.

I hurtled down the stairs, three at a time, desperately tugging at my trousers to avoid a 'touching-cloth' moment. I'd almost reached the bottom when I yanked the cord free and pulled them down. But it was too late. There was a noise like a 21-gun salute, which echoed deafeningly off the wood walls, and my arse just exploded, pebble-dashing the immaculate walls of the staircase. The fall-out went up the stair-carpet, over the floor – I even hit a lamp shade, from 4ft away.

I barged through the door and ran across the polished floor like a farm muck-spreader, shit flying in all directions. I looked as if I'd been hit by a shitstorm. By the time I actually got my arse on to the bog, I'd coated every single surface in the beautifully-furnished bathroom. Once I was sat there, I shat the equivalent of New Zealand's annual waste, and just sat there, pale and shaking (and covered in shit).

There wasn't much I could do, so I just squelched up the

stairs like a forlorn mud-man, and jumped into the nearest bed I could find. Exhaustion took over, and I fell into a deep – though slightly smelly – sleep.

Unfortunately, the Japanese bird had to get up early in the morning to go to work. The hysterical screams and heart-rending sobs which rang out from the stairs that day will stay with me for ever.

CHAPTER 15

If my long-standing love affair with narcotics was going from strength to strength, other relationships were going from bad to worse. With three failed marriages so far, you may have thought that I'd learnt my lesson, but I still couldn't really work out where I was going wrong.

I met this beautiful girl in Austria, absolutely bloody gorgeous, with dark eyes and long black hair. (Even those who can't find anything else in my favour are forced to admit I can pull some stunning women – it's that old Cockney charm.) Anyway, I wasn't touring or recording for a while, so I shacked up with this piece in Salzburg. I didn't start wearing leather shorts or take up yodelling or anything like that, but the time we had together there was spent far more constructively, if you catch my drift.

Once again, though, I was doing a lot of drinking while I was there and I think, as time went on, things pretty much went downhill faster than an Olympic skier. It all came to an end at a show we did a bit later – I forget where – when we had the mother of all rows in the dressing room before the gig.

Cliff, our guitarist, came into the dressing room and found me out of control, just screaming hysterically at this girl, with a bottle in my raised hand. He was convinced I was going to glass her with it, so he stepped in and calmed things down. Maybe I'd have hit her with it, who knows. Thank Christ, we never found out.

Anyway, we've got to do this show, and there's about 1,500 people waiting out in the venue, but I'm still fucking steaming after this row. My mood isn't helped by the fact that I've once again got a mixture of whisky and cocaine coursing through my system, mixing with adrenalin to create a lethal cocktail. My memory of the evening is a bit hazy, but the band insist that during the show I threatened to kill the girl in front of all those people, and that I was screaming abuse at her from the stage, effing and blinding like a madman. All in all, probably not one of my best nights.

It got worse, though. The drugs were affecting my mind more than ever at this stage, and they were certainly affecting the way I acted. I could be happy as you like one minute, and turn into a raging animal within seconds.

This Jekyll and Hyde transformation occurred several times during one particular tour. It was a one-off tour in Japan, which was basically a reunion of the heavy metal band Praying Mantis.

I think it was to mark an anniversary of the new wave of British heavy metal or something, but the event was being backed by a big record company, and they'd got two of the original Praying Mantis guys together, along with my good self on vocals, and my old Iron Maiden comrades Dennis Stratton and Clive Burr on guitar and drums respectively.

It was actually more of a Maiden reunion than anything else, but when money's being thrown at you, you don't quibble. Besides, I think the current incarnation of Maiden would have thrown a fucking fit if we'd called ourselves anything like that.

So, they get all of us guys together, and lock us up in a rehearsal room in Tottenham, supposedly to learn the Mantis material, but mainly to keep us (well, me) out of trouble until we were supposed to go out to Japan.

Well, I fucking hate rehearsing. Always have. It's all right for the other guys to stand about banging on about D major chords and syncopated beats, but my singing is a one-off; I only really come alive in front of a baying crowd of fans. I can't just stand around singing the same song over and over, it bores the tits off me.

And when I get bored, believe me, trouble starts. So it did on this occasion and, once more, it would all end in tears. While we were farting about with this project, I'd got friendly (yeah, again!) with one of the record company executives, a pretty young Japanese girl.

We'd seen each other a few times, been out for dinner and that, but it was nothing really serious, we were more like friends. Well, I can say that now with the benefit of hindsight, but at the time I suppose I got the hump when she didn't fall at my feet every time she saw me. Yeah, I know, but that was the way my mind worked at the time, with all the drugs and whatever.

I think the stress was starting to get a bit much as well around then, because the tour meant basically learning a whole set of songs from scratch, and performing them live.

So I perhaps got a bit obsessed with this girl, and that's when things got a bit out of hand. I found out where she lived, and I went round there. She wasn't in – I think she'd gone out with some friends or something – so I left a message on her answering machine.

I went to a nearby pub and had a drink, then another, then another. You just know how this is going to turn out, don't you? The last (and most pissed) message I'd left on her machine was basically a threat that she'd better come round to the pub to see me, or else. She obviously didn't want me causing any trouble, so she came round, scared to death.

Well, I was in no fit state to listen to reason, and I lost my rag right there in the pub. I was shouting and yelling at her, and the staff there called the police. I followed her to her house and basically forced my way in, which is when we had another row, with the drink fuelling my irrational rage.

What happened next I'm deeply ashamed of, and I regretted it the instant I'd done it. I would hate for anybody to think for one minute I'm trying to glorify it or whitewash it, because I've already said that I'd rather chop my own hand off than hit a woman again. The fact is that I attacked her, right there in her own house, punching her repeatedly in the face. This woman is a tiny little thing, about 7st; and there's this 15st monster giving her a beating.

She was already frightened, and she ended up in a bit of state. Her face was cut and bruised, and she had to be taken to hospital. She was understandably shaken by the whole affair, and she must have been terrified of me after that, because she avoided being alone with me from then on.

I can't explain why I acted like that, nor the fact that it's not the first time it had happened. But as if that wasn't bad enough, the whole scenario was repeated when we actually got out to Japan.

Our rooms were on the same floor of this hotel where we were all staying, and I must have been keen to see her on her own again, perhaps if only to apologise or make amends for what had gone on before.

That's all very well, but it's best not to have a skinful of booze and several lines of charlie before you go on such a delicate mission, because chances are you'll fuck up again.

And that's exactly what happened. I followed her up to her room one night, and forced my way in. We ended up having an almighty scene, with me shouting at her at the top of my voice, and her cowering and screaming. Once again, I'm ashamed to admit that I started laying into her, but this time the other band members had heard the commotion, and came running upstairs to break it all up.

Dennis and the other guys were absolutely disgusted with me, and I don't blame them. I was bloody disgusted with myself. It sobered me up like ice-cold water. Once again, I apologised and begged her forgiveness, but the damage had been done, you could tell.

If I could turn the clock back, I would. There's no positive spin you can put on that stuff, and I wouldn't want to try. It's difficult for me to write frankly about things like that, but I hope people will at least give me credit for having the honesty to admit it, and face up to what I did.

I'll say it one more time – I'm very, very sorry.

As if that wasn't bad enough, I was getting extreme grief from a Continental bird around that time, but on this occasion the fight was on home ground. I'd met this Italian girl, and she'd become the latest love, as we'd moved in together back in London. I'd given her a load of old flannel about owning all these vineyards and villas around the world, and she seemed to have gone for it. She came with us on tour a few times, and we had a right laugh together.

But, as usually happens (yeah, you can see a pattern emerging here, right?) romance turned into hostility, and hostility eventually turned into violence. She ended up spending one Christmas in Whipps Cross Hospital, and as a result, I spent it in the nick. My manager had to come and stand bail for me, to get me out of jail in time to play a show in Plymouth on Boxing Day. Same shit, different day, right?

When she recovered from her injuries, this bird actually ended up taking out a restraining order against me, which prevented me from coming anywhere near her. So she's in the flat (my flat, mind you) and I'm temporarily homeless.

So I've gone round to the flat to pick up my stuff, and I find that she's dumped several thousand pounds' worth of Armani suits out into the backyard, like a bundle of fucking rags. Of course, there's another bad scene, and in between calling her every name under the sun, I decide to leave the fucking suits there and, in my rage, I even took a piss on them for good measure. Was there any rational explanation for this behaviour? No, there wasn't. Did it make me feel better? Yes, it did.

In between these traumatic episodes, other romantic encounters were carrying on as normal. There was one girl in Brazil who I befriended ... well, let's just say she was just one of the most fantastic creatures you've ever seen in your life.

When I met her, I immediately had this feeling that I never wanted to leave Brazil again, that I'd be happy just staying there with her. We spent a short time together while I was there, and all the time I'm with her, my tongue's just hanging out, she was just this fantastic vision of beauty.

I met her family and all that, and I ended up staying on for about a month. I saw a lot of her during that time, and it was one of those ones where you just get this feeling that it's going to be a bit special.

She was actually still at college, and while I was there I was probably a bad influence on her, because we'd be up partying until 5.00 in the morning, and she'd go off to her classes the next day.

I remember once giving her about 50 quid's worth of roses, which is a hell of a lot of money over there, and I can still see her, just swamped in amongst all these flowers. Another vague memory I have of being with her was visiting a police chief's house. I think he must have been a friend of her family or something.

Now, I'm on best behaviour, because this bloke's probably aware of my reputation as a debauched rock singer, so I've made sure to get rid of any drugs on my person before I've gone to meet him. Turns out I needn't have bothered. You could have knocked me down with a fucking feather when he lines up a load of coke on his kitchen table, and invites us to help ourselves. Like those sheriffs I met in the States, he wasn't averse to a bit of the old white powder himself. Apparently, it came from various dealers who he'd arrested, and it had sort of got 'lost' between the raid and the police station. I tell you — send me to any country, anywhere in the world, and I'll find the drug-dealers, pimps, conmen, you name it. It's like a fucking instinct.

In the end, I had to go back to the UK for rehearsals, so me and this bird drifted apart, which was a shame. It's one of those situations where you wonder what might have been, and realise you'll never really know.

On the opposite end of the evolutionary scale, though, some of the biggest and ugliest wildebeest ever to walk the earth were hanging around me and the guys in the band, like flies round a particularly fascinating turd.

We were doing a show in Belgium, and our drummer Steve Hopgood has picked up this bird who's just the most hideous beast you've ever laid eyes on. She looked like Arthur Mullard with a wig.

Anyway, this half-woman, half-animal has got its claws into Steve, and they're on the way back to the hotel for a fuck. Now, the bad news is, she's got a friend. If the first one was a bit rank, well, she looked like Cindy bloody Crawford next to the friend. This bitch has got without doubt the fattest arse I've ever seen, while possessing all the physical allure of a sack of shit.

I know which way this evening's going to turn out, and it's like one of those car-crashes in slow motion, where you can see what's going to happen, but you can't stop it. Me and Steve are sharing a room. This means, of course, that yours truly is going to be stirring this great hog's pot before the night is over. It was a thought which made my blood run cold. You wouldn't know whether to fuck it, or harpoon it.

So, we're back in the hotel room, and Steve is in bed with his bird, and they're shagging away like a couple of rutting rhinos. This other tart has jumped into my bed, and she's lying there like half a ton of nutty slack. I just looked across at Steve, as if to say, 'What the fuck is this monster in my bed?' but he's already at work on his bitch, so it looks as if me and the pig are an item.

So I've crept into bed beside old Frankenstein, and she's lying there on her back stark naked, clearly expecting the works, too. Fucking hell.

After about 20 minutes of half-hearted fiddling about with her saggy great tits, I whisper to Steve, 'Do me a favour, will you, mate ... come over here and shag this, it's fucking horrible!'

You'd have thought that would have spoilt the air of romance, but neither of these women seem to speak much English. Steve's still got his hands full, so I go for the B-side – I turn Lardy over and give it to her up the arse, which at least spares me the ordeal of having to look at her face. She's there squealing and biting the pillow as I'm 'scuttling' away (if you're in the music industry, you'll be familiar with the phrase) with my face screwed up into a grimace at the horror of the whole thing. I'm jamming the old chap up into her flabby great arse, but she's so fat, I can't tell which crease is which. It was a case of pump once, and ride the waves ...

So, for the next hour or so, me and Steve keep up a joint running commentary of the sexual abuse we were putting our partners through. We were like two football commentators in the press box at a match – all we needed were sheepskin coats and lip-mikes.

There was another sad tart who Graham Bath (our guitarist) picked up in Barcelona, and this one just wouldn't shut up. All the time she was with us, day and night, she just kept yapping on – she was driving me up the fucking wall.

In the end, I snapped, and I grabbed hold of her, and pushed her into one of the hotel rooms, and locked the bloody door. She's probably still there now, the silly bitch.

Graham had a talent for picking up the worst sort of scabby old tarts on tour, but he'd surpassed himself with this one. She was just the ugliest cunt you've ever seen, she looked like the sort of wino junkie you'd see in shop doorways in Oxford Street, passed out in a pool of vomit.

One of the other guys was in the room that first night while Graham's giving it to this slag, and she's doing all sorts, getting him to piss on her, and licking his arse out all night, apparently. The other bloke's trying to get some sleep, while this dirty bitch is there with her tongue stuck up Graham's hairy arse.

But the prize for saddest cow of all time must go to the legendary groupie in America, who gave every member of Killers a hand-job, and then went on to do all the road crew, as well. The boys were all lining up, giggling, and there she was, down on her knees, wanking away. She was a bit of a pig, and I don't think she normally got much, 'cos she actually seemed to be enjoying it.

We got her T-shirt off, and she was just kneeling there in her huge white bra, patiently tugging off one cock after another. I think it's a pretty fair bet to say she'd had a drink or two that night.

Then, cheering, we got her bra off as well – so she's there with these massive great bare tits swinging round, still furiously wanking everybody off. 'Course, the end result of all this hard work was that she ended up absolutely covered with spunk. It was running down over her face and tits, her hair was fucking matted with it, it was bloody gross.

Having serviced all the boys, I think she must have ended up getting shagged by some of them as well and, like a bad smell, she's still around when we're getting up the next morning. The only thing is, she's still got this semen matted in her hair, and it's dried solid. She probably went home to her husband or boyfriend that day, but Christ knows what she must have told him. Like I said, sad cow or what?

There are some women who let other people take advantage of them, and yet there are others who take control of a situation and turn it to their own advantage. A girl who was definitely a member of the second group was this prossie from Paris who I came across years ago while I was with Iron Maiden.

Now this girl was in a league all of her own. I first saw her in this strip club over there, during a night on the town after a show. Me and Dave Murray had gone to this club, and we're watching open-mouthed as this girl does stuff that two young London lads had never even dreamt of, let alone seen. For example, she'd stick this cigar up her fanny, draw smoke from it, and blow bloody great smoke rings in the air. Fuck me, were we impressed, or what. I think me and Davey were bloody fighting over her at one stage.

Later, I was sitting in one of the booths and she came in, and draped herself over my lap. It was like a scene from your ultimate sexual fantasy – this gorgeous French tart, just about to shag your brains out. She pulled up her dress with one hand – no underwear, funnily enough – and unzips my trousers with the other hand.

In one smooth action – I'm guessing here that she'd done this sort of thing before – she got my dick out, shoved it up inside her snatch, and started merrily bouncing up and down on my lap like a fucking rabbit.

Just to prove what a truly class act she was, she rounded off a truly memorable evening with yet another trick. She bent over and – get this – proceeded to take a piss, right there on stage. This was no ordinary piss, however – it shot out in a massive stream about 10ft long, shooting from one side of the stage to the other. My jaw dropped yet again – I just couldn't believe it. Definitely my type of girl. I'm not sure she's the sort you'd want to take home to your mother but, let's face it, life would never be dull with her at home, would it?

*   *   *

Can I just say, at this stage, that I consider myself very much a man's man. I've nothing against queers as such, but the thought of any bloke getting his tool anywhere near my dirt-box just makes me want to shit. Just thought I'd point that out, right here and now.

The reason I draw this to your is that I was once caught in a compromising position with a bloke in New York but, as usual, there was a bit of a story attached to it. We were supposed to be doing this gig in the Big Apple but, for some reason, it got cancelled. When this sort of shit happens, you can go fucking mad and smash the place up (I've tried that), or you can use your time off constructively, and go out and look for drugs, which is exactly what I was doing.

I'd arranged to meet this dealer in an alleyway leading off a back street. When I arrived, it was dark, and there wasn't a soul around. We met up there, agreed this drug deal, and he handed the stuff over to me. Just as I stuffed it in my pocket, out of nowhere I hear this police siren, which is so loud it feels like my head's going to split open.

The panic button really goes off in a situation like this, because if you're caught with that much fucking coke on you in the States, they're probably going to suspect you of dealing, and you're looking at a few years of hard time in a State Penitentiary.

So, quick as a flash, I grabbed hold of the dealer's head, and forced his lips on to mine, pretending to give him a snog. I swear, the cops looked down the alleyway, thought we were two fags just getting up each other, and walked off in disgust. OK, it didn't come naturally, and I had a bit of a nasty taste in my mouth, but it was a whole lot better than the alternative. Once again, a result.

Without a doubt, though, one of my strangest ever encounters was a famous episode that occurred in Sheepshead Bay, New York, a few years back. Even thinking about this one now just blows my fucking mind.

It happened around Christmas time, and I think we'd just finished a tour, so I was at a bit of a loose end. For some reason, I was staying in a motel in Sheepshead Bay over the holiday season, by myself. I think a couple of the guys had stayed on after the tour, but they'd fucked off with birds and that. I think Cliff may have offered to come over for part of the break, but I probably got a bit stroppy and told him not to fucking bother.

So there's me on my tod in this place. It was a bit like something you'd see in an American road movie, all cheap wood panelling and exposed brick. Like a sort of downmarket Las Vegas-type of joint. It goes without saying that I got bored shitless in no time at all. I got absolutely wankered several days on the trot, when all I did was drink myself into a fucking stupor.

I had a shitload of charlie on me, so I was snorting up all the time as well. This had the effect of giving the whole experience a slightly dreamlike quality, as if I wasn't really there, that I was watching someone else. Days blended into one another as I just lay around and slobbed out, indulging myself in endless substance abuse.

On Christmas morning, I rang the kids back in England, just to check that they'd got the presents I'd had sent over to them. I probably went a bit over the top in the old Christmas shopping, as if to make up for not actually being with them. Speaking to them on the telephone made me feel even more depressed, to be honest. It probably made me even more aware of being thousands of miles away from home and family, just lying in a motel room, by myself.

I decided to make an effort to join in with the Christmas spirit, and I went down to the lounge bar for a drink. I was standing at the bar with a large Jack Daniel's in front of me, just staring into space and minding my own business for once, when I became aware of a party getting under way in the lounge.

As I turned around, the room seemed to be filling with a large group of middle-aged people, chatting, ordering drinks and generally getting into the festive spirit. They were typical middle-class Americans, White Anglo-Saxon Protestants, church-goers, whatever. I must have stood out like a sore thumb amongst them, as they stood around in their polyester slacks and knitted jumpers. They didn't know who I was, but I can remember thinking that these were the sort of people who'd probably fucking shit themselves if little Bobby bought an Iron Maiden record, or, God forbid, little Billie-Jo managed to get herself shagged by someone like me.

Decent, God-fearing folk – some of them may even have been members of the PMRC, the fucking ridiculous parents' organisation that tries to get heavy metal records banned on account of their (laughable) Satanic content. I must have stood out like a white zit, with my leathers, tattoos and earrings, and yet among the general chatter I heard a voice at my shoulder, saying, 'Are you on your own?' and I turned around to see this woman standing at the bar beside me.

I didn't really know what to think, and I must have looked a bit surprised as I turned around to look at her. She was petite, in her mid-forties, reasonably attractive in a mumsy kind of way, and a little bit on the stout side. She had a sort of grey rinse hairdo, and she looked like the kind of woman who baked cakes for the kids' fêtes, sat on committees, and wore a nightie in bed. She looked as if she'd take a dim view if her husband came home pissed from the golf club and wanted to shag her, she was that type.

She had these glasses on that made her look like a sort of Christian librarian, and she was dressed in an ultra-conservative flowery dress. As she introduced herself to me and I bought her a drink, we must have attracted some stares among the other party-goers, looking like two people who would never have a single thing in common.

But anyway, I thought, 'What the hell ...' so we had a few more drinks and started getting to know each other. Beneath the prim exterior, I think there was a naughty side itching to come out, to be honest. She told me at one point that I had 'lovely eyes', which considering at that point that a combination of whisky and cocaine had made my eyes look like pissholes in the snow, was quite a bold statement. She was either pissed or a bit mad, but frankly I was beyond caring.

She seemed to get a kick out of who I was, and what I'd done, and as I spoke to her about being in bands and touring and that, it was obvious this was a world which she knew absolutely fuck-all about.

At one point, I can remember the song 'Tie a Yellow Ribbon' was playing on the sound system, and there were all these couples twirling slowly around the dance floor. My new friend asked me if I wanted to dance, and before I had the chance to say no, she'd caught hold of my hand and pulled me out on to the floor.

This might seem an odd thing for a professional musician to say, but I fucking hate dancing. You will never get me to dance at any sort of party or function – I hate making a total cunt of myself. Anyway, it's hardly me, is it? Would you really expect to see me boogying around the floor at some bloody disco? Exactly.

And yet here I am, former lead singer of the world's top heavy metal group, slowly gyrating with a middle-aged woman to 'Tie A Yellow Ribbon' in a New York motel! Talk about getting yourself into some strange situations – I couldn't fucking believe it.

But if I thought that was a bit strange, it would get even more weird before too much longer. I can't remember what the hell we were talking about exactly, but we seemed to be getting on all right, and as the party wound down, she came back to my room.

Now, I wasn't really sure what to expect, but she was up for it, big time. She even tried a little coke to loosen her up, as we lay on the bed. Before you know it, she's down on her knees, this prim Mrs Middle America, she's got my cock out and she's giving me a vigorous blow-job. Just imagine that, the 'Beast' of heavy metal legend, being violently sucked off by a Washington Wife type! Fucking hell.

As her greying head bobbed up and down on my lap, I realised, too, that what she lacked in expertise, she certainly made up for in enthusiasm. I got her up on the bed, and pulled her dress up around her waist, revealing these very prim and proper white knickers. I pulled them off her, placed her ankles on my shoulders, and was just about to plunge the old chap into her, when fuck me if the bastard phone didn't ring.

We both almost jumped out of our skins, and looked at each other, as if to say, 'What the hell are we doing?' Anyway, it killed the romantic moment stone dead. As I spoke on the phone, she got up off the bed and started sheepishly pulling her knickers on and, by the time I'd finished, the mood had gone, really. I sent her off in a cab, and wished her a happy Christmas.

Talk about fucking timing! If someone hadn't phoned just then, I'd have been banging her all night! I wonder where she is now, and if she remembers her brief stint as a rock groupie? I only hope she hasn't told her husband.

*   *   *

As someone who's likely to be tempted off the straight and narrow every now and then, I think America was probably the worst place in the world I could have chosen to live during the Nineties, and LA in particular.

Everywhere you went, there was champagne, cocaine ... and fanny crawling all over you. I had VIP passes to top clubs, dealers ready to bring over some charlie at any hour of the day or night, the full five-star celebrity treatment. It was like having a licence to commit crime.

During one particularly excessive day in LA, I managed to buy a house and a motorcycle – I can't remember why or how, but there you go. If you're taking cocaine all the time with all the rest of these party animals over there, these sort of things actually seem quite normal.

I met this bird once at the infamous Rainbow, where half the world's rock stars hang out when they're in LA. Now this bird was class, she was like some sort of Californian fantasy. It was as if she'd stepped out of one of David Lee Roth's videos – all tits and teeth.

We've met up there and got chatting, and she's invited me to meet her the next night at the Four Seasons, a really posh hotel in Beverly Hills. The next night, I've had a shower, shit and a shave – not necessarily in that order – and got my best gear on to go out and meet this girl. Left my old woman at home, but there you go, what she doesn't know won't hurt her. (Well, it might now, come to think of it – sorry, darlin'.)

A massive limo draws up outside my apartment, and this uniformed chauffeur leaps out. 'Are you Mr Di'Anno?' When I nod, he's practically kissing my ring-piece, ushering me into the back of this Cadillac and fussing over me. I'm a bit wary and, as we drove through the LA streets, I kept my hand on the handgun I kept in my belt, just for comfort.

Anyway, we arrive at the Four Seasons, and I'm shown up to this fucking fantastic suite, where she's staying. This guy in a uniform brings up a big cold meat buffet, with champagne on tap. So I'm sitting there in this five-star suite, having it large, and chucking £100 champagne down my neck as if it was Special Brew.

Time gets on a bit, and this bird's late now. The phone goes, and it's her, saying she's been held up, and she'll be another hour or so. So I say fine, and settle back to slurp more champagne, happy as a pig in shite. The next thing I know, there's a delivery being dropped off outside the door. It's a package, addressed to me. When I pick it up, there's a message on it, saying how sorry she is for the delay. I open it, and there's five big bags of cocaine inside.

Well, I don't need asking twice. I carve it up on the table and start snorting it up. What with drinking and doing coke, I lose track of the time, and when I next look at my watch, three hours have gone by.

The phone rang again before long, and she's on the other end, sounding all flustered. 'Paul, I'm downtown and I've been busted!' she says. 'The cops are taking me in!'

It turns out she was mixed up with some really heavy people, and she's got picked up with a load of coke on her. She's in deep shit, looking at some serious jail time; but my first worry is whether she's going to say anything to them about me.

The shock stuns me out of my stupor, and I run around the room, grabbing my things and hiding any sign that I'd been there. I grabbed the bags of coke – well, I didn't want them going to waste – and I fucking legged it. The staff at the Four Seasons – a hotel which would not have approved at all – must have wondered what the hell was happening, as I legged it out of the lobby – it was like something out of a film. See what I mean about me and trouble? Rest assured, we'll always find each other.

CHAPTER 16

I'm a bit mad. Now the more astute among you will probably have realised this fact long before this stage of the book but, nevertheless, it's a fact.

The truth is, I've been told that I have a chemical imbalance in my brain. In layman's terms, that means you're a bit nuts. In my own case, it means I'm either feeling lower than a worm's arsehole, or I think I'm fucking Superman. I'm also schizophrenic as well, so it's a bastard to buy Christmas presents for me, really.

There was a bit of a problem over a visa application a while back, and the visa office in Britain refused to give me the paperwork I needed to go on a tour. The conversation went something like this:

My manager: 'Why won't you give him a visa?'
Bloke at visa office (who'd interviewed me): 'Because he's mad.'
My manager: 'Fair enough ...'

With me, it's full-on – all or nothing. I've been so high I felt I was going to explode, like when Maiden played the Reading Rock festival for the first time, or both our albums went into the charts at Number One.

On the other hand, I've slumped in a heap in a hotel room, saturated in drink and drugs, and just wanted everybody else in the world to fuck off and never bother me again. I just felt as if I hated everybody, especially myself. I've often felt I was fighting a one-man war, with everybody else on one side, and me on another.

Behaviour which seems bizarre to most people seems perfectly natural to me. A guy I knew had a new car, a beautiful BMW, and he was worried it was going to get nicked. For a few nights, I crouched in the back seat as it was parked outside his house, with a bloody great Bowie knife in my hand. I'd just sit there in the darkness, waiting for a burglar to come along, so I could rip his fucking throat out. Normal behaviour? You tell me what's normal ...

Funnily enough, it's often other people's problems which trigger me off. I read newspapers and watch the news on TV, and when I see pictures of kids in Africa or India just starving to death 'cos they've got no fucking food, a wave of misery just comes over me. I feel absolutely bloody helpless, 'cos there they are suffering, and I can do absolutely fuck-all about it.

I think the same when I read about the war in Afghanistan. The situation there has been going on for fucking years, and no cunt's going to do anything to help the people there. They're just left to starve, poor fuckers.

Even in the Western world, where at least we've got food to eat, there's still a lot of sadness. I'd say about 95 per cent of people are lonely as fuck, with absolutely no one to turn to if they needed help. All these people need is a bit of love. If I can see it, why can't other people? Why doesn't anybody do anything? It keeps me awake at nights.

I've always had a dark side, which is fascinated by the morbid side of life. I can remember as a kid having a hamster as a pet. I accidentally knocked the box down off its shelf and the little thing died. I was absolutely gutted but, being a morbid little fucker, I sort of mummified it, and gave it a proper burial, next to a little tree. I went to visit that grave every day for about two weeks.

In the end, my curiosity got the better of me, and I dug it up. It was all rotten and disgusting, but I just wanted to see what it looked like.

I suppose I've always had a fascination with death, but I've never been able to work out why one race of people want to kill another race of people. Just because you don't like someone's beliefs, religion or whatever, it just doesn't seem a good enough reason for murdering complete strangers, whoever they are.

I'm not afraid of dying – there have been a few times in my life when I thought I was going to die, but I wasn't afraid. I have contemplated suicide a couple of times, but I don't think I could ever go through with it. I don't think most people would have the bottle to do that, to be honest.

If I'm afraid of anything, it's leaving this earth without having provided for all my children, so they'll be all right when I'm gone. It might sound strange when so many of my relationships have ended so unhappily, but I still want them to be proud of me. I don't want to be an embarrassment or a burden to them.

Just when I'm feeling at my lowest, when everything seems at its most black, there is always something to pull me out of it. Usually, it's my family. They're a very down-to-earth bunch, my mum and dad and my sisters, and one of them will always say something or do something to make you laugh, and it just lifts you up out of whatever depression you were in. It's that working-class East London thing, I suppose. There's always someone worse off, and all that.

Just as the family kept me from getting too big for my boots when I became famous, so they still keep me on the straight and narrow now. But I think they understand the pressures I face, and the effect it's had on me. A cousin of mine said to me recently, 'You've been all over the world, Paul, but the world's been all over you, too ...'

I honestly believe that. I've had a great time, travelling and doing what I enjoy and all that, but the more famous you become, the less space you seem to have for yourself. I've been very lucky, but I've paid a price for it.

*   *   *

I don't know whether it's a symptom of madness, but I always like to do the unexpected, to keep people guessing. Just when they think they've finally got me sussed out, I go and do something which just leaves them breathless. Whether they're breathless with shock, admiration or disgust, frankly, doesn't matter.

You'll have noticed a pattern throughout this book – as soon as things show any sign of settling down into a routine, I shake them up, turn them upside down, and start all over again. When things are going well, I have an uncanny ability to fuck them up beyond repair. When things start to get even the slightest bit dull, I put such a spanner in the works that the whole machine is fucked completely.

So, when I'd been back in England for while, and people here had just gotten used to having me around, I decided to get married again. Now I can guess what you're saying to yourself right now, 'What the fuck did you want to go and do that for again? Do you never learn?'

Yeah, right — that's what everyone said at the time, and plenty more besides. People who'd already lost count of all my wives were having to fork out for yet another wedding present, and the more cynical among them were setting odds that it wouldn't last. I think you could have got 8-1 on less than a year at one point; and if you'd had a flutter at that SP, you'd have had a result.

The case for the defence is that she was achingly beautiful — all doe eyes, long black hair and cheek bones you could cut your food with. She was Bulgarian, and I met her when I was doing some shows over there. I can just remember thinking that she was the most fantastic vision of beauty I'd ever clapped eyes on.

She looked like one of those really exotic birds from the James Bond films; you know, one of the ones who's either going to cop it before the opening credits, or whip a Bowie knife from out of her drawers and waste every fucker in sight.

Well, she didn't do either of those, but she did enough to completely bowl me over. There have been quite a few dramatic moments in my life, as you'll have gathered, but this was one which will always stay with me. We'd done a couple of songs, and we were about to start a third, when the crowd just seemed to part, and there she was, staring at me.

We held each other's gaze for a good few minutes, and I think the guys in the band were getting a bit worried, thinking, 'What the fuck's Di'Anno doing?' But I just couldn't take my eyes off her, it was as simple as that. My heart was racing – I couldn't speak. I was just numb.

After the set, I got myself introduced and, from there on, the Di'Anno charm was full on, full blast. We spent hours chatting, like you do when you meet someone fascinating for the first time; and it was like a scene out of a movie, just the two of us there talking away and laughing.

We went on to a club, and we just had a wild time. I was drinking Bulgarian raki, which should carry a skull and crossbones on it, it's so lethal. But however much I drank, I still wasn't pissed. I was so preoccupied with her, I was just staring into her eyes, telling her how lovely she was, and explaining over and over that she was the fittest bird I'd ever seen.

And she seemed to feel the same way! She was telling me that she thought I was a nice man, and that she liked me very much, all in this really sexy broken English. I had goosebumps all over and a raging horn like a tent peg – it was like your ultimate sexual fantasy. A drop-dead gorgeous girl – and I can't emphasise enough just how bloody gorgeous she was – who was coming on to me, as fast as I could come on to her. Fucking hell!

I felt fit to burst, you know that feeling when you think you're the king of the world and you can do anything? I drank a complete bottle of Jack Daniel's and some more raki, and ended up standing on a table in the middle of this club, singing the Shaggy song 'Mr Lover Lover' at full volume. Not a subtle form of courtship I grant you, but it does the trick.

Bloody hell, was she impressed. I don't think she'd seen anyone carrying on like that before, but it didn't seem to put her off – quite the opposite. We went back to my hotel room, but while we slept in the same bed, I didn't fuck her. I respected her too much for that – this was no rough-as-a-badger's-arse groupie; she was something else.

She was obviously a good influence on me, because during the rest of the Bulgarian tour, while the other guys were getting completely wankered on booze every night (well, there's not much else to do – you can't get hold of any coke in Bulgaria), I was restraining myself, resting my voice, and just spending all my time with her. I didn't want to let her out of my sight for a second. I think I was afraid that someone would see this 'perfect' girl and snatch her up. I wanted her, and I'd have killed anybody who got in the way of that.

It felt right, and it felt like it was meant to be. The only trouble was, of course, that she lived in Sofia, and I was back living in London. I was due home in a few days, and I spent every available minute in her company, trying not to think about going home and leaving her behind.

When I go for something, I go for it 100 per cent, and I was completely and utterly heads over heels in love with this bird. I felt she was right for me, that she was the one I'd been fucking about looking for all these years, and that I'd finally found the one thing that would bring all my antics to a close.

While I was there, the press seemed to pick up on the story, and I opened the morning newspaper one day while we were having breakfast, and there's my face splashed all over the showbiz column, with a headline that said something like: DI'ANNO GETS BULGARIAN GIRLFRIEND!

I don't know how they got to hear about it, but i showed her the article and she laughed. I said, 'I wish this was true!'

She replied, 'It can be, if you want ...' Fuck me, the hairs on the back of my neck stood on end. Did I want her to be my girlfriend? Does the Pope shit in the woods.

The first challenge was to get her over to Britain. Once I'd gone back, this became my all all-consuming quest. It just felt wrong that we were apart – I felt her rightful place was with me, wherever I happened to be, and she certainly seemed to feel the same way.

While all my mates were taking the piss, saying I'd finally lost the plot altogether, I was spending hours and hours on the phone to her, running up thousands of pounds in phone bills. I think I was on the phone to her at least once a day for around six months. She was a smart girl – both her parents were university lecturers, so she was no dummy – and it seemed as if she felt exactly the same way about me as I did about her.

When I do things, I don't do them by halves. Whether its drink, drugs, violence, you name it – I'll jump in feet first, and worry about the details later. I've always been a brush-strokes sort of bloke, you know, leaving the details to other people.

I've always trusted my instincts, and even when I've been 100 per cent wrong, as I have been on quite a few occasions, I've never regretted it for a second. Would you rather be lying on your death-bed thinking, 'Christ, I made a complete cunt of myself over that bird ...' or would you rather be tortured by doubt for ever, thinking, 'I wonder what would have happened if me and that bird had got it together ...?'

You only get one chance at these things, so I screwed up my courage and asked her to marry me. Even allowing for the distance between us, and my less-than-unblemished record in this department, she didn't hesitate for a second.

This helped to smooth the way for the whole immigration

process, allowing her to enter Britain legally, although, I swear I'd have smuggled her in underneath a lorry if I'd had to. There was just no way I could allow us to be apart for a day longer.

It was still a pain in the arse, though, I had to apply for a visa for her, sort it all out with the Home Office, cut through all the red tape – it was horrendous, and it cost me fucking thousands. Mind you, I didn't think about the money at the time. I'd have done it if it had cost millions, without missing a heartbeat. I loved her that much.

When I'd finally got the whole mess sorted out, and the time arrived for her to leave her home in Sofia, though, I found out about a phobia she has – flying. I certainly don't think she'd ever been on a plane before, but she made it clear she wasn't going to start now. Instead, she got on a bloody bus, would you believe, which took her from the coach terminal in Sofia to Victoria Station in London, via the Czech Republic, Poland, Germany and everywhere else in between.

It must have been like hell on wheels, being cooped up in a coach all that time. I'd have gone off my fucking rocker, and ended up killing someone. I don't know why she had this problem with flying, I'd have paid to have her brought over by helicopter if necessary, but instead she had to endure this three-day ordeal on the road.

I was waiting for her at Victoria, and when she stepped off this bus, I didn't even recognise her. The poor little darling, she looked like she hadn't had a square meal in weeks. I just wanted to gather her up in my arms, get her home and feed her.

When she'd finally arrived in Britain, we tied the knot at Walthamstow Register Office, when this Bulgarian beauty became the latest Mrs Di'Anno. There was a slight confusion, as I'd stupidly asked several of my mates to be the best man, but they managed to sort it out amongst themselves without any unpleasantness.

So we moved into a flat in Walthamstow as man and wife, and for a while everything seemed rosy. You'll notice my use of the words 'for a while' there, because – and this may not come as a huge surprise to you – it didn't actually stay that rosy for very long.

The truth of it was that she just couldn't cope with me. There are very few – if any – who can, but the task of keeping me under control every hour of every day was just way, way out of her league.

It was like Leyton Orient trying to hold Inter Milan to a goalless draw – it just wouldn't happen. Drugs were still fucking my mind up big-time and, once again, that same old monster would materialise and scare the shit out of her. It was as if one part of me was this normal, ordinary sort of bloke, and the other a raging, uncontrollable psychopath. The scary thing was, I could go from one to the other within the space of a minute.

Once again, my life was falling apart. My band had just split up (yet again) and I'd had a really serious falling-out with the guys – Steve, Cliff, everyone. So I was in a constant state of rage, which just needed the slightest nudge to be unleashed at full force. It was like there was this permanent black cloud hanging over me, 24 hours a day.

I had money problems as well. All my cash was tied up in legal wrangles and international transfers and God knows what else, which basically meant I was skint. I don't mean a few quid short, I mean shit-or-bust on a Nick Leeson-type scale. The high living of previous years when I'd spent $10,000 in one shopping spree seemed a long way off at that time. I honestly thought I'd end up kipping under the arches at one point.

On top of all that, I'd fallen out big-time with my management (again). All of this was piling on top of me and, of course, it was once again my new bride who had to suffer the onslaught of madness. And when I flipped, I really fucking flipped. Again there were rows, and again there was violence. There'd be the mother of all screaming matches, me throwing things and breaking furniture, and she'd usually end up getting hurt. And I mean hurt.

There was just no way she was anywhere near prepared for a nightmare like that, and she really retreated into her shell. She was a stranger in a foreign country, with only me to hold on to and, more often than not, the bloke that she'd married had disappeared anyway.

It must have been a living hell for her, and she had no one over here to turn to. At one point, I was virtually keeping her a prisoner in the flat, as I was so scared that she'd leg it.

One day, when I was away on tour, she finally decided she could take no more, and she just ran away. I think she'd had just about as much as she could take, and she panicked. She actually ended up on my mum's doorstep, crying and carrying on about me. She said that I'd threatened to have the Mafia kill her brother if she ever left me, and she was desperate to have my mum persuade me to call off the 'contract'.

She must have made arrangements to get back home from there, because she'd fled the country by the time I came back off the tour. The Di'Anno curse had struck again. Once again, I'd had everything within my grasp and, once again, I'd managed to let it all slip through my fingers.

I was heartbroken – absolutely inconsolable. It made it all the worse, knowing that I'd no one to blame but myself. With all that had happened over the past few months, this just put the tin hat on it. I could have seen it coming, and I really should have; but thinking about how we'd been, and how much we'd wanted to be together, just made me feel physically sick to my stomach.

I was living through one of my darkest times at this point – paranoid, suspicious and painfully distant from anyone. I just felt the world was out to get me. It was like staring over a cliff edge at this point, not being able to see any way around it. I tried to get her back, I even went over to Bulgaria a couple of times to see her, but it was useless. She was gone.

I can look back now, and say, 'Well, that's life Paul – shit happens,' but I didn't feel like that back then, I can tell you.

The next thing I heard was one Christmas Eve, a couple of years later, when I got a letter from her. She started off saying that she hoped I was well and all that, and then went on to say she had some bad news for me – she'd met someone else. By that time, I was well and truly back to my old ways anyway, so it didn't hit me like I thought it would, to be honest. It was like she'd been gone for so long that she ceased to exist.

I was back ravaging helpless groupies and dipping my wick into any warm, wet fanny I could find, so she could fuck right off, as far as I was concerned, now. I was that worried, really.

Thinking about it now, as I write this, perhaps I was a little bit choked, under all the bravado, because I'd really felt at one time that we were going to spend the rest of our lives together, but there you go. I wrote back to her, giving her a load of old bollocks as usual.

We kept in occasional touch for a while, actually, just a few telephone calls here and there, all pretty friendly. Then, the next thing I know, I got a phone call out of the blue from her.

She said that she wanted all the divorce stuff all sorted out as soon as possible, because she wanted to get married again.

I asked her where she was phoning from, as she sounded quite close, and she told me she was in Kent! I asked her what the fuck she was doing in Kent, and she told me she was picking potatoes! Ask a stupid fucking question!

CHAPTER 17

So, I'm still making music, and I'm still enjoying it. That's the bottom line really, that's the only thing that's brought me through the roller-coaster ride you've just read.

I still enjoy doing shows, and although it takes me away from the people I love – my families and children – it brings me to the other love of my life, the fans who've been with me through Iron Maiden, Di'Anno, Battlezone and Killers. I can't emphasise this enough - if it wasn't for that lot, I'd have fucked off out of it long before now.

The novelty of touring wore off a long while ago, but I still feel the need to get myself out there and prove myself to an audience. That's what keeps me going, through all the airports, tour-buses and hotels which make up 22 hours of daily grind. The two hours you actually spend on stage make up for all of that, that's what you live for.

All that other stuff I could walk out on tomorrow – the

interviews, the meetings with record company people, the promotional appearances and shit like that, it wouldn't matter to me if it all ended right now. The only bit I'd miss is actually writing and performing music.

Many of the fans who come to my shows now weren't even born when I started my career, but then that's all the more reason to give 'em a show, rather than rely on past glories. You've got a job to do, you've got to get on with it.

You've got to remember, this is the crowd's big night out. They've come to be entertained. For one night, they're leaving their job or college or school behind, to enter the world of heavy metal music. They're looking for an escape, a rush of adrenalin, a taste of excitement. They don't want to see you under par, or hear you whining about missing your family, for fuck's sake.

Do the women still come? Well, yeah, they do. Do I still take advantage of what's on offer? Well, yeah – wouldn't you?

Do I feel I've been given the recognition I deserve? Well, no, probably not, but I suppose most people would feel that way about themselves, wouldn't they? The songs I wrote in Iron Maiden were massive international hits; I've proved I can still write and perform cracking songs, with some big record contracts and enough gruelling tours to finish me off for good.

The life I've led has brought me into contact with some of the most fantastic people in the world, and it's given me the biggest kick of all to have played a role in their lives in some way, however small. If I've taken someone's mind off whatever was pissing them off before they turned the stereo on, that's a job well done in my book.

But if I've made many friends, it goes without saying that I've made even more enemies. You can't live the life that I have for the last 25 years without trampling a few people underfoot, and I've probably trodden on more than most.

I read an interview recently with an American music mogul, and he said that someone who is universally liked is probably a very mediocre sort of person. That sort of sums it up for me, really. Call me what you like – and after reading this book you probably will – but you can never, ever call me mediocre.

My manager says I have two talents in life – singing and pissing people off. And God, he should know. He's the poor sod who's got to come along behind me clearing up the mess I've left, repairing any bruised egos, defusing any confrontations, containing any tantrums, and so on and so on.

It's true that I have a rare talent for really pissing people off – it just comes naturally. We played a really big festival in Europe just recently, and I got a bit out of order after the show, having a go at a few people and that.

We'd just done an absolutely blinding set of in-your-face heavy metal music, like it should be played, and I think I was still high on adrenalin. Apparently I upset some people backstage with my attitude or whatever, but fuck 'em, I say.

I'd had a few drinks, so I probably was getting a bit antsy, but I didn't smack anybody or get arrested, so that's got to be a result, really. You could say they got off lightly, compared to past episodes. Perhaps I'm mellowing, in my old age.

If I've any complaints at the moment, it's really about the state of the music industry in the UK. It's just died a fucking death, if you ask me. There's nothing much here that I'd want to listen to, to be honest. We just don't have any world-beaters at the moment. Every time I come home to Britain, it's just got worse and worse. I find it a bit depressing, having lived through the era that I have, and actually been in at the start of the Eighties heavy metal explosion.

The music world that I entered a quarter of a century ago has changed beyond all recognition, in terms of quality, songwriting, record companies ... you name it. I've slagged off manufactured boy bands until I'm blue in the face, but it's not really the guys' fault. They just do what they're told, and take the money. Well, you would at that age, wouldn't you? Of course you fucking would. Sing when you're told, dance when you're told, take a fucking shit when you're told.

If you're going to act like an accountant, then go and be a fucking accountant, and stop pretending to be something you're not. I'm not perfect, I'm not a rocket scientist or anything like that, but whatever anybody ever says about me, I'm genuine – the real deal. Everything I do is 1,000 per cent from the heart, always has been.

If you're just interested in making money, you should fuck off out of the music industry altogether. Become a boring twat, have a wife and two kids and end up hating yourself and your life. I've had a great life, and I wouldn't change it for anybody else's, ever.

The bottom, top and every other line with these people is money, as it always has been. If people can make a few quid out of bands like that, they're going to sign up a few dozen, squeeze them dry, and then drop them. That's the way it works.

All this means that there's less places for up-and-coming bands to play, so those bands with real potential don't get spotted. If there hadn't been a Ruskin Arms, Iron Maiden may not have hit the big time like we did. (Me and Davey Murray could still be sharing that fucking squat. Ugh!)

But no one seems to be doing anything about this, they're just letting the situation get worse. The policy of 'pay-to-play', where groups had to finance their own gigs, was a bloody disaster for live music. Like so many other bad ideas, it was imported from the States.

It just means that rich kids, whose daddies can afford to set them up with all the gear, can now get all the breaks, whether they deserve it or not. Kids who're prepared to struggle up the hard way with endless roadwork and year after year of bloody graft can just fuck off, it seems.

People think that Iron Maiden sprung from nowhere, but nothing could be further from the truth. It's the usual story that when they see you on *Top of the Pops*, they think you're an overnight sensation. Well, we were an overnight sensation – years of overnight fucking journeys from the arse end of nowhere through the night back to London, in order to do our day jobs.

It wasn't just the shows either, there was the money needed to keep the whole thing going. Most of the money we were paid in those early days went to buy amps, PA systems, vans, you name it. And you weren't talking about huge fees back then either, just beer money split five ways.

I think the band came perilously close to breaking up altogether at one point, when some cunt nicked all the gear from the truck. Everybody on the London music scene thought that was curtains for Maiden, but – once again – I have to give Steve Harris credit for sticking with it when lesser men would have thrown the towel in, and getting the band out of the shit to a point where it could come back, stronger and more determined than before.

But while it was a bloody struggle back then, I think it would be nigh on impossible now, I really do. There's an apathy towards British bands, both from the media and the paying public, which makes it all but impossible for even the good ones to break through.

It even affects me now. My current band haven't really played that many gigs in the UK, just because it would take so much money and grief to make it happen. I'd love to do three nights at the Marquee in London, or somewhere like that, just for our fans here who've stuck with us. Come to think of it, I'd love to do a full UK tour, if only for the many friends that we all have here, to see us in action, all revved up. Just to prove I can still do it.

I feel as if I've been exiled abroad for most of my career, mainly because the reception I've got from press and industry people in the States has been so much better than the UK. The fans are solid, but the other stuff isn't. The only reason I got such a major recording deal with BMG, was the fact that I was based in the States. If I'd been in Britain at the time, I don't believe it would have happened.

While we're on the subject, I really don't know what I've done to make the British music press hate me, but while the reviews of my albums have always been great, they've never missed a chance to take a pot-shot at me in other articles and features, usually about leaving Maiden, drinking, taking drugs, getting married, getting married again, and so on. Come on, chaps, I'm still here, ain't I? That's an achievement in itself, isn't it?

In fact, I've often thought that there was this big conspiracy against me within the music industry, both among the press and the record labels. This was a few years ago when I was doing a lot of drugs, so perhaps it was them making me paranoid, I don't know. But it just seems that whenever I try to do something, I find a door slammed in my face. It may be my reputation again, I just don't know.

There was one particular grievance I had which festered over a number of years with a music journalist. His name is Dave Ling, and he'd written a review about me in Kerrang! magazine, I think it was, which was less than flattering.

OK, fair enough, he's paid to say what he thinks, otherwise he's not doing his job, I understand that now. I don't expect hacks to be crawling up my arse, after all. But back then, when I was all fucked up, I took it really personally. I saw him soon afterwards at a club, and I chased him out of the club on to the street, ready to kick the fuck out of him. He legged it away from me, and I chased him through the London traffic like a hound after a fox, and he only got away by leaping on to a moving bus. If he hadn't, he would have got it, big time.

I didn't see him for a few years, but when I did, I realised what a complete cunt I'd been, and I apologised to him. We had a good chat, and we're actually great mates now, which we should have been all along, really. He's probably one of the best music journalists in the country, so more power to his elbow. We're on the same side, after all.

My profile in the UK is still very low, compared to Europe, the USA and Japan.

But having said that, I think my professional peak is still ahead of me. There's no reason why I can't carry on for a good while yet. And while I've had Number One albums with Iron Maiden, and one of the later Killers albums was voted one of the best heavy metal records of all time, I still think the best is yet to come.

I think too many people judged me by my first solo album

when I'd left Maiden (and looking back now, I must admit, it did maybe leave something to be desired) but I make music to please myself, not to worry about sales or charts and shit. If you don't like it, fuck you, that's my attitude.

And have I calmed down as I've got older? No, not at all. I'm still getting into exactly the same sort of trouble that I was 20 years ago; probably worse, if anything.

Let me give you an example of the sort of shit that still happens. I'd been seeing this bird who worked as a hostess in a West End club. She was a good girl, took it up the arse and everything, so you know, definitely one to be treasured. And she swallowed as well – a man can't ask for much more in a woman in my book.

Anyway, I'd been seeing her on and off for a while, in between tours and recording commitments. Nothing heavy, just a few drinks, a few lines, and some pretty wild sex sessions which left both of us feeling we'd gone 12 rounds. The sort where you shag her senseless, and you both lose the power of speech afterwards.

Anyway, I'd just come off a tour round Europe, so when I came back to London, I popped down to the club where she worked, just to surprise her. I'd never actually been there before – we always met somewhere else, which I could understand. When you're not working, you're not working – you'd never see me doing karaoke, now would you?

So I've gone down there, you know, giving it the big rock star bit with tales of fantastic exploits in foreign lands, and I'd brought her a huge bottle of really classy champagne as a present. But before I could give it to her, I notice she seems a bit edgy. Not unfriendly exactly, but like she'd prefer it if I'd warned her I was coming. I was just about to find out the reason for this....

The head doorman, a big, tasty-looking geezer, was giving me the evil eye as I spoke to this bird. I later found out they'd actually been a steady item for a couple of years, and were actually living together, but she'd neglected to tell me about this little fact.

So he sees this shaven-headed, heavily-tattooed monster chatting his old woman up, and he's not happy. He must have thought she was in some sort of danger or something, because he comes steaming over to us when I put my arm around her shoulders.

Now, fair enough, I'd have reacted exactly the same way in his shoes, but Di'Anno wasn't completely aware of the full facts as this tricky situation began to unfold. I just saw a big lump looking for trouble.

If he'd known I'd been giving it to her up the tradesman's for the past six months, he'd have been even more upset, I suppose, but that's neither here nor there.

I still didn't know what was happening when he picked me up by the scruff and swung back to knock the living shit out of me. Through instinct, I ducked out of the way, and his meaty great fist whistled over my head. I could feel the breeze on my scalp.

My shell-shocked mind registered that another one would be coming along any minute, and advised that I should take avoiding action ASAP. So, almost without thinking, I swung a heavy right at his chin, aiming for the sweet spot where the jaw meets the throat.

I clumped him all right, but in all the kerfuffle, I'd completely forgotten about the large bottle of champers in my right hand. It clanked into him like I was christening the QEII, glass and champagne spraying everywhere. Blood is pissing out of his head, and he's got one or two quite nasty-looking shards of glass sticking out of his face, so all in all, it's been quite a bad night for him. First, he's seen this ugly fucker groping his bird, and now he looks like he's been in a road accident.

Once again, quite a crowd has gathered by this time (where do these people come from? Have they got fucking scanners?) and I decide to leg it. Explanations would have seemed pretty lame, really, given the circumstances. Not surprisingly, I never saw her again; but fuck me, she was worth it.

*   *   *

While that particular lovely lady had the pleasure of being fucked hard up the arse by my good self, there are people around who've done the equivalent to me. There are people who've fucked me over down the years in a variety of ways, and for a variety of reasons.

You know the type – practically crawling up your arse when they meet you – 'Oh my God! Paul Di'Anno! I love Iron Maiden!' Then as soon as your back's turned, they immediately try to screw you for every cent they can get their grubby little hands on.

The music industry is a pretty murky sort of world at the best of times, and if you have any sort of success at all, there's usually a crowd of sharks circling around you before you can say 'Jaws'.

I was protected from that to a certain extent when I was in Maiden, and I've worked with some people since who were as good as gold, as I've said; but I've also come into contact with some pretty heavy-duty people – the sort you don't really want to piss off if you don't fancy being fitted for a concrete overcoat.

I nearly always managed to piss them off anyway, naturally, just by being my usual exuberant self and leaving a trail of mayhem behind me wherever I went. Hurricane Paul, that's me, reducing the best-laid plans of record companies and tour promoters to ruins, just by doing whatever I fucking like. And if they don't like it, they can shove it up their arses, because I'm the one people are paying to see.

Negotiations over contracts don't usually take very long when I'm involved. A few minutes of me screaming abuse at them, and they're either calling for security or bolting for the nearest exit. There's something about flabby-arsed businessmen which brings out the worst in me – I don't know what it is.

When I see some lardy fucker reclining in a custom-made leather chair, with his Gucci loafers up on a polished oak desk (all of which I paid for) I want to jump over it, grab him, and stuff his head up his fat arse.

Similarly, when there are rows with concert promoters, tour managers or whoever, I can usually solve it in seconds. The UN should be employing me as a peace envoy – I'd be fucking dynamite in world affairs. There's no need for a big conflab if the PA isn't right, or the dressing rooms aren't ready. A smack in the mouth or a chair over the head usually brings people around to my way of thinking, and my tours tend to go pretty smoothly as a result. People who work with me say they encounter far fewer problems with venues as a result of this hands-on style.

There's a few guys, though – and they know who they are – who still owe me big time. There's one in particular, quite a big noise in the business, who owes me hundreds of thousands of pounds from work my band has done for him.

He won't pay up, and he just hides from me, hoping I'll go

away. Well, I'd give up all that money just to have a few minutes in a dark alley with him, the thieving fucker. Would he pay if I held a gun to his head? You fucking bet he would. After he'd shit himself.

Don't think I've forgotten, mate. I'll just drop in one of these days for a chat.

CHAPTER 18

Before you start thinking I've taken up the pipe and slippers these days, it ain't that bad – I'm performing with my band, bigger and better than ever before, and I've been touring over the last year to crowds I haven't seen the like of since the early Maiden days, to be honest.

Ironically, despite my years of drinking and smoking, my voice is stronger, more powerful and simply better than it ever has been. It's something which I've always taken for granted, for better or worse. The best I can hope for is that my music makes people happy. It certainly makes me happy, and it's about the only thing I can really do – I'm not really any good at anything else.

Some of the best songs I've written have had the most emotion behind them. 'Remember Tomorrow', which was a real favourite for Iron Maiden fans, has a special meaning for me, because I wrote it for my grandfather. I re-recorded it in later years, because I didn't feel I did it justice when I was in Maiden.

Songwriting gives me an outlet for things which I find too painful or private to talk about. You can say a lot in a song, because it's personal to you – it's only you that knows what it really means. How do I feel when I hear my songs now? Proud, I suppose, because they'll always be there – no-one can ever take them away from me.

I have calmed down a bit I suppose, I don't fly off the handle quite so much. If I don't like someone I'll still tell them, whereas before I'd twat them first and ask questions later. The reason for this is that I'm happier than I've ever been at any time in my life. This may be due to my finding other reasons to live for, instead of my own selfish pleasure.

One of these is the Children of Hope charity in Argentina, which I've become involved with. It's based in Buenos Aires, and cares for children with brain trauma. When I was shown around there by the angel of a woman who runs it, I just couldn't handle what I was seeing – I'd never seen anything like it before.

I was on my way back from Argentina – I can't remember where I was going – and I just broke down on the plane, just burst into tears. Anything I can ever do for those kids, I'm there. I hope I'll be able to make a significant contribution in the future – it's the least any of us can do.

The major factor, though, in the change that's come over me, is the discovery of my faith. After the time I spent in jail, I was forced to take stock a bit, I suppose, just take a long hard look at myself and what I was. It didn't happen overnight, it was a gradual process, but I found myself wanting to know more and more about the faith of Islam, and the teachings of the Koran.

I'd always been interested in religion, and I'd read the Bible, but it didn't really get me going, you know? I don't know about the Greatest Story Ever Told, but I'd fucking love the royalties!

A friend of mine in London, who's a Muslim, introduced me to the teachings of the Koran, when he gave me a copy to read one day. If the Bible is for beginners, the Koran is the real deal – there was far more in there that I could actually relate to.

And so, I adopted the Muslim faith. Slowly and surely, I began to take up the ways of Islam, in order to try and become a better person. I'm not a good Muslim – I've got a beer in my hand as I'm writing this – but I'm at least making some effort to find out about the world around me, and the spiritual world around that. There wasn't a blinding flash of light one day, or a moment of extreme clarity, or anything like that; more a gradual leaning to try and educate myself.

Of course, the world went into shock over the attacks on the World Trade Center in New York, and Muslims were made out to be the lowest form of scum the world over. Yes, it was a shocking attack, and no, there can never be any kind of excuse for taking human life on that scale. When I saw the pictures on TV, I just couldn't comprehend the enormity of it all. But to tar all Muslims with the same brush is not only ignorant, it's deliberately misrepresenting the facts. It comes down to racism, as it always does. This was just the excuse some people had been waiting for.

It's the typical British mentality – we are right, so everybody else can fuck off. Islam has been oppressed by the West for God knows how long, and nobody's ever given a shit about it or even recognised the fact. When you mention Muslims to British people, they think of guys in beards with Kalashnikovs. Well, that's not the story – never has been. It's about a faith, a cause, and there aren't too many of them about these days.

Most people wouldn't know a cause if it kicked their front door in and fucked their wife. They can't see anything beyond a new BMW or a bigger house. That's where life starts and ends for most people; it's me, me, me.

Not long ago, we had a guy in my local mouthing off about it, saying that Muslims were a bunch of psychopaths who'd like to take over Britain and get rid of the Church of England altogether. Well, I fucking lost it with him, the gobby fucker.

I lamped him so hard he flew backwards over a table, sending glasses, chairs and people flying everywhere. There was absolute mayhem in the pub, with people screaming and running out of the way. As the guy landed on his back, I jumped on him, took my keys out, and slashed his throat with them before anyone could stop me. Blood was pouring from his throat down all over his clothes and on to the floor. It took several of the regulars to drag me off him, and he was a sorry-looking piece of shit when they lifted him up. I would have fucking killed him if they'd let me.

I know its not very 'PC' and, of course, I can see the irony of trying to kill someone who says your religion is too violent, but there was no way I could let that pass. There are just some things you don't say. Especially to me.

*   *   *

Today, when I still spend much of the year travelling to shows all over the world, I think more and more about putting down some permanent roots. I know it's long overdue, but it's taken me this long to get this far, for reasons which must be obvious.

I suppose everyone has a favourite place, a place where they feel safe, and where they feel wanted. For me, that place is the country of Brazil. I am completely in love with the country and its people. There's hardly a day goes by when I'm there that I'm not moved almost to tears by their affection for me, and their kindness to me.

I've got family ties there as well – several members of the ever-growing Di'Anno brood were born and raised out there (yes, with yet another girlfriend, before you ask!) and I suppose that's given me an emotional tie with the place, for starters.

I can't do enough for the people there; any time they want me, they've got me. Giving your all on stage has always been an emotional experience, it's about wanting people to like you. But the reception we get there is so electric, so atmospheric, it's beyond belief. It just explodes.

In the early days of Battlezone, one of the first incarnations of the band went out there on tour, and the reaction we got in the shows was just out of this world. They were just foaming at the mouth with excitement. We actually broke the Brazilian record for the number of shows played by a Western band at that time – I think Deep Purple had done eight or so shows the year before, but we did around 30. I think we could have done 300. Fuck me, it was like we'd died and gone to heaven. In all my career, both with Iron Maiden and as a solo artist, I've never known gigs like them. They had to call in extra security, because people were getting pushed through plate-glass windows in the crush. It was like Beatlemania times 20, just pure hysteria.

My bodyguards were crowding around me so I wouldn't get crushed, and it actually got quite scary at one point, because all you could see was this huge mass of people, all pushing forward like they were at some kind of religious festival or pilgrimage. There were hands all over me, they virtually tore the shirt off my back.

When you receive that sort of welcome, well, it was a turning point, it really was. People say that they were sitting in a jail cell or something, and they had a blinding flash, and 'Boom! – God came into my life!' Well, that never happened for me. I spent day after day, night after night, looking at the fucking wall of my jail cell in LA and, believe me, the fucker never showed up. Not once.

But arriving in Brazil that time was the closest I've ever had to those sort of moments – the sort that make you think differently in some way about yourself. It felt like I'd been there before somehow, or I belonged there in some way. At this stage in my life, I can usually take all that fame cobblers or leave it. I'm a normal bloke – if I can work out what being normal is – and I do normal things. I just want to play music and get on with it; that's it.

But even now, I can't get my head around it, when I'm in Brazil, and people queue up to shake my hand, or ask for an autograph or something like that. When I go to sign records in shopping malls and they have to draft the local police force in to keep order or something like that, I mean, it's fucking unbelievable. I just can't get to grips with it, even after all these years in the music business, and after everything that's happened to me – I just think, 'What the bloody hell is going on?'

Sometimes you've been booked to do a personal appearance for an hour, and you're still there after four. It's just beyond belief. Don't get me wrong, I bloody love it – who wouldn't? – but it'll do your head in if you start believing it all.

I'm still a bit scared of all that to be honest, 'cos that was the thing that fucked me up when I was in Iron Maiden; you know, letting it go to my head and that. There's a feeling of power you get, when people are cheering, chanting and calling out your name. If you've never experienced it – and not that many people have – it's impossible to describe.

I've also got a lot of really good friends in Brazil, so it may just be the place that I head for in the near future, when I want to unpack my bags after a world tour. I was over there a couple of times last year, working on some new songs with a guy named Paulo Turin, a very talented guitarist who's played with my band in the past. I flew out to Sao Paulo specially to see him at the start of last year, and we talked over some of the old times, swapping stories about life on the road.

He seems to remember lots of unsavoury stuff which I got up to over the years — it's like he's got some sort of photographic fucking memory or something. He was telling me how we were all on a tour-bus together once, and I was eating out this girl's pussy in the back seats, while everybody else watched.

Apparently we'd drunk a shitload of booze between us, and she was sitting on the seats, all squealing and giggling, with her skirt up around her waist, her knickers off and my head between her thighs, lapping away at her fanny.

I'll leave you with that particular image, because I think it roughly sums up the book you've just read. People have often said that I'm a bad influence on the young people who buy my records. This story will probably confirm that, but I don't really give a shit. All the religious twats and parents' groups who've said I'm the son of Satan have always been talking out of their arse, as far as I'm concerned. Ask yourself this — would Satan really choose to raise his kid in Chingford?

Anyway, for all those people who still think I represent the Dark One, here's a final message: FUCK YOU!

CHAPTER 19

In Their Own Words ...

Anonymous Music Industry Executive: 'Paul Di'Anno? He's a fucking animal ...'

US Immigration Spokesman: 'I don't ever want to hear Paul Di'Anno's name mentioned again ...'

British Visa Office: 'The reason we're not giving him a visa is because he's mad ...'

Anonymous Police Source: 'I can confirm that there are currently at least six warrants outstanding in the UK for Mr Di'Anno's arrest. These involve alleged offences involving assault and battery. We're extremely keen to talk to Mr Di'Anno concerning these matters.'

Arnie Goodman (former manager): 'I first met Paul Di'Anno when I had a chain of record stores, which had been involved in importing early Iron Maiden records into America.

'We'd got several hundred fans there wanting to see them, and while the other guys in the band were signing records and meeting the fans, Paul was in the bathroom with his head down the bowl, being sick all over the place. It seems he'd been partying the night before on booze or drugs or whatever, and he was in a hell of a state.

'Nevertheless, Paul was an important part of that band, and there are many people today who say that he's the best singer they've ever had. Certainly, the only Iron Maiden albums I really listen to are the ones he sings on. He was an important part of that whole heavy metal movement, and you can never take that away from him, but it was as if he outstayed his welcome in the band.

'His trouble is that he will say the first thing that comes off the top of his head to people, which can cause huge problems for him and everyone else. Some guys tell lies because they're going to gain from it but, with Paul, it's as if he does it just for the sake of it. He told some girl when he was over here that he was going to send a helicopter for her, which was clearly ridiculous, but she actually bought into that, and believed him.

'I've always thought he has tremendous potential, and he should be a huge star today, but he's not a band leader; he'll listen to the other guys in any band he's in, and just go along with them. I think the fact that he hasn't had a world-class band around him since he left Maiden has held him back, and I also think that the first solo album he did actually did more to damage his career than anything else he could have done.

'It was more of an AOR record than a heavy metal record, and he lost a huge amount of credibility over here in the States as a result of it. A lot of people went to see him play, but I think they were disappointed. Also, he's cancelled a lot of shows for very bad reasons, which you just can't do, really. Either he's been out all-night drinking, or he's been doing lots of drugs or whatever, but you just can't do that, because people will turn their back on you.

'Paul's problem is he'll go through money like no one else; if a cheque came in for him for $15,000 it would be gone two days later – he'd have spent it in various ways, he has no ability to think of the future.

'I realised he'd finally lost the plot just after he landed a really big record deal with BMG. This was his best – and last – chance to make a great comeback. It was a big-budget record, around $150,000, but in the middle of recording in New York, what does he do? He goes off and gets married again, which only lasted about a month anyway.

'Now instead of worrying about getting married, the guy should have been worrying about making a great record. I think BMG got a sniff of what was going on, and obviously thought, "The guy's a liability ..." This has always been Paul's problem – his reputation goes before him.

'After that, we dropped the band from our management, and I heard he'd gone to Los Angeles, where he was living with another woman, while he was still married to the other one. He knocked this new woman around pretty bad, and got thrown in jail, and after that they wouldn't let him back into America again.

'He's certainly a great singer, and I don't think he's necessarily a bad guy, but put him in front of two people and then he's got an audience, and he becomes a very different person. I don't know how the guys in Iron Maiden feel about him, and I'd love to see them get together again to do a few tracks with him, but I guess they've had even more problems with him over the years than we did.'

Steve Hopgood (drummer): I love Paul to death, he's been one of my best mates, and we've spent some of the best times in our lives in each other's company.

'I've probably seen more than anyone the craziness that surrounds Paul; all the drinking, drug-taking and general mayhem he causes. He's an amazing bullshitter; I've heard him tell people he's Australian, Brazilian, Italian – even Aborigine, if you can believe that. He's always highly amusing, and he loves nothing better than to hold court in front of a crowd of people, telling them all these stories and that. Most of them aren't true, but it doesn't matter, really.

'He's an Ozzy Osbourne sort of character, he always does just what you least expect him to – which means at least that life is never dull when he's around. He's a lovely bloke, extremely generous, he'd do anything for you. But the trouble usually starts when he's been drinking or doing cocaine. It's like a couple of bottles of Jack Daniel's bring out the devil in him, and then you never know what's going to happen. Once he starts, there's no stopping him.

'He'll leave a trail of devastation behind him like a fucking hurricane. Hotel rooms will get trashed, backstage areas will get smashed up – when Paul's on a bender, everything that's standing will get fucking flattened!

'He got so pissed before a show we did once that he had to be helped on to the stage. Once he was up there, he couldn't stand up by himself, fell head-first into the amps, and just lay there in a heap, unconscious.

'I shared a room with him once at a hotel, and I woke up suddenly in the middle of the night, because I can hear the sound of running water. I turn on the light, and there's Paul standing up in the middle of the room with this big grin on his face, pissing into the fucking wardrobe! He was so drunk he didn't know where he was!

'Same thing happened at a truckstop somewhere in the States when we pulled up in the tour-bus. Paul goes off to have a piss up against a wall, and just falls asleep there standing up, leaning his head against the wall, with his dick still in his hand!

'Mind you, drink or drugs can send him completely off his head. He was signing some autographs once, and this fan casually remarks to him that he preferred the first solo album to the second. It wasn't really a criticism, the guy was obviously a fan, and he was just making an observation, just to strike up a conversation, I suppose.

'Paul just goes fucking mental. He screams at him, "You fucking cunt!" and punches him full in the face, just lamped the guy for no reason. Paul's a big bloke, and the guy just crumpled. I thought that particular incident was, well, not really in order, shall we say.

'He's bad news around women as well, really. He's really charming and women love him; it's just when they get more involved with him that things go wrong. There was this one girl out in Austria who faked her own death to get away from him, apparently. Just did a Reggie Perrin, got her family to pretend she'd died, just so he wouldn't come after her. To this day, he still thinks she's dead.

'He's been in other trouble, as well. We had the bizarre situation when we were preparing one album that we were writing the music for in England, and sending tapes over to Paul to write the lyrics to, because he was in jail in Los Angeles. He'd been arrested for trying to kill his girlfriend with a knife, along with possession of firearms and cocaine, and he got four months in the County Jail.

'When we next tried to get into the States to do some gigs, they refused to let Paul through US Customs because he was a convicted felon. There was no way they were going to let him into the country – he was officially banned from America.

'What made things all the more embarrassing was that we were supposed to be playing a gig at the Foundation Forum, a big music festival in Los Angeles, and Bruce Dickinson – the guy who replaced Paul in Iron Maiden – was also going to be appearing there! What the hell he must have thought, I don't know.'

Graham Bath (guitarist): One of the best-known legends about Paul Di'Anno is the drunken brawl that he had with his guitarist, when he kicked the guy's front teeth in. Well, that particular legend is absolutely true, and I know, because I was that guitarist.

'We were in America, and we'd all been drinking all day. We were all really pissed, and everybody was in a funny sort of mood, because we'd had some trouble with the road crew. I was pretty drunk, and once we'd dropped this member of the crew off at an airport, I got into an argument with Paul back on the tour-bus.

'The details are a bit hazy, because we'd had so much booze, and Paul had been doing loads of coke as well. Somehow, though, we ended up fighting in the seats of the bus. I pinned him between the seats, with him bent over double, and this really got him mad, because he was trapped, and couldn't move. He was screaming and spitting at me, really going berserk.

'He went absolutely schizo, shouting, "Right, you cunt, outside, now!" So we trooped outside, and everybody's watching. Steve, our drummer, has got a video camera and he's filming it all – it's a bit of a joke really.

'There then followed the most pathetic fight you've ever seen, with me in my drunken state throwing punches which missed him by a mile, and him doing the same. He's still shouting at the top of his voice, going absolutely mental, and eventually he's got hold of my hair and he's pulling it, until he's got me on the ground.

'So I'm sitting up on the floor, still absolutely pissed, not really knowing where I am, when he really loses it, and things suddenly turn serious. He comes running at me, and kicks me full in the face as hard as he can. I fall back, and there's blood everywhere. My face just caves in. My nose was completely split open, and my front teeth were shattered.

'Steve puts down the camera when he realises things have got a bit out of control, and the band pull Paul away. A minute later, he wriggles free, still in a rage, and comes up and kicks me in the head again. That's when I lost consciousness. Airport security turn up, and demand to know what's going on, and there's chaos as everybody stands around yelling and shouting.

'The strange thing was, neither of us could remember what the row was about, and we were both laughing about it the day after. I know Paul regretted it the minute he'd done it; in fact, I think he was actually quite upset about it when he sobered up.

'We made a joke of it the next night on stage. I appeared on stage wrapped in toilet roll, as if I was covered in bandages! I think that night Paul had a row with Steve, so the whole thing started all over again.

'On another occasion, I made the mistake of inviting Paul and his band to crash out at my house when I was living in Wales. They'd just played a gig in Cardiff, and they came back for a party.

'At some stage in the party, someone (and I don't know who, but I've got my suspicions) took a shit in a baseball cap which had been lying around the house, with the result that almost the entire house ended up smeared in human shit. Walls, carpets, furniture, everything. I got chucked out of the house soon after, not surprisingly, so thanks for that, Paul!

'When I joined Battlezone and got to know him better, me and the guys had some pretty fucking wild tours, with all the drinking and partying that was going on. It was just getting really out of control, it was just wild.

'And when you'd got this bunch of guys back at the hotel, just drinking and taking drugs with women they'd picked up after the show, there would be Paul right in the thick of it, holding court in front of an audience.

'He loves to entertain, he has to be the centre of attention; and when he isn't the centre of attention, he'll do something to make sure that he is. He is a really funny bloke, he's had me crying with laughter with all these stories about what he got up to when he was in Iron Maiden and everything. You know, "Well, me and Harris did this, and me and Murray did that ..." and so on.

'The great thing about Paul is that he's such a bullshitter; he'll sit there telling people a load of old rubbish, but you'll laugh anyway. With all those people around him, he's happier than a dog with two dicks, really. He turns into Fuckeye Jones, one of his comic characters, and he'll be there all night, then.

'And finally, at the end of the night, he'll be leading the charge, running around and knocking on people's doors to see if they've got any coke. I've seen him sell a £400 gold bracelet at the end of a long night, just to get some more drugs.

'He was getting a lot of money from Maiden at the time, and he's just the most generous bloke with his money, he'll buy you stuff whether or not you actually wanted it.

'The annoying thing about him is, if you've all had a really heavy night (and he'll have drunk fucking gallons of Jack Daniel's) he'll always be the first one up, washed and shaved, banging on everyone's door to wake them up, yelling, "Come on, Bathy, you cunt, wake up!"

'I left him in a hotel bedroom with two girls once, just chatting and snorting coke, and I went off with another girl. I came back around lunchtime the next day, and he was still in the same fucking position – I swear he hadn't moved, he was still going on and on.

'When I came in, he looked up, took a final snort of coke, and said, "Right, that's me – I'm fucked!" and just fell back on to the floor with a crash, and passed out.

'Nice one, Paul!'

Anonymous musician: We were touring with the band Killers, and we stayed in this really posh hotel. We were downstairs having breakfast, and we realised that Paul was nowhere to be seen.

'A short while later, we heard this commotion out in the lobby – there's always a commotion with Paul – and the hotel manager is out there going mad. He's shouting, "Who is staying in Room 109?"

We all quickly realised it was Paul. The manager's going berserk, he's calling the police and there's a hell of a row going on. Paul is still nowhere to be seen.

'We all went upstairs to take a look at what was going on, and we peered inside the room where Paul had been staying. It was really scary – the room was completely trashed. A huge vase of flowers had been thrown across the room and smashed, there was shit all over everywhere, and the furniture had been overturned and thrown about.

'This wasn't the normal hotel room trashing that rock stars get up to, this was like something a madman would do. On the walls there were these huge swastikas carved into the paint – everybody was, like, "What sort of person could do this?"

'Well, we knew, didn't we?'

Bob Muck (friend): I was actually with Paul Di'Anno during one of the most famous episodes in his life – when we tried illegally to smuggle him back into America.

'He'd been to jail and got kicked out of the country, so there was just no way he could fly straight over there from England; they'd have just arrested him on sight.

'But tour promoters and record companies obviously needed to see Paul back in the States, so we came up with a plan to get him across the border without the authorities finding out about it. We took him to Toronto, and then up to Niagara, where we planned to drive across the American border, posing as tourists.

'Now, we're both big, mean-looking guys, covered in tattoos, and I honestly don't think anyone would have let us into their country even if we were wearing fucking nuns' costumes. So our "disguise" didn't work ...

'On top of that, the driver we'd hired to take us across in a rental car had a stash of marijuana on him, which he hadn't told us about. So this dummy was planning to smuggle drugs into the States, on top of all the other shit!

'Before we got to the border, we stopped at a Denny's restaurant for a bite to eat. So nobody knows who we are, but Paul is just rock 'n' roll all the time, you know, he's getting pretty loud. Pretty soon, the waitress serving us has found out who he is – well, she's so starry-eyed, she pours coffee all over the table, and all over my pants. She just can't believe she's serving the famous Paul Di'Anno, of Iron Maiden fame! She'd have gotten on that table and let him screw her then and there, you know?

'So, once we've managed to get him away from her, we get back into the car and drive to the checkpoint, along with crowds of other tourists. But there's immediately a problem. The cops had obviously gotten wind of what we were up to, because they all appear out of nowhere, surrounding the car, with their billy sticks drawn. They're all shouting and yelling at us, and we knew we were really in the shit.

'We'd paid a $5,000 deposit on the car, and I remember thinking we were gonna lose that if the cops pulled the car to pieces. They were shouting and hollering at us as they dragged us out of the car and roughed us up – you know how Yankee cops are – and they just slapped the cuffs on both of us and marched us away.

'Our driver had stuffed the marijuana down his pants and,

for some reason, they never found it. They asked him a few questions, but once they realised he wasn't part of the plot, he was free to go.

'They questioned me and Paul and, for some reason, he told them he was from South America. They obviously thought we were part of some drug cartel, smuggling narcotics into the States, because they got really mad, threatening to beat the shit out of us.

'What made it worse was that I was running a punk label at the time, and I had papers on me with names on them like 'MDC', which stands for Millions of Dead Cops. They kept asking what these papers were, and what the letters stood for!

'Once they discovered Paul's British ID, though, they realised he was the former singer of Iron Maiden, and they were like, "Wow, we bagged a rock star!" I think he even signed a couple of autographs for them, they were so proud of themselves. They said to him, "Well, you're the big rock star, trying to smuggle yourself into America, but we got you! We got you!" Paul just laughed, and said something cheeky like, "Yeah, well, if you leave a rat in a maze long enough, it'll find the bloody cheese, won't it?"

'After a while holding us there, they turned us around and kicked us out of the States, so we had to go back into Canada. We didn't really know what to do, as this meant the tour that had been planned was cancelled.

'So we drove back to Toronto, and Paul hung out with me there for a few days. We went to a few bars, and he got a new tattoo, we had a pretty good time. He's a good guy actually, one of the easiest guys I've ever worked with. The only trouble was, wherever we went, there'd be hordes of people coming up to him and wanting to shake his hand, or get an autograph. We couldn't go down Toronto's main drag without him being surrounded by people.

'Then there were the women. They just wouldn't leave him alone. Wherever he went, they were just all over him. I remember thinking, "Damn! Why didn't I take up singing when I was younger?" I'd never seen so many women in my life, but Paul was obviously used to it.

'One day, I took him to a local bar and, at first, we just sat there having a beer, without anybody knowing who he was. Then the bar-owner recognises him, and he can't believe that Paul Di'Anno's in his bar!

'He says, "Hey, Paul, what do you want to drink, man? It's on the house!"

'So Paul replies, "I'll have six Jack Daniel's, and six bottles of Molson, please!"

'The guy goes off to get it, and Paul leans over the bar, and shouts, "Oi! Come back!" He gestures at me. "You haven't asked what my friend's having ..."'

Pete Newdeck (drummer): 'We were doing a show in Slovenia, and it's going great — the crowd are really into us, and they're acting as if Paul is God. All of a sudden, in the middle of the show, there's this guy down the front who catches Paul's eye.

'For some reason, he gets down off the stage and confronts this guy, slapping him a couple of times and shouting abuse at him, before giving him a full-blooded punch in the face. It was quite nasty, and totally unnecessary. The guy didn't seem to have done anything to Paul, as far as we could see.

'What made it worse, we found out after the show that the

guy was autistic or something like that, which could explain why Paul thought he was behaving a bit oddly, not that that's any excuse for what he did.

'We all confronted him about it afterwards, and asked him what the hell he was playing at, and he just said, "The guy kept looking at me!"

'So were the rest of the crowd, Paul...'

Lea Hart (current manager): 'A few years ago, I'd been commissioned by a Japanese record company to produce an album featuring British heavy metal musicians. They gave me a list, and one of the names on it was Paul Di'Anno. Me and Paul had known each other for a long time, and I tried to get in touch with him to tell him about the record. The trouble was, nobody seemed to know where he was living. I finally tracked him down via a pub in Walthamstow, where they all seemed to know him very well, so he obviously hadn't changed that much.

'Paul adopts a local pub, gets barred, talks his way back in the next night, and repeats this process every week of the year. He gets barred from pubs like you or I change our shirts ...

'Anyway, when I met up with him, he agreed to participate in the album. I needed to send him a tape of the song he'd be doing, so he gave me his address. It was actually the address of his parents' house in Chingford, which isn't too far from me, so I said I'd drop it round.

'At our meeting, I'd noticed that Paul wasn't really looking too great. I thought maybe he was down on his luck a bit, as he seemed a bit scruffy and dishevelled. Despite this, though, he told me how well he was doing, and how many homes he had around the world, including one in Beverly Hills and one in Malibu. He told me about his vast collection of Harley Davidson motorcycles, and the six Dobermans he kept as pets.

'Once he'd had a bit to drink, he went on to explain his family history. He claimed that his father was dead, and that his mother had re-married a guy from Australia, who'd been captured during the Second World War and kept in a POW camp, where he'd been tortured by the Japanese. I was intrigued, to say the least ...

'A few days later, I nipped round to Paul's parents' house, and parked up outside. It was pitch dark, and chucking it down with rain. It's a really big four-storey house, with a large garden. Now there's no light outside, so as I approach the garden gate, I'm thinking about those Dobermans. I was wondering whether I could outpace them in running for the gate, and decided I probably couldn't.

'So I tiptoed into this dark garden, listening intently for growls or barks. As I got closer to the house, I could hear this faint, high-pitched yapping sound. Now I'm not a dog expert as such, but I do know that Dobermans don't yap. "If that's a Doberman," I thought, "he's got a really serious throat problem, and his five mates must be asleep."

'Feeling a bit more confident, I walked up to the door and rang the bell. A man answered the door and, from between his legs, this tiny little sausage dog zoomed out and started licking my ankles.

'The man – who I now know to be Paul's father, and who is a really lovely bloke, by the way – said that Paul was down the pub, but he probably wouldn't be long. He invited me in to wait for him, and I followed him into the kitchen. He starts making me a cup of tea, and I feel a bit awkward, because I don't really know what to say.

'What's worrying me is that this bloke was once tortured by the Japanese, and now here I am, representing a Japanese record company, which is employing his son. It was like that Fawlty Towers episode; I was trying to think of something to talk about, without mentioning the war!

'I tried to make some small talk, so I said, "How do you get on with the weather over here?"

'He looked a bit puzzled, and replied, "Same as everybody else, I suppose ..."

'I decided to try a different tack. "Do you miss Australia at all, then?" I asked cheerfully.

'He looked completely blank. "Australia? I've never been to Australia! I'd love to take the missus there, but we haven't got a passport between us. Closest I've been to the southern hemisphere is Bethnal Green, mate!"

'I tried to cover my tracks. "Well, it's the accent, Cockneys sometimes sound like Australians, don't they?" Meanwhile, I was thinking, "Thanks Paul, you cunt ..."

'When I later came to manage Paul, there was another situation that sticks in my memory. He'd gone out to Bulgaria to do some shows, and while he was there, he fell in love with some girl he'd met. Paul falls in love on a regular basis, but he insisted this one was different. When he came back, he said he wanted to marry her, and he started trying to get her into Britain.

'It later transpires that he told this girl all about his homes all over the world, his fleet of cars and the maids who waited on him hand and foot. This girl was obviously swept up in all of this, as I think the first night she slept with Paul in his hotel room was the first time she'd ever been in a hotel. Apparently, they get Dallas repeats over there, and she thought he was some sort of JR Ewing character.

'When she did come over, it certainly wasn't to a Dallas lifestyle; all she got was a few visits to hospital with broken ribs, a broken arm and heavy bruising.

'I first met her when I went round to see Paul one day. He was living in a flat in Walthamstow at the time, and he'd called me that day, saying that he wasn't feeling too good. He told me that he was broke, and that he couldn't afford to eat. Now when Paul says that, he means he doesn't have enough money for cocaine and Jack Daniel's.

'I certainly wasn't going to give him cash just so he could get hold of some charlie and a bottle of Jack, so instead I went round to my local Tesco's to do some shopping. There are these really cheap super-value meals, which are like 8p per can. They're just beans or something – all the old tramps and drop-outs buy them. I bought loads and loads of them, and took them round to Paul's in a plastic bag.

'You should have seen his face fall when he saw what I'd brought him. He looked like someone had pissed on his bonfire, big-time. I was struggling to keep a straight face ...

'Trying to hide his disappointment, he invited me in and, as I walked into his flat, I saw this young woman on her hands and knees in the middle of the floor. It wasn't what you think – she was fully clothed, with a bucket of dirty water by her side. The strange thing was, she had this little toothbrush in her hand. She'd only just arrived in the country, and she'd obviously found out that JR Ewing was not all he seemed. Either that, or he'd given the maids the week off.

'You never know with Paul, but my mind boggled. I asked the obvious question: "What the fuck is she doing?" He swiftly replied, "What do you think she's fucking doing? She's cleaning the floor!"

'Paul, people say a lot of things about you, but you do have charm, mate.'

Tony Incigeri (former manager): 'We brought Paul Di'Anno over here to the United States to do a tour when he had the band Battlezone, after he'd left Iron Maiden. Now bringing a band over from Britain – in fact, from any foreign country – is a very time-consuming, expensive business, because they all need to be cleared by immigration, and to have working papers for the time they're here.

'I dealt with their drummer, Steve Hopgood, on this, and he sent over all the information about the guys in the band. Almost immediately, there was a problem. Officially, Paul Di'Anno didn't exist. Our immigration lawyers could find no record of a UK passport being issued in that name.

'I rang Steve, and said, "What's going on?" He told me that Paul's real name is Paul Andrews, a fact which he'd only just found out for himself. When we put the application through in that name, there were no problems.

'When I spoke to Paul, he told me that he'd had to change his name, after he'd gotten into a little trouble, but insisted that Di'Anno is his real name, and that the immigration guys must have got it wrong. Well, these guys don't get things wrong very often, so there was Paul's first lie – he wasn't being totally honest with me.

'Before I'd signed up Battlezone to come over, I'd spoken with Iron Maiden's manager, Rod Smallwood, and he'd warned me about Paul. "He's a nice guy, but you'll have problems with him," he told me, but I chose to ignore this warning. I thought maybe there was some bad blood there or something, so I went ahead anyway.

'I think Paul liked the fact that I'm Italian and from "the neighborhood", so to speak, because he always claimed to be Italian himself. He liked my accent, the way I talk; I think he got a kick out of it.

'When I went to meet him off the plane, the first thing I see is that he has this bottle of Thunderbird in his hand. I don't know if they sell it over there in Britain, but it's the sort of stuff you see bums on the street drinking over here. So I wonder to myself what the fuck's going on with this guy.

'We're driving back from the airport, and he pulls a huge bundle of money from his pockets, about $5,000 dollars. I said to him that he shouldn't be carrying around that sort of money, that I should maybe put it in a bank for him, but he hangs on to it.

'I found out that money was for drink and drugs. Within a few days, he'd blown the lot on bourbon and blow, and he was ringing me asking to borrow some more. He'd been buying everybody drinks; friends, fans, band-members, everyone. I think some girls had hit on him for some money in a bar as well, and he'd given it to them. I was in another bar with him one day, when he insisted on buying the entire bar a drink. He just gave the bartender a big wad of cash, and told him to get everyone a drink. He was really a very generous guy.

'But when he rang me asking for more money, I told him that I'd warned him this was going to happen. I said to him, "You've pissed all your money away, so now you're going to have to live on your per diem [daily allowance] like everybody else. You don't like it, that's too fucking bad ..."

'We had some cash problems at that time anyway. Some of the dates had to be cancelled through lack of ticket sales, and it didn't help when one of the guys wrecked the van they were using. It was his first time driving it and, of course, he was used to driving on the other side of the road, so he crocked it.

'The guy who'd hired us the van was a friend of mine, and it was a big pain in the ass, because we had to hire another one, which was much more expensive. The tour manager ended up putting the charge on his credit card.

'Before the tour is too far in, I'm something like $10,000 in the hole. The tour manager's having to use his credit card again, and we're really having some problems. Steve Hopgood gets an offer to join another band, Jagged Edge, and comes to me to tell me that he wants to leave.

'I persuade him to stay for a while longer, as we still had quite a few dates to do; so he agrees, and we travel to LA for the next few shows. I travel out from New York to see them, and they're pretty good. But I find out that they haven't been that good in the previous shows, as people tell me they were all bombed, and Paul looked like he didn't give a fuck any more. He'd been indulging heavily in drink and drugs out there, and his head was all over the place.

'He had some moments of clarity, when he realised what he was supposed to be doing, that this was his job, but he'd tell me all these fantastic stories – he always had a story. He also seemed to have a never-ending list of ailments. One day he'd be limping, the next he'd be holding his head, or his arm, or whatever. I christened him Paul the Crutch!

'Anyway, one day, out of the blue, I learn that Paul and

Steve have just checked out of the hotel and flown home. They still had around 25 dates to do, but they just upped and left. I've lost all this money, the tour manager's put around $7,000 on his credit card, and they're gone. There was nothing else I could do – we had to abandon the shows, and I had to arrange for the other guys to fly home.

'If I'd have got my hands on Paul then, I'd have fucking strangled him. I really wanted to kill him.

'A while later, I spoke to him on the phone, and he said that he was sorry. I told him that I would work with him again, that I still liked him, and he told me that he liked me, too. But I warned him, "Paul, when you next get some money, I don't care whether it's from Iron Maiden or record deals or what; it's got to go straight back into our fucking pockets over here, because we've lost out, big time!"

'I do think Paul's a nice guy, really. It's just that his head is all over the place, all the time...'

Anonymous roadie: There was an incident with one of Paul's wives – I can't remember exactly which one. We were on tour in Germany, and she joined us out there on one of the dates, and she brought along her parents, so they could met their new son-in-law. I think they probably got quite a shock when they saw him, but he made it ten times worse. They were Italian, and Paul assumed they couldn't speak any English. He was breathtakingly rude to them, saying things like, "Fuck off, you pair of mother's cunts!" He thought it was really funny, and was laughing about it (I think he'd had quite a lot to drink). I just thought, "How can you be such a twat?"

'Once again, the relationship ended in disaster. He beat

her up and put her in hospital one Christmas Eve, and he got arrested. The band had a gig to play on Boxing Day, so his manager had to go and bail him out. This girl's parents had to fly over to pick up their daughter, just so they could take her away from him. '

Ann-Marie Buchanan (friend): My first impression of Paul, when I met him in London, was that of someone who was very, very loud and also very drunk. I thought he was American, because he'd just come back from living in Los Angeles at that time, and he had this silly American accent. I just thought he was someone who was very brash and loud.

'I saw him again a few months later, at the Astoria club. There was this drunk bloke who kept trying to trip me up all night, and when I turned round to give him what for, there was Paul standing there looking at me. He still had this silly accent!

'I kept in touch with him for a while after that, because he used to ring me up out of the blue from all these faraway places, and announce that he was coming to see me. We were just mates, there was never anything romantic between us – I was spared that.

'One day, he rings me up and announces that he's coming back to England for a while, and could he come and stay with me? So he turns up, and we became flat-mates after that, as he just never left!

'We had the wildest nights out. With Paul, there was always copious amounts of alcohol, and lots and lots of drugs. We'd start off at the George on Charing Cross Road, and end up at the Marquee club, just drinking and drinking.

'Everything was free – people would come up to him and ask for autographs or to have their photos taken, and they'd be buying him drinks all night. At some clubs loads of people would offer him drugs, and he'd be completely off his head. All the clubs we went to let us in for free, and ushered us up to their VIP rooms, where we'd be well taken care of.

'I have to say, though, Paul was actually a very good flatmate. Not a lot of people know this side of him, but he used to do all the cooking, and he'd do the shopping for me, and even clean the place up! You'd never know whether he was going to be around or not, because he'd disappear for weeks on end, and then ring you from the other side of the world.

'He used to look after me, though, in all sorts of ways. I was having boyfriend trouble, so he used to hold my hand through it, and make sure I was OK. I was suffering from an abcess at one point, too, and I think he was really concerned about me, making sure I took care of myself. Mind you, his idea of taking care of myself was making sure I drank at least a glass of brandy every night before I went to bed!

'We moved to Walthamstow, and then I moved over to West London, and so I left him back at the flat, because there was still some time left on the tenancy. This was around the time that he'd come back from Bulgaria, and was trying to get this girl from over there to come to Britain and marry him.

'We lost touch a bit for a while after that, although I kept hearing all these stories about him – drinking, getting married, taking drugs, fighting, getting into trouble, all sorts of things. I don't know if these were all true, but there were always loads of stories flying around about Paul.

'When I did get to speak to him a few years later, I really got the impression that he'd given up. It seemed that things had stopped happening for him, and that he couldn't really be bothered any more. I know he'd upset a lot of people over the years – I was one of them, as he left the flat owing me a hell of a lot of money, and leaving me with a £600 telephone bill to pay!

'He has a really bad reputation as a drinker, drug-taker and fighter, but I think I got to know him better than most people over the years, and I saw a softer, gentler side. He can be very charming.

'I know his family is extremely important to him, especially his son and his mother; and he was very good to me while I was having a few personal problems, he really helped me through it.

'One of my best memories of him is of going for a night out, going to the pub and then on to a club, and just getting so drunk I can't remember anything about what went on. He was just drinking and taking drugs solidly through the night, like he'd been doing it all his life. He could just go on for ever. I had to get up to go to work the next day and, as I walked out of my room, I came across him passed out on the floor of the living-room. I was so mad at him for leading me astray like that, I just kicked him in the head as he lay there and shouted at him, "You bastard!"'

Paulo Turin (guitarist): 'My favourite memory of Paul Di'Anno dates back to a tour we did in Brazil. We had some time off, and we met these girls on the beach. Women really seem to go for Paul, I've seen him with some incredibly beautiful girls, and one of these girls seemed to be attracted to him.

'She was quite young, and she was almost certainly a prostitute, and they seemed to be getting on really well. Paul is very charming to women; it's only when he marries them that everything goes wrong, as he has done five or six times.

'Anyway, we're going to the next show on the tour-bus, and

this girl is with Paul. I noticed that Paul had a bottle of tequila, and when I looked again a bit later, I saw it was empty.

'When I look over again, I see that Paul has disappeared, and the girl seems to be sitting there by herself. Then I looked over the top of the seat, and noticed Paul's head right up her skirt, between her legs. He's got her panties off, and he's licking out her pussy, right there on the bus, with everybody on board watching him! We just couldn't stop laughing at what he was doing, but he didn't seem to care, he just carried on.

'She was moaning and sighing and wriggling around, and he was there with his face between her thighs, just lapping away!

'That was the tour when he learned to say the word "cunt" in Portugese which, for some reason, he thought was really funny. He would say it over and over to everyone he met, shouting it when testing the microphone at soundchecks and things like that, without realising how offensive the local people were finding it.

'Another story from that same tour also sticks in my mind, which was a gig we played, where things got pretty wild. The crowd were just going absolutely crazy, and the bouncers at the front started to get a bit rough, pulling people out and so on.

'While we were all playing, Paul saw this happening, and he just went completely nuts. He dropped the microphone on to the stage, so there was this deafening crash which echoed through the PA system, and he just dived head-first from the stage into the middle of these bouncers.

'There were about 15 of them, and they were all absolutely huge, like real body-builder types. But Paul didn't seem to care – he was just beside himself with rage. He jumped on the biggest one, who was about double his own height and weight, and starting punching him hard in the face.

'He was hysterical, screaming, "You fucking cunt! You don't treat my audience like that!" and so on. The guy's face was quite cut up, he was getting badly hurt. Once the fight had been broken up, after this massive struggle, and they finally got Paul off this guy and back on stage, he was still yelling and screaming at them.

'The funny thing was, after the show, this big bouncer came up to Paul and apologised for what he'd done!'

Cliff Evans (guitarist): I remember doing a show with Paul over in Greece, it was back in '95, or something like that, and we were on a tour wit_ Zodiac Mindwarp, Metal Church and Vicious Rumours.

'Zodiac, who was a crazy fucker himself, just couldn't believe what Paul was getting up to – he'd never seen anything like it, there was no way he could keep up with him. There was this one particular show we were doing, I think we were second on the bill. On the day of the gig, Paul had gotten hold of a bottle of Jack Daniel's at around midday, which is just the worst news you can have, really. It always means trouble for everybody – it's just a case of when.

'So, knowing it was all bound to end in tears, I politely suggested to Paul that perhaps he shouldn't drink too much, as we're due on stage in a few hours. Well, I might just as well have saved my breath. He told me to shove my fucking head up my arse, or words to that effect, and poured half the bottle down his throat in one go.

'Once he starts, he can't stop, and every time I looked around after that, the level of whisky in the bottle had gone down and down. Then he gets hold of another bottle from somewhere, so he's on his second bottle of Jack, and it's still mid-afternoon.

'By the time the show's due to start, the venue is absolutely packed out, the audience is just jammed solid. They're obviously looking forward to the show, 'cos they're going wild out there, calling Paul's name and that. I was in the dressing room getting ready, when Paul crashes through the door, completely pissed out of his head, and promptly falls headlong over a table. By the look of him, he'd done a load of coke, too, which would just about put the tin hat on it, really. He's just lying there on the floor, grinning from ear to ear.

'So, I'm sitting there wondering how the hell we're going to do a show with him in that state, when someone comes through to tell us that we're due on stage. So the band troop out towards the stage with our instruments, and with two guys holding him up, Paul stumbles along behind us.

'We walk out through the crowd and, almost immediately, I notice some sort of disturbance behind me. As I turn around to see what's going on, all hell is breaking loose. Paul was wearing these rosary beads (he was going through his Catholic phase at the time – it was his latest religion of the month, after Muslim, Jewish and bloody Aborigine ...) and someone from the crowd has grabbed at them, the necklace has broken, and they've gone all over the floor. There's fucking rosary beads everywhere.

'So Paul has gone absolutely fucking mental, screaming and crying, and he's dived back into the dressing room, and reappeared with a gun. Fucking hell, the place went mad. Everybody in that section of the crowd just screamed and ducked for cover, trying to get out of this madman's way.

While I was recovering from the shock of this, Paul's waving this gun at the guy who broke the beads, threatening to kill him and that. "You're dead ... you're fucking dead!" he was screaming in his face.

'We had this roadie who was working for us at the time who was obviously well used to mad people with guns. He's taken the gun off Paul, and managed to prevent him shooting one of his own fans. Meanwhile, we've gone up on to the stage, and we're standing around like spare ones at a wedding. We're absolutely shitting ourselves at this point, because we just don't know what he's going to do next. It was the feeling that things had really gotten out of control, you know? Thanks to Paul!

'We're all looking around for him, both the band and the audience, and it turns out he's got lost in the dark and can't find his way to the stage. At one point he's stumbling around the mixing desk at the back of the hall, asking the sound guy where the stage is. Bear in mind there's only one hall in this venue – if he'd just turned around, he would have seen the stage right behind him.

'The crowd are gobsmacked – they can't believe it. After what seemed like ages, he's finally helped up on to the stage, there's about three or four steps there, and he's got up them on his hands and knees, still completely off his head. Once he's finally managed to get himself stood up there, he tops the performance by falling head-first into the amplifiers. We're all looking at each other, not knowing what to do, because he doesn't look capable of talking, let alone singing.

'The crowd are loving it, they can't believe their eyes either, but this is real rock 'n' roll entertainment to them, they're going ape. So we start to play, and Paul is just about managing to make some sort of a noise into the microphone, and when he forgets the words, he just points the microphone into the audience, so the crowd can sing along.

'He's shouting at the top of his voice, but not really making much sense. At one point, I seem to remember he told the crowd they were all a bunch of inbred cunts, but hopefully the language barrier would have prevented too many of them from understanding that.

'He's so pissed, he can't stand up for too long, so he sinks to his knees, leans on the monitor for support and just carries on singing like that. It looks like we've got a dwarf for a singer. The crowd are going berserk; they don't even seem to mind that you can't see him from more than a few rows back.

'Zodiac Mindwarp is watching in admiration from the side of the stage, with this huge grin across his face. He thinks it's the best thing he's ever seen. And funnily enough, we were sort of getting away with it, until Paul decided to address the crowd in Greek. Someone had given him something to read out, and he's drunkenly searching through his pockets for it, fumbling around.

'He produces this dog-eared little bit of paper, and reads out what's on it, in a dodgy (and very slurred) Greek accent. It must have made some sort of sense, because people were nodding, but God only knows what he was saying.

'Once we'd managed to crash our way through the gig, Paul really let rip then. At the after-show party, he's snorting lines of cocaine around 2ft long, and laying into the drink like there was no tomorrow. He was just like a fucking animal. I think he was up all night, celebrating a lucky escape.

'My other favourite story concerning Paul happened when we were playing a show in Rome. Paul was well into this whole Catholic thing, and he'd been banging on all through the tour about going to the Vatican to see the Pope.

'He was going on and on about it – he said it would be the greatest day of his life, that everything that had ever happened to him was preparing him for this special day.

'We were all quite interested in going to have a look, so we walk up this long road which leads to the Vatican. Every 20 yards or so, Paul would fall to his hands and knees and start wailing and sobbing, saying how grateful he was for this special opportunity, going to the Vatican and that. Tears are streaming down his face, the whole bit. He's got his rosary beads, and he's going on and on about being a Catholic, and about how this is his life's ambition.

'Only trouble was, when we actually got to the gates they wouldn't let him in! He was wearing shorts, and that was against the rules, apparently!

'So while we were inside looking around, he had to wait outside, standing there like a lemon!. Luckily, he hadn't had a drink, or I'm fairly sure we'd have seen a punch-up at the Vatican.'

Dennis Stratton (guitarist): My first memory of Paul is shortly after I joined Iron Maiden, when we were recording the first album. It was in 1979, when the band had just signed to EMI, and I'd been brought in to complete the line-up. I was the oldest member of the group, so everything was very new; we were just five young fellas with a father figure, Rod Smallwood, who managed us.

'I was recording my guitar pieces in the studio separately, so it was a few days before I got to meet Paul. I'd met Dave Murray, the other guitarist, at the Ship pub in Wardour Street the week before, along with bass player Steve Harris and Rod.

'So I'm at Hollywood Studios, working out some riffs with Steve and Dave, and Paul walks in to do some vocal tracks. We shake hands, and the first thing he says to me is, "You're a West Ham supporter?" I told him I was, so that was something we had in common. Then straight away, he starts to rub me up the wrong way, saying with all his usual tact and diplomacy, "I don't suppose you've tried 'Phantom of the Opera?'

'This was a song from that album which was extremely complex, with lots of harmonies and time changes and that, and he obviously thought I hadn't learnt it yet. In fact, I'd spent an entire afternoon learning the song a few days before, so I could already play it, and I did so in the studio. He came up to me afterwards, all surprised, and said, "You did know how to play it!"

'And that was Paul all over, really; he'd say something without really thinking about it, and piss people off without meaning to. This happened especially in the later years, when he'd had a few beers.

'My first impression of Paul was that he was a bit of a rebel. If everybody else said one thing, or went one way, he'd deliberately say the other, or go the other way, just to be different. I think the rest of the band got a bit tired of it after a while, you know, with him just going against the grain all the time, often over silly little things.

'Like all frontmen, he liked to be the centre of attention, and he liked to impress people. He could be a bit cheeky and, as I say, he had this talent for winding people up, whether it was wearing a pork pie hat on stage (Rod Smallwood was a bit pissed off about that) or slagging off Judas Priest when we were on tour with them (Priest were very pissed off about that).

'The thing about Paul is, it was never malicious. He could do anything, and still does, and people still forgive him. They just say: "Oh, that's Paul." Back then, everything was all new and exciting, and he hadn't really gotten too heavily into the drink or drugs, but when I've come across him since, there have been a couple of times when he's got more than a bit out of order, and I've had to step in.

'It's like he's got some sort of identity crisis, like he's a sort of Jekyll and Hyde character. He's a great mate to have, you can have a good meal or drink with him, and he's a great laugh, but you can catch him on another occasion, and he gets aggressive and upsets people. It's like he's lots of different people, and you don't know which one you're dealing with.

'He's certainly a colourful character, and while we've had our differences over the years, I've never had a real problem with him. He knows I won't take any shit from him!'

Tanya Almor (friend): 'I don't know if Paul's schizophrenic, but in the 20-odd years I've known him, I still don't really know who the real Paul Di'Anno is!

'He doesn't give anything of himself away, but I think underneath it all, he's basically a pretty good guy, really. He does tell all these outrageous stories though – we used to call him Paul Di'Other One, because he would just bullshit you all the time. We used to say you could tell when Paul was lying, because his lips were moving!

'Apparently, he was the same when he was at school – if you said you had something, he'd have ten of them! We've almost had a brother-and-sister type relationship over the years, but I haven't seen him too much in the last few years because I'm a lay minister at a church out in Hollywood, now.

'I've heard all the stories about him being violent to his wives and girlfriends, but I never really saw that. I've seen him so incredibly drunk, though, that I've just had to pour him into my car to get him home. He used to say his back teeth were floating!

Rob Angelo (guitarist): I was a member of Iron Maiden in the mid-Seventies, so I was actually in the band before Paul joined. After I'd left, I saw them play a gig in North London, and you could tell they had it – whatever it took to make it big. And whatever you need to be a rock star – Paul not only had it, he had buckets of it!

'He struck me as being different from the rest of them – he had short hair, which was very unusual in those days. I got talking to him after the gig and he seemed like a real character, but it wasn't until later that I discovered what a complete lunatic he is.

'Maiden asked me to go back soon after that, but I was in another band by then, who had a record deal, so I decided against it. I think I was still a bit sore about being kicked out of the band before, so I told Steve Harris to stick it when he asked me back again. I'm probably the only person ever to have done that!

'I met up with the guys from Maiden again when I was a member of the group Praying Mantis, and we supported them on their British tour. One of my favourites memories from that time, and one which says it all about Paul really, was when we went to Huddersfield.

'Huddersfield had a special significance for us, as it's the home town of Rod Smallwood, Iron Maiden's manager. We're on the way there on the bus, and a few of us said, "Let's wind Rod up, and fuck about as much as we can!"

'So me and Paul decide to go shoplifting! We went up and down the high street, nicking sweets and everything we could lay our hands on. Once we'd got tired of that, we went back to the hotel, and headed straight for the bar.

'It was a really posh hotel, with all these stags' heads and suits of armour, and the bar was full of wealthy-looking businessmen. Of course, we got really pissed, and I can remember Paul's voice was getting louder and louder, fucking this, and cunt that. You can always hear Paul's voice over everybody else's and he was in full flow that day. I was embarrassed, and I was as pissed as he was!

'It was bad enough us being there anyway, with all our long hair and leathers, and these businessmen just started leaving, 'cos they're really offended – yet everybody's too scared to say anything to him.

'So we're there in a hell of a state, and we've still got a show to do! I can't remember how we actually got to the gig, or how we managed to get on stage – the whole thing is a blur. Of course, when it's over, Paul immediately goes back to the bar with the others and starts again. I just can't handle this by now, I'm absolutely fucked, and pretty soon I've gone off to bed.

'I can remember waking up in the middle of the night, because of this fucking awful racket that's going on downstairs. I go outside to see what the hell's going on, and I see this scene of pandemonium in the lobby. There's these two mannequins dressed up as a bride and groom which have obviously come from some sort of display in the hotel.

'Several members of the two bands are taking it in turns to take them up to the top of the stairs and chuck them over the balcony, to see them crash down on the floor below. Needless to say, I can see Paul right in the bloody thick of all this!

'It was obvious that the staff had given up trying to get them to be quiet, and the noise they were making was like fucking bedlam. We all got a bollocking from Rod the next day about our appalling behaviour. He accused us of acting up deliberately because it was his home town. As if we would, Rod!

'There were other outrageous incidents on that tour, like the time in Bristol when Paul got an airgun and shot up all the lights and windows in this concert hall where we were going to be playing.

'I couldn't believe he was doing it! Everybody would know who'd done it; he didn't make any secret of the fact he had this gun with him. It was just schoolboy stuff really, acting like a kid! There'd be this food laid on every night in the dressing room, and there would always be a huge food fight; it would end up smeared all over the walls or dumped on someone's head. It was just a laugh, there was nothing malicious about it.

'I saw him occasionally after that, usually at clubs like the Music Machine or the Marquee. There was this London rock scene going on, and you'd see people hanging out there like Lemmy from Motorhead, Gary Holton from the Heavy Metal Kids, and the guys from the Sex Pistols.

'I wasn't that surprised when I heard later that he'd been kicked out of Maiden, because I don't think they were ever really at ease with him or his image. Steve Harris is quite a strait-laced sort of guy, and Paul's just the opposite – he'd just fuck about, and go wild all the time.

'With respect to the bloke, Paul's got this self-destruct button, and I think he would just go mad on drink and drugs whenever he could, lurching from one disaster to another, so it was only a matter of time before they got pissed off with him, really.'

Anonymous roadie: There's a world-famous groupie in Japan, who's known as 'Yukari the Super Sucker'. She's said to be the oldest groupie in Tokyo, and she's very well known to thousands of rock musicians, road crews and the like, over many years.

'Professionally, she works full-time as a prostitute in "Soapland", which is the red-light district in the Shinjuku area of the city, where she entertains hordes of middle-aged Japanese businessmen every day.

'Her title pretty much says it all, but for those who've led a sheltrered life, she is reputed to be the best blow-job in Japan, although you have to say that the years haven't been kind, and she looks as rough as fuck.

'We were on tour over there with Paul's band, and he'd made it known to the road crew (all platinum card holders to Yukari's workplace) that he'd be very interested in testing out those famous lips for himself.

'The arrangements were made, and Yukari phoned to say that she'd be delighted to give Paul's little furry friend an Oriental shampoo. Apparently, she was a bit tied up (!) that week, but she promised if he came down to Soapland, she'd give him "the best brow of his rife ..."

'So, Paul and his entire entourage rushes across town to open an account with Yukari (and leave a deposit!) In the limo, Paul was so anxious to get there I thought he might give himself a blow-job if the driver didn't get a move on.

'Eventually, we arrive in Soapland, and an usher gives us a glossy magazine (this is a Japanese tradition) which has photographs of all the girls, along with prices and details of their specialities. There's a well-touched up picture of Yukari there, explaining her particular party piece, as if anyone needed to be told.

'Even with special effects. she did look bloody old. I couldn't help thinking we'd have done better with a copy of *Playboy* and a box of tissues, but Paul is in there like a shot. He disappears behind this door, and we all settle down to wait. Now in my experience these things can take some time, so we started chatting amongst ourselves.

'Less than ten minutes had passed, when the door flies open, and an obviously distraught Paul comes flying out, flushed and sweating. He's doing up his trousers, and running for the exit.

'When we asked him what was wrong, he replied, charmingly, "That fucking fish-eyed cunt! I'm giving it to her in the gob, and her fucking false teeth all fall out on the floor!"

'It was a fantastic time for all of us, though, just coping with this massive phenomenon, and I think we were all walking around all the time waiting for the bubble to burst, when it would all be taken away from us.'

Randy Wolpin (booking agency CEO): 'We booked Paul Di'Anno for a US tour in 2000, and everybody was really excited about it. There are a lot of Paul Di'Anno fans over here, and they were waiting to see him in concert.

'But one week before the band were due to arrive, we were contacted by the immigration authorities, who said that Paul was being refused entry to the United States. Apparently, it was to do with the American Embassy in London, who'd discovered there had been violations in California, which hadn't been mentioned on the visa application. They also said Paul had generally not told the truth on his application.

'We tried to appeal, but they said we'd have to do it via

Scotland Yard in London, and that it could take eight to ten months. The whole tour got cancelled. We had to ring every single promoter, explaining why the shows weren't happening. I even got Paul to ring some of them himself.

'We were so desperate, I even had this idea of sending Paul to Canada, and sneaking him across the border, but it failed, and he got arrested and thrown into jail again. It was a disaster! '

Clive Burr (drummer): 'Paul had already been in Iron Maiden for a while when I joined the group, and my first impression of him was that he was a really nice guy, good to work with, and always a true pro on stage.

'He was a real star even then, you know. He always loved being the centre of attention, and while he was never the most diplomatic of people, when he did have rows with the management or whoever, it was just him saying he wasn't going to be told what to do.

'He was a real laugh, a typical East Londoner, and that made him very easy to get on with, for me.

'I could tell, in later years, though, that his attitude had changed slightly, and that he was no longer 100 per cent happy with the band or what it was doing. It was subtle, there were no big wobblers or anything like that, but it didn't come as a massive shock when him and the band went their separate ways, put it that way.

'I take my hat off to him, though, as he's done a hell of a lot, and he's a real survivor – the fact that he's still around is a miracle, considering his colourful life offstage and all the stuff that's happened. I haven't kept in touch with him as often as I'd like, but I've heard on the grapevine when shit's been happening.

'But good on you, Paul – keep it up, mate, keep it firm and keep it happening!'

ACKNOWLEDGEMENTS

My very special thanks to the following people:

Dale Webb and Lea Hart, John Blake Publishing, Killers (Cliff Evans, Darayus Kaye, Pete Newdeck and Marcus Thurston), Torgrim Oyre, Robert Mills, Arnie Goodman, Nicko of NOTB, Steve Hopgood, Graham Bath, John Wiggins, Paulo Turin, Pat Begent and The Intrepid Fox, Beverly, Conan, Emily, Juanitta, Conchita, Maisie, Marinya, Julian Pratt, Ian Camfield, all at The Royal Standard, special BIG thanks to Mum & Dad, Darren, Sharron, Michele, Kelly, Cheryl, Jason and all the kidz, Atilla, Nicki, Soggy, Sharon Skidz, Flo, Kev, Dick, Big Dave, Leanne Duncan, James, Sarah Cari, The Inbredz, Paddy, Sarah and Kerry & all at The Alehouse, Fast Eddie Clarke, Mariko Fujiwara, Junk – DNA, Gabriel Gonzales, Jeriko and Los Chicos de la Esperanzo in Buenos Aires, Rod, Andy & all of Iron Maiden, Phil Campbell, Brian

Adams (Eagle Rock), Hatch Farm Studios, Nick Smith & John Burns, Pauli Tsarion, Libby, Stuart, Emma, Kav, Angel, Trina, Marc Angel, Ricky, Mozza, Trev the DJ, French Greg & Philipe of NOTB, Frank Cristoph, Clive Burr, Andrew Kisser & Sepultura, The Manifesto Bar-Brazil, all at Spitfire Records, Felix Reisch, Martin Popoff, Jeff Keller, Darren Edwards, Godsize, Bill Liesegang, Pete Jupp, Steve Overland, Revision, Chinchilla, Shuff, Gary Sharpe Young, Rodney Moffit, St Moritz Club, JR, Peter Steinbach, Bob at Muck Records, Debbie Bisceglia, Leonardo Santos, Robert Skoog, Bart Metalheart, Cesar & Daniel, Richy/Heavy's, Henk Mol, Bob Skeat, Rick Wills, Ray Callcut, Steve Grimmet, Steve Parry, Craig Simcox, Micke Martensson & Roger in Sweden, Marcos Cardoso, Andresa, Beatrix, La familia Cabron, Alex, Gustavo, Andrea, Rafael, Roberto, Silvano, Renato, Sebastion, Carla, Andresa and all of my Brazilian family, Kostas Kyriakakis, Ann-Marie, Club Rockers, Adam Parfitt, Victoria Bullock, John Blake, Morten Stromberg and the Brothers, Tanya, Becky Ross, Gino, Nancy, Eddie Mercado, Randy Wolpin at Poochi, Paul 'Woodchuck' Roberts (the best bro), Mum and Dad Roberts, all the disabled seamen, Diana Tchavdarova, Arve Thomas, Espen & Brynjulv, Tony Incigeri, Wild World Productions – sorry if I missed anyone out.